✸✸✸ Forbes
TRAVEL GUIDE
Formerly Mobil Travel Guide

CANADA

ACKNOWLEDGMENTS

We gratefully acknowledge the help of our representatives for their efficient and perceptive inspections of the lodgings listed. Forbes Travel Guide is also grateful to the talented writers who contributed to this book.

Copyright © 2010 The Five Star Travel Corporation. All rights reserved. This publication may not be reproduced in whole or in part by any means whatsoever without written permission from Forbes Travel Guide, 200 W. Madison St., Suite 3950, Chicago, IL 60606; info@forbestravelguide.com

CANADA
★★★★★

2

ISBN: 9-780841-61414-7   Manufactured in the USA

10 9 8 7 6 5 4 3 2 1

TABLE OF CONTENTS

CANADA ★★★★★

STAR ATTRACTIONS

If you've been a reader of Mobil Travel Guide, you will have heard that this historic brand partnered with another storied media name, Forbes, in 2009 to create a new entity, Forbes Travel Guide. For more than 50 years, Mobil Travel Guide assisted travelers in making smart decisions about where to stay and dine when traveling. With this new partnership, our mission has not changed: We're committed to the same rigorous inspections of hotels, restaurants and spas—the most comprehensive in the industry with more than 500 standards tested at each property we visit—to help you cut through the clutter and make easy and informed decisions on where to spend your time and travel budget. Our team of anonymous inspectors are constantly on the road, sleeping in hotels, eating in restaurants and making spa appointments, evaluating those exacting standards to determine a property's rating.

What kind of standards are we looking for when we visit a proprety? We're looking for more than just high-thread count sheets, pristine spa treatment rooms and white linen-topped tables. We look for service that's attentive, in-dividualized and unforgettable. We note how long it takes to be greeted when you sit down at your table, or to be served when you order room service, or whether the hotel staff can confidently help you when you've forgotten that one essential item that will make or break your trip. Unlike other travel ratings entities, we visit the places we rate, testing hundreds of attributes to compile our ratings, and our ratings cannot be bought or influenced. The Forbes Five Star rating is the most prestigious achievement in hospitality—while we rate more than 8,000 properties in the U.S., Canada, Hong Kong, Macau and Bei-jing, for 2010, we have awarded Five Star designations to only 53 hotels, 21 restaurants and 18 spas. When you travel with Forbes, you can travel with confidence, knowing that you'll get the very best experience, no matter who you are.

We understand the importance of making the most of your time. That's why the most trusted name in travel is now Forbes Travel Guide.

STAR RATED HOTELS

Whether you're looking for the ultimate in luxury or the best value for your travel budget, we have a hotel recommendation for you. To help you pinpoint properties that meet your needs, Forbes Travel Guide classifies each lodging by type according to the following characteristics:

★★★★★These exceptional properties provide a memorable experience through virtually flawless service and the finest of amenities. Staff are intuitive, engaging and passionate, and eagerly deliver service above and beyond the guests' expectations. The hotel was designed with the guest's comfort in mind, with particular attention paid to craftsmanship and quality of product. A Five Star property is a destination unto itself.

★★★★These properties provide a distinctive setting, and a guest will find many interesting and inviting elements to enjoy throughout the property. Attention to detail is prominent throughout the property, from design concept to quality of products provided. Staff are accommodating and take pride in catering to the guest's specific needs throughout their stay.

★★★These well-appointed establishments have enhanced amenities that provide travelers with a strong sense of location, whether for style or function. They may have a distinguishing style and ambience in both the public spaces and guest rooms; or they may be more focused on functionality, providing guests with easy access to local events, meetings or tourism highlights.

★★The Two Star hotel is considered a clean, comfortable and reliable establishment that has expanded amenities, such as a full-service restaurant.

★The One Star lodging is a limited-service hotel or inn that is considered a clean, comfortable and reliable establishment.

For every property, we also provide pricing information. All prices quoted are accurate at the time of publication; however, prices cannot be guaranteed.

STAR RATED RESTAURANTS

Every restaurant in this book comes highly recommended as an outstanding dining experience.

★★★★★Forbes Five Star restaurants deliver a truly unique and distinctive dining experience. A Five Star restaurant consistently provides exceptional food, superlative service and elegant décor. An emphasis is placed on originality and personalized, attentive and discreet service. Every detail that surrounds the experience is attended to by a warm and gracious dining room team.

★★★★These are exciting restaurants with often well-known chefs that feature creative and complex foods and emphasize various culinary techniques and a focus on seasonality. A highly-trained dining room staff provides refined personal service and attention.

★★★Three Star restaurants offer skillfully-prepared food with a focus on a specific style or cuisine. The dining room staff provides warm and professional service in a comfortable atmosphere. The décor is well-coordinated with quality fixtures and decorative items, and promotes a comfortable ambience.

★★The Two Star restaurant serves fresh food in a clean setting with efficient service. Value is considered in this category, as is family friendliness.

★The One Star restaurant provides a distinctive experience through culinary specialty, local flair or individual atmosphere.

Because menu prices can fluctuate, we list a pricing range rather than specific prices. The pricing ranges are per diner, and assume that you order an appetizer or dessert, an entrée and one drink.

STAR RATED SPAS

Forbes Travel Guide's spa ratings are based on objective evaluations of more than 450 attributes. About half of these criteria assess basic expectations, such as staff courtesy, the technical proficiency and skill of the employees and whether the facility is clean and maintained properly. Several standards address issues that impact a guest's physical comfort and convenience, as well as the staff's ability to impart a sense of personalized service. Additional criteria measure the spa's ability to create a completely calming ambience.

★★★★★Stepping foot in a Five Star spa will result in an exceptional experience with no detail overlooked. These properties wow their guests with extraordinary design and facilities, and uncompromising service. Expert staff cater to your every whim and pamper you with the most advanced treatments and skin care lines available. These spas often offer exclusive treatments and may emphasize local elements.

★★★★Four Star spas provide a wonderful experience in an inviting and serene environment. A sense of personalized service is evident from the moment you check in and receive your robe and slippers. The guest's comfort is always of utmost concern to the well-trained staff.

★★★These spas offer well-appointed facilities with a full complement of staff to ensure that guests' needs are met. The spa facilities include clean and appealing treatment rooms, changing areas and a welcoming reception desk.

★★
★★ CANADA
★★
★

ALBERTA

ALBERTA IS A RICH FRONTIER—CANADA'S ECONOMIC BOOMTOWN, THANKS TO PROFITABLE oil sands—and home to some of the continent's most awe-inspiring scenery and outdoor adventure. Here you'll find sweeping plains, towering Rocky Mountains, sparkling emerald lakes, cowboys and cattle ranches, champagne powder snow, a colorful gold rush heritage and some of the most delectable steak in the world.

Alberta boasts the widest variety of geographical features of any province in Canada, including badlands rich in dinosaur fossils, rolling prairies and vast forests. All along its western border are the magnificent Canadian Rockies, which encompass six national and provincial parks, including the legendary Jasper and Banff.

Enter Alberta, which is easily accessible from Montana, from Waterton Lakes National Park and drive north to Calgary where you'll intersect with the Trans-Canada Highway. The view of the Rockies from the Calgary Tower and the excitement of the Calgary Stampede, a 10-day event held each July, are not to be missed. From Calgary, drive northwest to Banff, Lake Louise and Jasper National Park for some of the finest mountain scenery, outdoor activities, resorts and restaurants on the continent. Heading due north from Calgary and visit Red Deer, a town famous for agriculture, oil and its beautiful parkland setting. Farther north is the provincial capital, Edmonton. A multicultural city noted for its oil, Gold Rush past, parks, cultural celebrations, magnificent sports facilities and rodeos. Northwest of Edmonton, Alberta provides paved access to Mile 0 of the Alaska Highway at Dawson Creek, British Columbia. There is also paved access to the Northwest Territories— Canada's northern frontier land.

Drive southeast from Calgary and enter an entirely different scene: cowboy-and-Indian territory. Fort Macleod brings you back to the early pioneer days. Lethbridge is famous for its replica of the most notorious 19th-century whiskey fort, Fort Whoop-Up, and the Nikka Yuko Japanese Gardens. Farther east, visit Medicine Hat, known for its parks, pottery and rodeos. Don't go to Alberta without plenty of space on your camera's memory card.

BANFF

See also Calgary, Lake Louise

As early as 1885, Albertans knew what treasure lay in their backyards. The Banff Hot Springs Reservation was incorporated to protect the steaming, healing grottos abundant to the area, and by 1887 that vision was expanded to become Rocky Mountains Park. Today, the vast recreation area is known as Banff National Park—Canada's first national park, the second in North America and only the third in the world. A UNESCO World Heritage site, the park covers 2,564 square miles (6,641 square kilometers).

Banff comes alive each summer with its music and drama festival at Banff Centre. In winter, the Rockies provide some of the best skiing on the North American continent. A fantastic blend of both culture and natural beauty, Banff offers exciting nightlife, sleigh rides, Western barbecues, gondola rides, boat and raft tours, concerts, art galleries, museums, hot springs, ice-field tours, hiking and trail rides.

Snowy peaks tower over glassy alpine lakes. Massive canyons carved out of plain landscapes and more than 1,000 prehistoric glaciers await eco-warriors and everyday shutterbugs alike. Animals are so plentiful that traveling throughout the province (and camping and outdoor eating) requires special care. Watch for bighorn sheep, mountain goats, moose, elk, deer and grizzly and black bears.

WHAT TO SEE
BANFF GONDOLA
403-762-2523; www.banffgondola.com
Take a gondola and travel up to 7,500 feet in elevation for spectacular vistas. Besides the beautiful views, there are gift shops and restaurants at the top. Admission: adults $29, children 6-15 $14. Daily.

BANFF NATIONAL PARK
403-762-1550; www.pc.gc.ca/pn-np/ab/banff
As Canada's first national park, Banff was initially famous for its hot springs, and visitors still flock here to check out the bubbling thermal waters at the Cave and Basin National Historic Site. The town is home to many of the park's resorts and lodges, perhaps the most notable being the opulent Fairmont Banff Springs, fashioned after a Scottish baronial castle. Upscale accommodations also can be found near the wondrous Lake Louise, its placid blue-green waters reflecting the sharply angled mountain peaks surrounding the shoreline. Budget-minded visitors to Banff National Park typically opt to sleep under the stars, with the park offering 2,468 campsites on a first-come, first-served basis. Banff National Park stands tall among the spectacular peaks of the Canadian Rockies as one of the premier year-round vacation destinations in all of North America. Downhill skiers and snowboarders come from around the world to Banff's legendary slopes, with three major ski resorts serving the area. The summer months bring boot-clad hikers eager to take advantage of more than 1,000 miles (1,600 kilometers) of trails that cut across diverse but consistently striking terrain, winding through open meadows and dense forests, and passing alongside ancient glaciers and glistening lakes. Other popular activities include mountaineering, fishing, canoeing, kayaking, golfing, horseback riding and wildlife viewing.
Admission: adults $9.80, seniors $8.30, children 6-16 $4.90. Year-round.

BANFF PARK MUSEUM
403-762-1558; www.pc.gc.ca/lhn-nhs/ab/banff
One of the oldest museums in Canada, you'll find displays of animals, insects and other collections found in Banff National Park. There is a reading room and hands-on discovery room.
Admission: adults $3.90, seniors $3.40, children 6-16 $1.90. Mid-May-September, 10 a.m.-6 p.m. Mid-May-September, daily 10 a.m.-6 p.m.; October-mid-May, daily 1-5 p.m. Guided tours: Mid-May-September, daily 3 p.m daily; October-mid-May, Saturday-Sunday 2:30 p.m.

BANFF UPPER HOT SPRINGS

403-762-1515, 800-767-1611; www.hotsprings.ca

Originally built in 1932, the therapeutic waters of Canada's most revered hot springs produce average temperatures of 100 F, with an expansive outdoor pool and rich selection of spa indulgences.

Admission: adults $7.30, seniors and children 3-17 $6.30. Mid-May-Mid-September, 9 a.m.-11 p.m.; October-mid-May, Sunday-Thursday 10 a.m.-10 p.m., Friday-Saturday 10 a.m.-11 p.m.

BREWSTER CANADA MOTORCOACH TOURS COLUMBIA ICEFIELD GLACIER EXPERIENCE

403-762-6700, 877-423-7433; www.brewster.ca

Tours take passengers onto the Columbia Ice-field for a glacier-bound excursion.

Admission: adults $49, children 6-15 $24. April-October; hours vary by season.

CAVE AND BASIN NATIONAL HISTORIC SITE OF CANADA

403-762-1566; www.pc.gc.ca/lhn-nhs/ab/caveandbasin/

This is the birthplace of Canada's national park system and a national historic site. Attractions include hot springs, an explorable cave, exhibits, trails, and a theater.

Admission: adults $3.90, seniors $3.40, children 6-16 $1.90. Mid-May-September, daily 9 a.m.-6 p.m.; October-mid-May, Monday-Friday 11 a.m.-4 p.m., Saturday-Sunday 9:30 a.m.-5 p.m. Guided tours: Mid-May-September, daily 11 a.m., 2 p.m., 4 p.m.; October-mid-Mary, Saturday-Sunday 11 a.m.

FAIRMONT BANFF SPRINGS GOLF COURSE

403-762-2211; www.fairmont.com/banffsprings

This spectacular 27-hole golf course is situated along the Bow River and framed by the majestic peaks of the Canadian Rockies. There is also a driving range, practice greens, and a pro shop.

Admission: prices vary. May-October.

JOHNSTON CANYON

16 miles west of Banff; 403-762-1550; www.banff.com

This is a self-guided, 3.6-mile (5.8-kilometer) hike through the scenic canyon allows you to view Ink Spots and six cool water springs.

ROCKY MOUNTAIN RAFT TOURS

403-762-3632; www.banffrafttours.com

These one- or three-hour float trips travel on the Bow River through Banff National Park.

Admission: varies by tour. Mid-May-September.

SUNSHINE VILLAGE

403-277-7669, 877-542-2633; www.skibanff.com

This legendary ski area offers more than 3,300 acres of terrain with an elevation of 8,954 feet (2,729 meters) and a vertical drop of 3,514 feet (1,071 meters). There is one high-speed eight six-passenger gondola, seven quad chairs, one triple chair, one double chair and two magic carpets. Enjoy the

onsite restaurants, lounges, ski and snowboard school, rental shop, day care, snowboard park and more.
Admission: adults $75.95, seniors $61.67, children 6-12 $25.95, children 13-17 $53.81. Mid-November-mid-May; hours vary by season.

SPECIAL EVENTS
ANNUAL BANFF/LAKE LOUISE WINTER FESTIVAL
403-762-8421; www.banfflakelouise.com
This two-week festival, including cultural events, winter athletic contests, a Town Party and bar socials, has been a Banff tradition since 1916.
Late January-early February.

BANFF SUMMER ARTS FESTIVAL
403-762-6301, 800-413-8368; www.banffcentre.ca/bsaf
Main stage productions and workshops in opera, ballet, music theater, drama, concerts, poetry reading and visual arts are central to this summer fest.
May-September.

BANFF WORLD TELEVISION FESTIVAL
403-678-1216; www.banff2009.com
While this event is primarily for industry networkers, the public can view some of the best international television free of charge.
June.

WHERE TO STAY
★★BANFF CARIBOU LODGE
521 Banff Ave., Banff, 403-762-5887, 800-563-8764; www.bestofbanff.com/bcl/
195 rooms. Restaurant, bar. Fitness center. Pool. Spa. $151-250

★★BUFFALO MOUNTAIN LODGE
700 Tunnel Mountain Road, Banff, 403-410-7417, 800-661-1367;
www.buffalomountainlodge.com
108 rooms. Restaurant, bar. Business center. Fitness center. $151-250

★★★BANFF PARK LODGE
222 Lynx St., Banff, 403-762-4433, 800-661-9266; www.banffparklodge.com
Stunning mountain views can be seen from any room of this full-service hotel located just two blocks from Banff's shopping district and near the Bow River. After a long day at play, enjoy a quiet dinner in the hotel's fine-dining restaurant, The Terrace. A casual dinner can be found at The Chinook where there are theme-night dinners that range from Italian to Western fare.
211 rooms. Restaurant, bar. Pool. Business center. $151-250

★★BREWSTER'S MOUNTAIN LODGE
208 Caribou St., Banff, 403-762-2900, 888-762-2900;
www.brewstermountainlodge.com
77 rooms. Restaurant, bar. Complimentary breakfast. Business center. Fitness center. $151-250

★★★THE FAIRMONT BANFF SPRINGS

405 Spray Ave., Banff, 403-762-2211, 800-540-4406; www.fairmont.com/banffsprings

A striking backdrop of snow-capped peaks and towering trees makes for a magical experience, with regal accommodations, luxurious amenities and plentiful activities—including world-class skiing and championship golf. The Willow Stream spa offers a well-rounded treatment menu to help guests further relax in this majestic setting.

768 rooms. Restaurant, bar. Business center. Fitness center. Pool. Spa. Pets accepted. Golf. Tennis. $251-350

★★★RIMROCK RESORT HOTEL

300 Mountain Ave., Banff, 403-762-3356, 888-746-7625; www.rimrockresort.com

Terraced into the side of a mountain in Banff National Park, this sophisticated hotel offers alpine vistas with world-class skiing nearby. A comprehensive health center and saltwater pools appeal to fitness-minded visitors, while the spa indulges all. Three dining establishments echo the elegance of the hotel while catering to a variety of tastes.

346 rooms. Restaurant, bar. Business center. Fitness center. Pool. Spa. $251-350

★★★ROYAL CANADIAN LODGE

459 Banff Ave., Banff, 403-760-6967, 800-661-1379; www.charltonresorts.com

In the serene setting of Banff, this small, rustic hotel charms with spacious guest rooms featuring high ceilings, Canadian maple furnishings, granite vanities and either gas fireplaces or views of the Alpine Garden. Evergreen, the restaurant, serves three meals daily and features Canadian cuisine, while the Grotto Spa includes a mineral pool and whirlpool and offers several types of treatments.

99 rooms. Restaurant, bar. Fitness center. Pool. Spa. $151-250

WHERE TO EAT

★★BALKAN

120 Banff Ave., Banff, 403-762-3454; www.banffbalkan.ca

Greek. Lunch, dinner. $16-35

★★★★BANFFSHIRE CLUB

The Fairmont Banff Springs, 405 Spray Ave., Banff, 403-762-6860;
www.fairmont.com/banffsprings/

The jewel of the lavish Fairmont Banff Springs, the Banffshire Club prides itself on having one of the most extensive wine cellars in Canada. Warm up with one of many single malt scotches in view of Sulphur Mountain and enjoy game dishes and a uniquely fresh, Alberta-inspired menu with hints of French cuisine.

French. Dinner. Closed Sunday-Monday. Reservations recommended. $86 and up

★★★BOW VALLEY GRILL

The Fairmont Banff Springs, 405 Spray Ave., Banff, 403-762-6860;
www.fairmont.com/banffsprings

Housed in the historic, castle-like Fairmont Banff Springs Hotel, this French

ALBERTA ★★★★

restaurant was recently remodeled to restore its romantic brilliance. The formal, special-occasion space is the property's signature dining room and offers the excitement of tableside preparations and nightly dancing.
French. Breakfast, lunch (Saturday), dinner, Sunday brunch. Reservations recommended. $36-85

★★BUFFALO MOUNTAIN LODGE DINING ROOM
Tunnel Mountain Drive, Banff, 403-760-4484, 800-661-1367;
www.crmr.com/dining-buffalo.php
American. Breakfast, lunch, dinner. Reservations recommended. $36-85

★★GIORGIO'S TRATTORIA
219 Banff Ave., Banff, 403-762-5114; www.giorgiosbanff.com
Italian. Dinner. $16-35

★★★LE BEAUJOLAIS
212 Buffalo St., Banff, 403-762-2712; www.lebeaujolaisbanff.com
A prestigious destination in a beautiful town, this restaurant is awash in fresh flowers, candlelight and mountain views. Comfortably formal service and occasional tableside preparations are a treat.
French. Lunch, dinner. Closed November-mid-December. $36-85

★★★THE PRIMROSE
300 Mountain Ave., Banff, 403-762-3356, 888-746-7625;
www.rimrockresort.com/primrose.html
High on Sulphur Mountain, this restaurant is the more casual dining option at the Canadian Rockies Rimrock Resort Hotel. Enjoy great views and straightforward, yet delicious cuisine.
American. Breakfast, dinner. $36-85

★★★SEASONS
1029 Banff Ave., Banff, 403-762-5531; www.rockymountainresort.com
This fireside café is housed at the Banff Rocky Mountain Resort and Conference Center in the heart of the Canadian Rockies. The atmosphere is casual, and the regionally influenced menu is broad. Views of the Rockies add drama to the experience.
American. Dinner. Closed Tuesday-Wednesday. $16-35

★★★TICINO
415 Banff Ave., Banff, 403-762-3848; www.ticinorestaurant.com
Named after the region in Switzerland that borders on Italy, this restaurant serves cuisine with influences of both countries. The bistro emphasizes hearty pasta, meat and fish dishes with a variety of local vegetables and herbs. The rustic Italian alpine room has attracted diners for more than 30 years.
Italian, Swiss. Dinner. $36-85

SPA
★★★★WILLOW STREAM SPA
405 Spray Ave., Banff, 403-762-6860, 800-404-1772; www.fairmont.com/banffsprings
Willow Stream Spa is a shining star in the world-class mountain paradise

of Banff Springs. This top-rated facility has it all, along with an outdoor whirlpool, an indoor Hungarian mineral pool and three waterfall-style whirlpools. A diverse treatment menu is available, offering therapies customized for reawakening, balancing, rejuvenating and revitalizing. Sport-specific treatments include massages designed for golfers and skiers, while those who want to enjoy their spa treatments together can do so in the specially designed couple's suite. A full-service fitness center offers guided hikes and fitness consultations in addition to its two pools, cardiovascular equipment and free weights.

CALGARY

See also Banff

The gateway to the Canadian Rockies, Calgary was founded in 1875 by the North West Mounted Police at the confluence of the Bow and Elbow Rivers. Surrounding the city are fertile farmlands and to the west, the rolling foothills of the Rockies. A city couldn't be more ideally situated for both economic luster and gawk value—lush ranchlands and profitable grain farming have made Calgary Canada's principal agribusiness center, while majestic peaks overlook the urban landscape.

Site of the 1988 Olympic Winter Games, Calgary offers endless pursuits for outdoor enthusiasts with world-class golfing, skiing, snowboarding, hiking, mountaineering and whitewater rafting in its foothills and alpine environs.

Powering Calgary's recent phenomenal growth is oil. Since 1914, the petroleum industry has centered its activities here. Today, more than 85 percent of Canada's oil and gas producers are headquartered in Calgary. Despite this influx of cash and ambition, Calgary retains a small town feel with a Wild West atmosphere well-demonstrated by the enthusiasm and pride that brims over during Stampede Week—arguably one of the most voracious parties in the entire country.

WHAT TO SEE
CALGARY SCIENCE CENTRE

701 11th St. S.W., Calgary, 403-268-8300; www.calgaryscience.ca

This centre features a Discovery Dome, astronomy displays, exhibitions and observatory. There are also self-guided tours as well as science and technology demonstrations.

Admission: adults $13.50, seniors $9.50, children 3-17 $9.50. Monday-Thursday 9:45 a.m.-4 p.m., Friday 9:45 a.m.-5 p.m., Saturday-Sunday 10 a.m.-5 p.m.

CALGARY TOWER

101 Ninth Ave. S.W., Calgary, 403-266-7171; www.calgarytower.com

The Calgary Tower is a 626-foot (191-meter) tower with a spectacular view of Calgary and the Rocky Mountains. There is also a revolving restaurant, observation terrace, lounge and shops to enjoy.

Admission: adults $12.95, seniors $10.95, children 13-17 $9.95, children 4-12 $5

THE CALGARY ZOO, BOTANICAL GARDEN AND
PREHISTORIC PARK

1300 Zoo Road N.E., Calgary, 403-232-9300, 800-588-9993; www.calgaryzoo.ab.ca

One of Canada's largest zoos, there are more than 900 animals here along with a botanical garden. The Canadian Wilds (25 acres) portion features Canadian ecosystems populated by their native species.

Admission: prices vary by season. Daily 9 a.m.-5 p.m.

CANADA OLYMPIC PARK

88 Canada Olympic Road S.W., Calgary, 403-247-5452; www.coda.ab.ca

The premier site of the 1988 Olympic Winter Games, this park features an Olympic Hall of Fame and Museum, plus winter sports facilities with one double and two triple chairlifts, a T-bar, ski school and rentals. Summer facilities include mini-golf, beach volleyball, a summer bobsled ride, mountain biking and softball.

Admission: varies by activity.

EAU CLAIRE FESTIVAL MARKET

200 Barclay Parade S.W., Calgary, 403-264-6450; www.eauclairemarket.com

Enjoy this two-story warehouse with boutique shops, specialty food stands, restaurants, bars and a five-screen cinema, including an IMAX theater.

EPCOR CENTRE FOR THE PERFORMING ARTS

205 Eighth Ave. S.E., Calgary, 403-294-7455; www.epcorcentre.org

The Epcor Centre for the Performing Arts is comprised of four theaters and houses the Calgary Philharmonic Orchestra, Theatre Calgary and other performing arts.

FORT CALGARY HISTORIC PARK

750 Ninth Ave. S.E., Calgary, 403-290-1875; www.fortcalgary.com

This vast riverside park is the site of the original North West Mounted Police (NWMP) fort at the meeting place of the Bow and Elbow Rivers. Abandoned in 1914, the site of the fort is now being rebuilt. An interpretive center highlights NWMP and Calgary history. Adjacent is Deane House, restored and opened as a restaurant.

Admission: adults $11, seniors and students $10, children 3-6 $5, children 7-17 $7. Daily 9 a.m.-5 p.m.

GLENBOW MUSEUM

130 Ninth Ave. S.E., Calgary, 403-268-4100; www.glenbow.org

Combining a museum, art gallery, library and archives all under one roof, Glenbow boasts more than a million artifacts and some 28,000 works of art in its vast collections. You'll find regional, national and international fine arts; displays of native cultures of North America and the development of the West; mineralogy, warriors, African and personal adornment. There is also a museum shop.

Admission: adults $14, seniors $10, students and children 7-17 $9.

Monday-Saturday 9 a.m.-5 p.m., Sunday noon-5 p.m.

HERITAGE PARK HISTORICAL VILLAGE

1900 Heritage Drive S.W., Calgary, 403-268-8500; www.heritagepark.ab.ca

This village recreates life in Western Canada before 1914 and features more than 150 exhibits; a steam train, paddle wheeler, horse-drawn wagon and electric streetcars.

Admission: adults $20, seniors $16, children 3-17 $15. Mid-May-September, daily 9:30 a.m.-5 p.m.

THE MILITARY MUSEUMS

4520 Crowchild Trail S.W., Calgary, 403-974-2850; www.themilitarymuseums.ca

The newly expanded Military Museums honor four Calgary regiments. There are films and traveling exhibits.

Admission: adults $6, seniors $4, children 7-17 $3. Monday-Friday 9 a.m.-5 p.m., Saturday-Sunday 9:30 a.m.-4 p.m.

ROYAL TYRRELL MUSEUM OF PALEONTOLOGY

1420 N. Dinosaur Trail, Drumheller, 403-823-7707, 888-440-4240;
www.tyrrellmuseum.com

This is the world's largest display of dinosaurs in a state-of-the-art museum setting. There are more than 35 complete dinosaur skeletons; a paleo-conservatory with more than 100 species of tropical and subtropical plants that once thrived in this region; and hands-on exhibits include interactive terminals and games throughout.

Admission: adults $10, seniors $8, children 7-17 $6. Mid-May-August, daily 9 a.m.-9 p.m.; September-mid-May, Tuesday-Sunday 10 a.m.-5 p.m.

SPRUCE MEADOWS

18011 Spruce Meadows Way S.W., Calgary, 403-974-4200; www.sprucemeadows.com

This is the only internationally sanctioned outdoor horse jumping show held in North America and it offers the world's richest show jumping purse.

SPECIAL EVENTS
CALGARY STAMPEDE

Stampede Park, 1410 Olympic Way S.E., Calgary, 403-261-0101, 800-661-1260;
www.calgarystampede.com

Billed as "The World's Greatest Outdoor Show," the Stampede has been held every year since 1912. Revelers gather with vivid enthusiasm for parades, rodeos, chuck wagon races, stage shows, exhibitions, square dances, marching bands and vaudeville shows.

Ten days in early July.

WHERE TO STAY
★★BLACKFOOT INN

5940 Blackfoot Trail S.E., Calgary, 403-252-2253, 800-661-1151;
www.blackfootinn.com

200 rooms. Restaurant, bar. Business center. Fitness center. Pool. Spa. Pets accepted. $151-250

★★★DELTA BOW VALLEY

209 Fourth Ave. S.E., Calgary, 403-266-1980, 800-655-8571; www.deltahotels.com

Guests have the choice of a room with a city, mountain or river view at this downtown full-service hotel, which is located east of the grand Canadian Rockies. Elements Bistro emphasizes regional cuisine and Canadian wines are featured.

394 rooms. Restaurant, bar. Business center. Fitness center. Pool. Pets accepted. $151-250

★★★THE FAIRMONT PALLISER

133 Ninth Ave. S.W., Calgary, 403-262-1234, 800-540-4477; www.fairmont.com/palliser

This palace-style building is a city favorite and its downtown location makes it a convenient base for business or leisure travelers. The hotel features traditional European styling and a skywalk connects it to the Telus Convention Centre, Calgary Tower and Glenbow Museum. The Oak Room and Rimrock restaurants feature a variety of savory treats, while guests with a sweet tooth can visit the weekly all-chocolate buffet.

405 rooms. Restaurant, bar. Business center. Fitness center. Pool. Pets accepted. $151-250

★★GREENWOOD INN CALGARY

3515 26th St. N.E., Calgary, 403-250-8855, 888-233-6730; www.greenwoodcalgary.com

210 rooms. Restaurant, bar. Fitness center. Pool. Pets accepted. $61-150

★★★HYATT REGENCY CALGARY

700 Centre St. S., Calgary, 403-717-1234, 800-233-1234; www.calgary.hyatt.com

This Hyatt's downtown location is ideal for both leisure and business travelers. Spacious rooms, vast amenities and 24-hour room service as well as a fitness center and indoor pool keep guests pampered. Relaxing dinners and small get-togethers can be had at Thomsons Restaurant and the Sandstone Lounge.

355 rooms. Restaurant, bar. Business center. Fitness center. Pool. Spa. Pets accepted. $251-350

★★★INTERNATIONAL HOTEL SUITES CALGARY

220 Fourth Ave. S.W., Calgary, 403-265-9600, 800-661-8627; www.internationalhotel.ca

This high-rise hotel is conveniently located in the heart of the city center within walking distance of area attractions. The hotel's onsite restaurant, 4th Avenue Cafe, features international cuisine and offers a children's menu. For lighter fare, head over to the 4th Avenue Lounge and order from the tapas menu.

248 rooms. Restaurant, bar. Business center. Fitness center. Pool. Spa. $151-250

★★★MARRIOTT CALGARY

110 Ninth Ave. S.E., Calgary, 403-266-7331, 800-896-6878; www.marriott.com

Situated in the heart of downtown Calgary, the Marriott is connected by skywalk to the Calgary Tower and Telus Convention Center and located near the Glenbow Museum and Calgary Zoo. An array of amenities and services

provides guests with the comforts of home.
384 rooms. Restaurant, bar. Business center. Fitness center. Pool. Pets accepted. $151-250

★★★SHERATON CAVALIER HOTEL
2620 32nd Ave. N.E., Calgary, 403-291-0107,866-716-8101; www.sheratoncalgary.ca
Many families choose the Sheraton Cavalier Hotel when staying in Calgary not only for its spacious guest rooms but also for its indoor water park. With a well-equipped business center and a cyber café onsite, the hotel attracts a number of business travelers as well. It is located 10 minutes from the airport and a complimentary shuttle is available.
306 rooms. Restaurant, bar. Business center. Fitness center. Pool. Spa. Pets accepted. $151-250

★★★SHERATON SUITES CALGARY EAU CLAIRE
255 Barclay Parade S.W., Calgary, 403-266-7200, 888-784-8370;
www.sheratonsuites.com
This downtown hotel facing Eau Claire Market is a great choice for both business and leisure travelers, and the indoor pool with waterslides is a hit with kids. Guest suites are spacious and dining options diverse at the Irish pub Fionn McCool's and Barclay's, an upscale-casual restaurant.
323 rooms. Restaurant, bar. Business center. Fitness center. Pool. Pets accepted. $251-350

WHERE TO EAT
★★★THE BELVEDERE
107 Eighth Ave. S.W., Calgary, 403-265-9595; www.thebelvedere.ca
Housed in the restored Union Bank building, this contemporary dining room has a plush, clubby feel. The restaurant offers a seasonal, unhurried experience featuring globally inspired, creative cuisine.
Seafood, steak. Lunch (Tuesday-Friday), dinner. Closed Sunday-Monday. $36-85

★★★CENTINI RESTAURANT AND LOUNGE
160 Eighth Ave. S.E., Calgary, 403-269-1600; www.centini.com
Fresh, seasonal food is prepared and served with passion at this Italian restaurant located in downtown Calgary's Telus Convention Center near many businesses and shops. On offer are housemade specialty pastas and an extensive wine list featuring 650 wines and 8,500 bottles.
Italian. Lunch (Monday-Friday), dinner. Closed Sunday. Reservations recommended. $36-85

★★THE KEG STEAKHOUSE AND BAR
7104 MacLeod Trail S., Calgary, 403-253-2534; www.kegsteakhouse.com
Steak. Lunch, dinner. Reservations recommended. $16-35

★★QUINCY'S ON SEVENTH
609 Seventh Ave. S.W., Calgary, 403-264-1000; www.quincysonseventh.com
Seafood, steak. Lunch (Monday-Friday), dinner. Closed Sunday Reservations recommended. $36-85

★★★THE RIMROCK

The Fairmont Palliser, 133 Ninth Ave. S.W., Calgary, 403-260-1219, 800-441-1414;
www.fairmont.com/palliser

Located in the landmark Palliser Hotel, this regionally influenced restaurant
has been serving guests for more than 80 years. The elegant dining room
is a popular choice for special-occasion dinners and for seating during the
lobby's Sunday buffet brunch.
Canadian. Breakfast, lunch (Monday-Friday), dinner, Sunday brunch. Reservations recommended. $36-85

★★RIVER CAFÉ

Prince's Island Park, Calgary, 403-261-7670; www.river-cafe.com

Canadian. Lunch (Monday-Friday), dinner, Saturday-Sunday brunch. Closed
January. Reservations recommended. Outdoor seating. $16-35

CANMORE

See also Banff

Canmore burst onto the tourist scene after hosting Nordic events during the
1988 Calgary Winter Olympics. Today, it is an authentic Alpine village that's
a destination for thrills and vistas, with a significant selection of exquisite
galleries and unique gift shops. Most of Canmore can be traversed within an
hour by foot; the town center surrounds Eighth Street (or "Main Street" as
it is known colloquially), originally a residential road boasting some of the
oldest architecture in the town.

Much of the area to the northeast of Canmore is located in a critical wildlife corridor that hosts bears, cougars, wolves and elk as they move between
habitats. A series of hiking and walking paths traverse this area, known as
The Benchlands, and are watched over by various stakeholders (Bow Valley Mountain Bike Alliance, the B.V. Riding Association and local hiking
groups) in order to protect wildlife and its habitat while providing high-quality recreational trails. Climbing is popular, with various sport and multi-pitch
climbs throughout the Bow Valley, and the area is a world destination for ice
climbing. Kayakers and canoeists can take guided trips with one of the many
local outfitters or independently navigate the surrounding rivers and lakes.
Caving enthusiasts will enjoy the extensive Rat's Nest Caves.

SPECIAL EVENTS
CANMORE ARTSPEAK FESTIVAL

Canmore, 403-678-6436; www.artspeakcanmore.com

Celebrate Canmore's artistic spirit at this four-day event featuring various
artists, an art walk, a literary festival, film screenings and street performers.
June.

CANMORE CHILDREN'S FESTIVAL

Canmore, 403-678-1878; www.canmorechildrensfestival.com

This two-day event provides an array of children's entertainment, including
acrobats, magicians, jugglers, music, theater, storytelling, crafts, stilt-walk-
ing, dancing, face painting and clowns.
May.

CANMORE FOLK MUSIC FESTIVAL

Canmore, 403-678-2524; www.canmorefolkfestival.com

This music festival is held annually on the Heritage Day long weekend in August at Centennial Park on the Stan Rogers Stage. The festival is the longest running music festival in Alberta.
August.

CANMORE HIGHLAND GAMES

Canmore, 403-678-9454; www.canmorehighlandgames.ca

Presented annually by the Three Sisters Scottish Society on Labor Day weekend, these games feature heavy lifting competitions, piping, drumming and highland dance events.
September.

FESTIVAL OF EAGLES

Canmore; www.eaglewatch.ca

This festival is a celebration of the Golden Eagle autumn migration over Canmore and the Bow Valley. The weekend celebration includes guided hikes, bird walks, interpretive displays, theatrical performances and guest speakers. Spotting scopes are set up at Canmore Collegiate High School.
October.

WHERE TO STAY

★★CHATEAU CANMORE

1718 Bow Valley Trail, Canmore, 403-678-6699, 800-261-8551;

www.chateaucanmore.com

93 rooms. Restaurant, bar. Business center. Fitness center. Pool. Tennis. $61-150

★★RADISSON HOTEL AND CONFERENCE CENTER CANMORE

511 Bow Valley Trail, Canmore, 403-678-3625, 800-395-7046;

www.radisson.com/canmoreca

224 rooms. Restaurant, bar. Business center. Fitness center. Pool. Pets accepted. $61-150

WHERE TO EAT

★★CHEZ FRANCOIS

1604 Second Ave., Canmore, 403-678-6111; www.restaurantchezfrancois.com

French. Breakfast, lunch, dinner. Outdoor seating. $36-85

EDMONTON

See also Calgary

As the capital of a province whose economic mainstays are petroleum and agriculture, Edmonton has the brash confidence of a major supplier of one of the world's most sought-after resources. Yet at its heart, this northern stalwart is rooted in a practical sensibility.

Established as a fort of operations during the fur trade era, Edmonton came into itself in the 1890s as a major supply depot for the Yukon gold rush—the highlight of the All-Canadian Route to the Klondike. Thousands of men stopped for days, weeks or months before making the final 1,500-mile push for gold. Many decided to stay and transformed a quiet village into a prosperous city. Each July the city celebrates this era with Klondike Days. Edmonton is a beautifully green city with more park area per capita than any other city in Canada, much of which is located along the banks of the North Saskatchewan River. Visitors enjoy a perfectly Albertan blend of outdoor adventure, shopping, sports, arts, culture, dining, recreation and a wide variety of world-class attractions. Canada's "Festival City" also offers a calendar full of annual events celebrating jazz, folk, symphony, theater, dance, visual arts, street performers, food and fun for every member of the family.

WHAT TO SEE
ART GALLERY OF ALBERTA
100-10230 Jasper Ave., Edmonton, 780-422-6223; www.artgalleryalberta.com
More than 5,000 works of contemporary and historical art from around the world live here at the largest art museum and longest-running cultural institution in Alberta.
Admission: adults $10, seniors and students $7, children 6-12 $5. Monday-Friday 10:30 a.m.-5 p.m., Saturday-Sunday 11 a.m.-5 p.m. Free Thursday 4-8 p.m.

CAPITAL CITY RECREATION PARK
9545 100 St. N.W., Edmonton, 780-496-7275; www.edmonton.ca
Winding through the city's river valley, this is one of Canada's most extensive park systems. Bicycle, walking and cross-country ski trails link the major parks featuring barbecue and picnic facilities and food concessions.

CITADEL THEATRE
9828 101 A Ave., Edmonton, 780-425-1820, 888-425-1820; www.citadeltheatre.com
This five-theater complex in downtown Edmonton is one of Canada's finest centers for the performing arts. There is a glass-enclosed atrium area and waterfall.

COMMONWEALTH STADIUM
11000 Stadium Road, Edmonton, 780-944-7400; www.edmonton.ca
This stadium was built for the 11th Commonwealth Games and now home of the Canadian Football League's Edmonton Eskimos. The Stadium Recreation Centre houses a gym, weight room and racquetball and squash courts.

DEVONIAN BOTANIC GARDEN
Highway 60, Edmonton, 780-987-3054; www.devonian.ualberta.ca/
This botanic garden includes an enormous, lush retreat including alpine and herb gardens, a peony collection and native plants, an extraordinary five-acre Japanese garden, nature trails, aspen and jack pine forests, a lilac garden, a butterfly pavilion and an orchid greenhouse.
Admission: adults $13, seniors $8.50, children 7-12 $3, children 13-17 $5. May-mid-October, daily.

EDMONTON QUEEN RIVERBOAT

9734-98 Ave., Edmonton, 780-424-2628; www.edmontonqueen.com
This riverboat runs along the North Saskatchewan River, which travels through many local parks. Packages include Sunday brunch, dinner or cruise only. May-October, Thursday-Sunday; hours vary by day.

FORT EDMONTON PARK

Whitemud and Fox Drives, Edmonton, 780-496-8787; www.fortedmontonpark.ca
Canada's largest historical park encompasses Fort Edmonton, the Hudson's Bay Company Post that gave the city its name. There are demonstrations, artifacts, costumed interpreters, steam trains and streetcar rides.
Admission: adults $13.50, seniors and children 12-18 $10.25, children under 12 $6.75. Mid-May-September; hours vary by season.

FRANCIS WINSPEAR CENTRE FOR MUSIC

4 Sir Winston Churchill Square, Edmonton, 780-428-1414, 800-563-5081;
www.winspearcentre.com
This is the home of the Edmonton Symphony Orchestra.

JOHN JANZEN NATURE CENTRE

7000 143 St., Edmonton, 780-496-2910; www.edmonton.ca/johnjanzen
This nature center features exhibits and events focused on nature in urban settings.
Admission: adults $2, seniors and youths $1.65, children $1.35. Hours vary by season.

OLD STRATHCONA FARMERS' MARKET

10310 83 Ave., Edmonton, 780-439-1844; www.osfm.ca
This is Alberta's biggest and best farmer's market. Shop for produce and local crafts at this indoor market.
Saturday 8 a.m.-3 p.m.

ROYAL ALBERTA MUSEUM

12845 102 Ave., Edmonton, 780-453-9100; www.royalalbertamuseum.ca
This museum features excellent displays reflecting the many aspects of Alberta's heritage. Exhibits on natural and human history include information about aboriginal peoples, wildlife, geology, live insects, dinosaurs and ice age mammals.
Admission: adults $10, seniors $8, students $7, children 7-17 $5. Daily 9 a.m.-5 p.m. Half-price Saturday-Sunday 9-11 a.m.

RUTHERFORD HOUSE

11153 Saskatchewan Drive, Edmonton, 780-427-3995; www.culture.alberta.ca/heritage/
This Jacobean Revival home was the residence of Alberta's first Premier and has been restored and refurnished to reflect the lifestyle of the post-Edwardian era. Costumed interpreters re-enact life in 1915 with activities such as woodstove baking, historical dramas, craft demonstrations and musical performances.
Admission: adults $4, seniors and children 7-17 $3. Mid-May-September,

Tuesday-Sunday 9 a.m.-5 p.m.; September-mid-May, Tuesday-Sunday noon-5 p.m.

TELUS WORLD OF SCIENCE-EDMONTON

11211 142 St., Coronation Park, Edmonton, 780-452-9100; www.odyssium.com
An entertainment hub with a 275-seat IMAX theater, dome theater, Star Theater and six exhibit galleries featuring the latest discoveries in science, astronomy and space exploration. There are aslo artifacts (moon rocks, telescopes) and space flight simulation to check out.
Admission: adults $13.95, seniors, students $11.75, children 4-12 $9.50.
Daily 11 a.m.-5 p.m.

VALLEY ZOO

13315 Buena Vista Road, Edmonton, 780-496-8787; www.valleyzoo.ca
The Valley Zoo features a wide variety of birds and mammals, fish and reptiles. There is a train, merry-go-round, pony rides, and paddle boats to keep children occupied when the animals are sleeping.
Admission: varies by season. Year-round.

WEST EDMONTON MALL

8882 170 St., Edmonton, 780-444-5200, 800-661-8890; www.westedmontonmall.com
Canada's largest shopping and entertainment complex features more than 800 stores, 110 eating establishments, 13 movie theaters, an aquarium, dolphin shows, a replica of a Spanish galleon, four submarines, a water park with wave pool and water slides, bungee jumping, an ice skating rink, casino, the Galaxyland amusement park with a 14-story looping rollercoaster, 18-hole miniature golf course and an IMAX Theatre. You could spend days here!
Monday-Saturday 10 a.m.-9 p.m. Sunday 11 a.m.-5 p.m.

SPECIAL EVENTS

CANADIAN FINALS RODEO

Rexall Place, 7424 118 Ave. N.W., Edmonton, 780-471-7210, 888-800-7275;
www.canadianfinalsrodeo.ca
This professional indoor rodeo decides the national championships.
Mid-November.

EDMONTON INTERNATIONAL STREET PERFORMERS FESTIVAL

Sir Winston Churchill Square, Edmonton; www.edmontonstreetfest.com
Catch performances by more than 60 international street acts at 1,500 free outdoor shows.
July.

FOLK MUSIC FESTIVAL

Gallagher Park, Edmonton, 780-429-1899; www.edmontonfolkfest.org
This folk music festival covers three days and is Alberta's largest outdoor music festival.
August.

FRINGE THEATRE FESTIVAL

10330-84 Ave., Edmonton, 780-448-9000; www.fringetheatreadventures.ca

Fringe fest brings dance performances, music, plays, mimes, and street entertainers to 27 stages in the parks and on the streets.
Mid-late August.

HERITAGE FESTIVAL

10125-157 St., Edmonton, 780-488-3378; www.heritage-festival.com

More than 75 cultures show Alberta's multicultural heritage in pageantry of color and music. Take part in music and dance performances; displays and demonstrations at more than 60 outdoor pavilions, plus arts and crafts and international cuisine.
Early August.

JAZZ CITY INTERNATIONAL MUSIC FESTIVAL

Edmonton, 780-990-0222; www.edmontonjazz.com

This festival features jazz concerts, workshops and other outdoor events.
Late June-early July.

WHERE TO STAY

★★★DELTA EDMONTON CENTRE SUITE HOTEL

10222 102nd St., Edmonton, 780-429-3900, 888-890-3222; www.deltahotels.com

This hotel is located inside the Edmonton City Centre West shopping mall, and it's connected to City Hall and the Shaw Conference Centre. Rooms have contemporary furnishings. Cocoa's Restaurant features continental cuisine with regional specialties and serves breakfast, lunch, dinner, Sunday brunch and late-night snacks.
169 rooms. Restaurant, bar. Business center. Fitness center. Pets accepted.
$151-250

★★★THE FAIRMONT HOTEL MACDONALD

10065 100th St., Edmonton, 780-424-5181, 866-540-4468;
www.fairmont.com/macdonald

This glorious château overlooks the scenic North Saskatchewan River Valley. From its formal high tea to its distinguished guest rooms and suites, this hotel recalls the charm of the Victorian period. Inventive nouveau cuisine is highlighted at Harvest Room, which also serves a Sunday brunch, and the Confederation Lounge is a nice spot for sipping a cocktail while soaking up the clubby atmosphere.
199 rooms. Restaurant, bar. Business center. Fitness center. Pets accepted.
$151-250

★★★THE SUTTON PLACE HOTEL

10235 101st St., Edmonton, 780-428-7111, 866-378-8866;
www.edmonton.suttonplace.com

Connected by a walkway to Edmonton City Centre, this hotel is within walking distance to Sir Winston Churchill Square and the Edmonton Art Gallery. Enjoy dinner at the Sutton Place's Capitals Restaurant with its à la carte menu or sip a drink or two at the open-air atrium of Central Park Lounge.
313 rooms. Restaurant, bar. Business center. Pool. Pets accepted. $61-150

★RAMADA INN AND WATER PARK EDMONTON SOUTH
5359 Calgary Trail, Edmonton, 780-434-3431,800-272-6232; www.ramada.com
122 rooms. Restaurant, bar. Pool. Pets accepted. $61-150

★★★THE WESTIN EDMONTON
10135 100th St., Edmonton, 780-426-3636, 800-937-8461;
www.thewestinedmonton.com
Conveniently located in downtown Edmonton, this hotel has a pedestrian walkway that connects to area attractions such as the Edmonton Art Gallery, Shaw Conference Center and Citadel Theater. Unwind at the gym or swim in the heated indoor pool. Pradera Café, the Westin's restaurant, focuses on regional and international cuisine.
416 rooms. Restaurant, bar. Business center. Fitness center. Pool. Spa. Pets accepted. $151-250

WHERE TO EAT
★★COCOA'S
10222-102nd St. N.W., Edmonton, 708-423-9650; www.deltahotels.com
French. Breakfast, lunch, dinner, late-night, Sunday brunch. $36-85

★CREPERIE
10220-103rd St., Edmonton, 780-420-6656; www.thecreperie.com
French. Lunch (Tuesday-Friday), dinner. Closed Monday. Reservations recommended. $16-35

★FIORE CANTINA
8715-109th St., Edmonton, 780-439-8466; www.fiorecantina.com
Italian. Breakfast, dinner. Outdoor seating. $16-35

★★★THE HARVEST ROOM
10065 100th St., Edmonton, 780-429-6424, 800-540-4468;
www.fairmont.com/macdonald
Located in the historic chateau-style Hotel MacDonald, this elegant dining room features contemporary Canadian cuisine using fresh, local ingredients. The outdoor terrace overlooks the North Saskatchewan River Valley.
Seafood, steak. Breakfast, lunch, dinner. Reservations recommended. $36-85

★★LA BOHEME
6427 112th Ave., Edmonton, 780-474-5693; www.laboheme.ca
French. Dinner, Sunday brunch. Reservations recommended. Outdoor seating. $36-85

★★★LA RONDE
10111 Bellamy Hill, Edmonton, 780-420-8366, 800-661-8801;
www.chateaulacombe.com/laronde.php
This restaurant sits on the rooftop of the Crowne Plaza Hotel Chateau Lacombe. The revolving room has incredible views of the surrounding city, and the cuisine makes good use of local ingredients. Dishes include bison ribeye with sage spatzle and maple-glazed arctic char.
Seafood, steak. Dinner, Sunday brunch. Reservations recommended. $36-85

FORT MACLEOD

See also Lethbridge

From a distance, Fort Macleod looks like any other town—but its rich history and national significance are apparent as soon as visitors wander through its streets. It is at a crossroads that once hosted Indian encampments, wagon trails and buffalo grazing grounds, in view of the Porcupine Hills that front the Rocky Mountains. Once known as Blackfoot Crossing, Fort Macleod became a North West Mounted Police barracks and trading post in 1874. From the fort spread the fame of the "men in red" who stamped out the illegal whiskey trade and kept rowdy gold miners in check—and who eventually became known as the Canadian RCMP.

The town gradually took shape alongside the Oldman River, named for the grandfather of Blackfoot mythology, and within easy view of the mountains. Fort Macleod draws you into a time when the North West Mounted Police, Blackfoot Indians and pioneer settlers were the only inhabitants. Main Street is dotted with gift shops, antique stores and restaurants that recapture this spirit.

WHAT TO SEE
FORT MUSEUM
219 25th St., Fort Macleod, 403-553-4703, 866-273-6841; www.nwmpmuseum.com
Experience the rich history of Fort Macleod, the first outpost in the Canadian West. Witness the history of the North West Mounted Police (the precursor to the national RCMP), plains tribes and pioneer life and enjoy the spectacle of the Mounted Patrol Musical Ride.
Admission: varies by season. May-November.

HEAD-SMASHED-IN BUFFALO JUMP INTERPRETIVE CENTRE
Highway 785, Fort Macleod, 403-553-2731; www.head-smashed-in.com
This UNESCO World Heritage Site celebrates 6,000-year-old Native American hunting techniques as interpreted by members of the Blackfoot Nation, built into the cliff where buffalo were herded to jump to their death.
Admission: adults $9, seniors $8, children 7-17 $5. July-early September, daily 9 a.m.-6 p.m.; early September-June, daily 10 a.m.-5 p.m.

REMINGTON CARRIAGE MUSEUM
623 Main St., Cardston, 403-653-5139; www.remingtoncarriagemuseum.com
This museum displays one of the largest collections of horse-drawn vehicles in North America with more than 240 carriages, wagons and sleighs. The gallery has interactive displays, multimedia productions and a carriage factory.
Admission: adults $9, seniors $8, children 7-17 $5. July-early September, daily 9 a.m.-6 p.m.; early September-June, daily 10 a.m.-5 p.m.

SPECIAL EVENTS
SANTA CLAUS PARADE AND FESTIVAL
Fort Macleod, 403-553-2500; www.fortmacleod.com
This is one of the oldest and largest Santa Claus parades west of Toronto. Last Saturday in November.

JASPER

See also Edmonton

Everywhere you turn in the resort town of Jasper, dramatic peaks crown the horizon. Established in 1907 in the heart of the Canadian Rockies, Jasper is one of Canada's largest and most scenic national parks—and unique in that the town of the same name is at its center, jointly governed by a municipal government and Parks Canada. In more than 4,200 square miles (10,878 square kilometers) are waterfalls, lakes, canyons, glaciers and wilderness areas filled with varied forms of wildlife. The park has year-round interpretive programs, trips and campfire talks as well as guided wilderness trips, a sky tram, skating, skiing, ice climbing, and rafting and cycling trips. While driving through Jasper, be prepared to be awestruck at every turn. Keep your camera poised—all the better if you've got a wide-angle lens for unmatched panoramas.

WHAT TO SEE

THE ICEFIELDS PARKWAY

800-252-3782; www.icefieldsparkway.ca

One of the most famous mountain highways in the world, the Icefields Parkway travels between Lake Louise and Jasper along the crown of the Canadian Rockies. The scenery is phenomenal: soaring peaks still under the bite of glaciers, turquoise green lakes surrounded by deep forests, roaring waterfalls and, at the very crest of the drive, the Columbia Icefield, the largest non-polar icecap in the world. Lakeside lodges offer canoe rentals, short horseback trail rides, whitewater rafting trips and excursions onto the Columbia Icefield in specially designed snowcoaches. Just off the highway, by the Athabasca Glacier, the Columbia Icefield Center provides information on the ice field and the glaciers (Mid-April-mid-October). Wildlife is also abundant: mountain goats, mountain sheep, elk, moose and bears are frequently sighted.

JASPER TRAMWAY

Highway 93 and Whistler Mountain Road, Jasper, 780-852-3093;
www.jaspertramway.com

Two 30-passenger cars take 1-mile trips up Whistler's Mountain. This is a vast area of alpine tundra with hiking trails, picnicking areas, a restaurant and gift shops at the summit.

Admission: adults $28, children 5-14 $14. April-mid-October; hours vary by season.

MALIGNE TOURS

Highway 16 and Maligne Road, Jasper, 780-852-3370, 866-625-4463;
www.malignelake.com

Take a narrated boat cruise on Maligne Lake to the world-famous Spirit Island. There are fishing supplies and boat rentals. as well as whitewater raft trips.

Admission and hours vary by activity and season.

MARMOT BASIN

Highway 93 A and Marmot Basin Road, Jasper, 780-852-3816, 866-952-3816;
www.skimarmot.com

Two quads, triple, three double chairlifts, two T-bars, magic carpet; patrol,

ski school, rentals, repair shop; nursery, three cafeterias, bar. Vertical drop 3,000 feet.
Admission: varies by season. Late-November-early May, daily 8 a.m.-5 p.m.

MIETTE HOT SPRINGS
Miette Road and Highway 16, Jasper, 780-866-3939, 800-767-1611; www.parkscanada.gc.ca/hotsprings
Located at Jasper National Park, there are two pools that uses water from natural hot mineral springs. The water is cooled a bit so it is comfortable and there is a lounging area where you might just see wildlife like bighorn sheep, black bear and deer. There is also a cafe and gift shop.
Admission: adults $6.05, seniors and children 6-16 $5.15. May-mid-October; hours vary by season.

WHERE TO STAY
★ALPINE VILLAGE
Highway 93A N., Jasper, 780-852-3285; www.alpinevillagejasper.com
48 rooms. Pool. Closed mid-October-April. $61-150

★★★CHATEAU JASPER
96 Geikie St., Jasper, 780-852-5644, 888-852-7737; www.mpljasper.com
This comfortable hotel is an ideal base for active travelers who enjoy skiing, snowboarding, snowshoeing and ice skating during the winter, and hiking and guided nature tours during the summer. Spacious rooms feature lovely views, while the hotel's in-town location makes it perfect for dining and shopping.
119 rooms. Restaurant, bar. Business center. Fitness center. Pool. $251-350

★★★THE FAIRMONT JASPER PARK LODGE
Old Lodge Road, Jasper, 780-852-3301, 866-540-4454; www.fairmont.com/jasper
The Fairmont Jasper Park Lodge is the sophisticated alternative in the Canadian Rocky Mountains. This rustic retreat consists of a series of cedar chalets and log cabins, with luxurious accommodations, fine dining and exceptional services.
446 rooms. Restaurant, bar. Business center. Fitness center. Pool. Spa. Pets accepted. Golf. Tennis. $151-250

★★LOBSTICK LODGE
94 Geikie St., 780-852-4431, 888-852-7737; www.mpljasper.com
139 rooms. Restaurant, bar. Business center. Fitness center. Pool. Pets accepted. $61-150

★★MARMOT LODGE
86 Connaught Drive, Jasper, 780-852-4471, 888-852-7737; www.mpljasper.com
107 rooms. Restaurant, bar. Pool. Pets accepted. $151-250

★★SAWRIDGE INN & CONFERENCE CENTER
82 Connaught Drive, Jasper, 780-852-6590, 888-729-7343; www.sawridgejasper.com
153 rooms. Restaurant, bar. Business center. Fitness center. Pool. Spa. Pets accepted. $151-250

WHERE TO EAT
★★★EDITH CAVELL DINING ROOM
Old Lodge Road, Jasper, 708-852-6052, 800-441-1414; www.fairmont.com/jasper
The gourmet fare, vintage wines and attentive service of Jasper Park Lodge's dining room are all eclipsed by breathtaking lake and mountain views. Settle in for a grilled steak or locally caught trout and take in the scenery.
French. Dinner. Reservations recommended. Jacket required. $36-85

LAKE LOUISE
See also Banff
The blue-green glacial lake reflects a mirror image of the Victoria Glacier when the sun hits it at the right point. At the shore, nestled at the base of the mountain, sits the Chateau Lake Louise, one of the most elegant and classic hotel landmarks on the continent.

Lake Louise is the third in the must-visit trinity of Banff and Jasper. Its central Rocky Mountain location, longstanding history and lively resort atmosphere make it both an exciting and scenic destination. During the summer, the sightseeing gondola takes visitors high over the town to Mount Whitehorn, where a lodge serves as an alpine home base for hiking, picnicking and exploration. Summer or winter, take in the fresh mountain air equipped with canoe, mountain bike, skis, snowboard, climbing rope or horse.

WHAT TO SEE
LAKE LOUISE GONDOLA
877-253-6888; www.lakelouisegondola.com
Ascend to 6,850 feet (2,088 meters) in 14 minutes to view Lake Louise Victoria Glacier and The Great Divide. There is a restaurant, cafeteria, deli bar; hiking trails and nature programs.
Admission: adults $25, children 6-15 $12.50. Mid-May-September.

LAKE LOUISE SKI AREA
1 Whitehorn Road, Lake Louise, 403-522-3555, 800-258-7669; www.skilouise.com
This is Canada's largest ski area with more than 130 runs on four mountain faces across 4,200 acres. The top elevation is 8,660 feet with a vertical drop of 3,260 feet. The area includes a gondola, six-person chairlift, three quads and triple chairlift. After skiing, enjoy a meal at one of their restaurants, a cafeteria, or bar. There is a rental shop, ski and snowboard school.
November-May, 9 a.m.-4 p.m.

MORAINE LAKE AND VALLEY OF THE TEN PEAKS
7 miles (12 kilometers) east of Lake Louise; www.pc.gc.ca
Towering mountain peaks frame the emerald green lake. There are hiking trails and a canoe rental.

WHERE TO STAY
★★BAKER CREEK CHALETS
Highway 1A, Bow Valley Parkway, Lake Louise, 403-522-3761; www.bakercreek.com
35 rooms. Restaurant, bar. $151-250

★★DEER LODGE
109 Lake Louise Drive, Lake Louise, 403-522-3991, 800-661-1595;
www.crmr.com/deer-lodge.php
73 rooms. Restaurant, bar. Business center. Closed early October-early December. $151-250

★★★EMERALD LAKE LODGE
1 Emerald Lake Road, Field, 250-343-6321, 800-663-6336;
www.crmr.com/emerald-lake-lodge.php
Located on 13 acres in Yoho National Park, the lodge has a formal dining room, reading and sitting rooms, conference facilities and a games room. The onsite restaurant, Mount Burgess Dining Room, serves rustic California cuisine with Native American influences and offers award-winning Canadian wines. There are plenty of activities from hiking and fishing in summer to skiing and ice fishing in winter.
25 rooms. Restaurant, bar. Business center. $151-250

★★★THE FAIRMONT CHATEAU LAKE LOUISE
111 Lake Louise Drive, Lake Louise, 403-522-3511, 866-540-44134;
www.fairmont.com/LakeLouise
This grand resort offers its guests a front-row seat to Banff National Park while overlooking the sparkling water of Lake Louise. Stunning panoramas are matched only by the sophistication and comfort offered inside, where European flair blends with Canadian hospitality.
550 rooms. Restaurant, bar. Business center. Fitness center. Pool. Spa. Pets accepted. Ski in/ski out. $251-350

★★★POST HOTEL
200 Pipestone Road, Lake Louise, 403-522-3989, 800-661-1586; www.posthotel.com
This historic alpine lodge shares the finer things with guests who savor gourmet European cooking, sip award-winning wines and sleep in total luxury. One of Canada's best ski areas is just a few minutes from the hotel.
96 rooms. Closed mid-October-mid-December. Restaurant, bar. Business center. Fitness center. Pool. Spa. Ski in/ski out. $251-350

WHERE TO EAT
★★★FAIRVIEW DINING ROOM
111 Lake Louise Drive, Lake Louise, 403-522-1818, 866-540-4413;
www.fairmont.com/lakelouise
This historic dining room, Chateau Lake Louise's original, is housed in a breathtaking Canadian Rockies location. One of several restaurants at the resort, the dining room serves classic continental cuisine during the summer months amidst original 1913 grandeur.
Continental. Breakfast, lunch, dinner. Reservations recommended. $36-85

★★★★POST HOTEL DINING ROOM
200 Pipestone Road, Lake Louise, 403-522-3989, 800-661-1586; www.posthotel.com
Tucked into the foothills of the Canadian Rockies is this gem of a dining experience. Set in one of Banff National Parks remaining historic log lodges, the Post Hotel Dining Room achieves an easy sense of old-fashioned charm

with majestic mountain views and a blazing stone fireplace. The exceptional cuisine is matched by a highly acclaimed wine list with more than 32,500 bottles and more than 2,200 selections.

Canadian. Dinner. Closed mid-October-mid-December. Reservations recommended. $86 and up

★★WALLISER STUBE
The Fairmont Chateau Lake Louise, 111 Lake Louise Drive, Lake Louise, 403-522-1818, 866-540-4413; www.fairmont.com

French. Dinner. Reservations recommended. $36-85

LETHBRIDGE
See also Fort Macleod

Lethbridge is one of the warmest and sunniest cities in Canada—and not just in terms of the weather. The community's pride for its recreation-driven lifestyle makes for a friendly, spirited and active community.

Originally known to the Blackfoot as Sik-okotoks or "place of black rocks," Lethbridge transformed from a coal-producing town to a lush parkland with gardens such as the Brewery Gardens at the western edge of town; Indian Battle Park, site of the last battle between Native American nations in North America; and Henderson Lake Park. In 1869, traders from the United States came north and built so-called "whiskey forts" in and around the future city site, the most notorious of which was Fort Whoop-Up. The arrival of the North West Mounted Police in 1874 soon stamped out the illegal whiskey trade and brought order to this rambunctious corner of the west. The rebuilt fort now steeps visitors in this wily heritage, and the flag that signaled the arrival of the latest load of whiskey is now the city's official flag.

WHAT TO SEE
ALBERTA BIRDS OF PREY CENTER
2124 16th Ave., Coaldale, 403-345-4262; www.burrowingowl.com

This living museum features hawks, owls, falcons and other birds of prey from Alberta and around the world. The interpretive center has educational displays and wildlife art. There are daily flying demonstrations and picnicking areas.

Admission: adults $8.50, seniors $7.50, children 3-5 $4.50, children 6-18 $5.50. Mid-May-mid-October, daily 9:30 a.m.-5 p.m.

FORT WHOOP-UP
Third Ave. and Scenic Drive, Lethbridge, Indian Battle Park, 403-329-0444; www.fortwhoopup.com

Step into southern Alberta history at this replica of a booming, circa 1870s whiskey trading post. There is an interpretive gallery, a theater and tours. Hours vary by season.

NIKKA YUKO JAPANESE GARDEN
Henderson Lake Park, Mayor Magrath Drive and Ninth Avenue S., Lethbridge, 403-328-3511; www.nikkayuko.com

Built to commemorate Canada's centennial in 1967, the authentic garden is a symbol of Japanese-Canadian friendship. The garden is an art form of peace and tranquility.

Admission: adults $7, seniors $5, children 6-17 $4. Early May-mid-October; hours vary by season.

SIR ALEXANDER GALT MUSEUM

502 First St. S., Lethbridge, 403-320-3898, 866-320-3898; www.galtmuseum.com

This museum features displays that relate to the early development of area, which include indigenous culture, pioneer life, civic history, coal mining, farming history, irrigation and ethnic displays.

Admission: adults $5, seniors and students $4, children 7-17 $3. Mid-May-August, daily 10 a.m.-6 p.m.; September-mid-May, Monday-Saturday 10 a.m.-4:30 p.m., Sunday 1-4:30 p.m.

WATERTON LAKES NATIONAL PARK

Highways 5 and 6, Waterton Park, 403-859-2224, 800-661-8888; www.pc.gc.ca

Waterton is a rare gem tucked into the southwest corner of Alberta where the great Rocky Mountains rise suddenly out of the rolling prairies. Amid the peaks are the lakes of Waterton, carved out of the rock by ancient glaciers and forming a blend of unusual geology, mild climate, rare flowers and abundant wildlife. In 1932, Waterton Lakes National Park was linked with neighboring Glacier National Park in Montana—the cross-border area is now known as Waterton-Glacier International Peace Park. Waterton spans 195 square miles (505 square kilometers) on the eastern slope of the Rocky Mountains, just north of the U.S.-Canadian border. Travelers from the United States can reach the park via the Chief Mountain Highway along the east edge of Glacier National Park (mid-May-mid-September). The trails are well-maintained and afford an introduction to much of the scenery that is inaccessible by car. The Red Rock Parkway goes from the town of Waterton Park to Red Rock Canyon after branching off Alberta Highway 5. A buffalo paddock is located on Highway 6, just inside the northeastern park boundary. You can also drive from the town of Waterton Park to Cameron Lake via the Akamina Parkway.

SPECIAL EVENTS
INTERNATIONAL AIR SHOW

Highway 5 S. and McNally Road, Lethbridge, 800-661-1222;
www.albertaairshow.com

The Canadian Forces Snowbirds are the highlight of this two-day air-show that includes several Canadian and international acts.

Late July.

WHOOP-UP DAYS

3401 Parkside Drive S., Lethbridge, 403-328-4491;
www.exhibitionpark.ca/whoopup.htm

This festvial features exhibitions, a rodeo, and a grandstand show.

Mid-August.

WHERE TO STAY
★★LETHBRIDGE LODGE
320 Scenic Drive, Lethbridge, 403-328-1123, 800-661-1232;
www.lethbridgelodge.com
190 rooms. Restaurant, bar. Business center. Fitness center. Pool. $61-150

★★PRINCE OF WALES
117 Evergreen Ave., Waterton Lakes National Park, 403-859-2231;
www.princeofwaleswaterton.com
86 rooms. Closed mid-September-early June. Restaurant, bar. $151-250

WHERE TO EAT
★★★COCO PAZZO
1264 Third Ave. S., Lethbridge, 403-329-8979
One of the trendiest spots in the area, this restaurant offers guests the best in
Italian food in a casual, cafe atmosphere. With a variety of pasta dishes to
suit every taste, fantastic red wine and a fun crowd, it is a delightful dining
experience.
Italian. Lunch (Monday-Saturday), dinner. Outdoor seating. $36-85

MEDICINE HAT
See also Lethbridge
Despite its industrious roots, Medicine Hat is the ideal environ for natural
bounty and beauty. Rich in clays and natural gas, the area was a natural site
for brick, tile and petrochemical plants—but its hot summer temperatures
make it ideal for beautiful market gardens and greenhouses.

The name Medicine Hat is a translation of the Blackfoot name Saamis,
meaning "headdress of a medicine man." Natural gas was discovered here
in 1883, and in 1909 the huge Bow Island gas field was founded, sending
the town on a production frenzy that lasted for generations—the gas fields
inspired the British poet Rudyard Kipling to refer to the settlement as "the
town with all hell for a basement."

WHAT TO SEE
CYPRESS HILLS INTERPROVINCIAL PARK
Highway 41, Medicine Hat, 403-893-3777; www.tpr.alberta.ca/parks
This park is an oasis of mixed deciduous and coniferous forests in the middle
of a predominantly grassland region. At a maximum elevation of 4,810 feet
above sea level, the hills are the highest point in Canada between the Rocky
Mountains and Labrador. The area offers a swimming beach, boating, canoeing, fishing, camping, a golf course, hiking trails and nature interpretive
programs.

DINOSAUR PROVINCIAL PARK
Approximately 25 miles west of Medicine Hat on Highway 1, then north on Highway
884, west on Highway 544, 403-378-4342; www.tpr.alberta.ca/parks
Discoveries of extensive fossil concentrations in this area in the late 1800s
led to the designation of this area as a provincial park and UNESCO World
Heritage Site. More than 300 complete skeletons have been recovered and
are now displayed in museums worldwide. The 22,000-acre park consists

mainly of badlands; large areas have restricted access and can be seen only on interpretive tours. Facilities include canoeing, fishing and camping sites; interpretive trails, and dinosaur displays (at the actual discovery site) along a public loop drive. There are also guided tours and hikes and amphitheater events.

MEDICINE HAT MUSEUM AND ART GALLERY
1302 Bomford Crescent S.W., Medicine Hat, 403-502-8580; www.highway3.ca
Displays depict the history of the Canadian West, featuring pioneer items, local fossils, relics and Native artifacts. The archives contain a large collection of photographs and manuscripts.
Admission: donation. Monday-Friday 9 a.m.-5 p.m., Wednesday 7-10 p.m., Saturday-Sunday1-5 p.m.

WHERE TO STAY
★★MEDICINE HAT LODGE
1051 Ross Glen Drive S.E., Medicine Hat, 403-529-2222, 800-661-8095;
www.medhatlodge.com
223 rooms. Restaurant, bar. Business center. Fitness center. Pool. Pets accepted. $61-150

RED DEER
See also Calgary, Edmonton
Midway between Calgary and Edmonton is Red Deer, beautifully positioned in the lush, green parkland of central Alberta. A wealth of recreation and cultural programs keep visitors charmed, including famed dinner theatres by Central Alberta Theatre. Attend rodeos and authentic agricultural exhibitions alongside world-class sporting events such as the Canadian Open Figure Skating Championship and the Scott Tournament of Hearts (curling).

In the early 1870s, the Calgary-Edmonton Trail crossed the river at Red Deer Crossing. With the coming of the railway, traffic increased, and a trading post and stopping place were established. When the Northwest Rebellion broke out in 1885, a small regiment was stationed at Fort Normandeau, which still stands on the outskirts of the city. The river was originally called Was-ka-soo See-pi, the Cree word for "elk," because of the abundance of these animals in the area. Early Scottish fur traders thought the elk was related to the red deer of their native land, hence the present name for the river and city.

WHAT TO SEE
CANYON SKI AREA
Road 384, Red Deer, 403-346-7003; www.canyonski.net
This ski area features a triple and double chairlifts, handle tow, a Nordic jump, ski patrol, a school, rentals and snowmaking. There is also a day lodge and bar. The largest vertical drop is 500 feet and there is also cross-country skiing. November-March, daily.

FORT NORMANDEAU
The C & E Trail and 32nd Street, Red Deer, 403-346-2010
This rebuilt 1885 army fort and interpretive center features displays of

cultural history with living history interpreters. There is a picnic area and canoe launch.
May-September, daily.

RED DEER AND DISTRICT MUSEUM

4525 47a Ave., Red Deer, 403-309-8405; www.museum.red-deer.ab.ca
This museum tells the story of the area, from the early First Nations settlements to the present. Also located here are Heritage Square and Red Deer and District Archives.
Monday-Sunday noon-5 p.m., Wednesday noon-9 p.m.

WASKASOO PARK

6300 45th Ave., Red Deer, 403-342-8159
This large River Valley Park extends throughout city and includes 47 miles of bicycle and hiking trails, an equestrian area, fishing, canoeing, a water park, an 18-hole golf course and camping sites. There are natural and cultural history interpretive centers.

SPECIAL EVENTS
FORT NORMANDEAU DAYS

Fort Normandeau, C & E Trail and 32nd Street, Red Deer, 403-346-2010
This festival features Native American ceremonies and dances, a parade and children's activities.
Late May.

HIGHLAND GAMES

Westerner Exposition Park, 4847 19th St., Red Deer; www.reddeerhighlandgames.ca
The annual games began in 1947 and feature highland dancing, piping and drumming and shortbread baking competitions.
Last Saturday in June.

WHERE TO STAY
★★★CAPRI CONFERENCE CENTRE

3310 50th Ave., Red Deer, 403-346-2091, 800-662-7197; www.capricentre.com
Although this full-service hotel is primarily booked by convention travelers, there are diversions for leisure travelers, too. Various types of rooms and suites are available. The hotel has a heated outdoor pool and deck, whirlpool, shopping concourse and the Capri Centre Spa & Health Club. Barbero's Restaurant is a great choice for a business lunch or quiet dinner, and guests can kick up their heels at Billy Bob's Country Music Dance Hall or take a breather at Bellini's Lounge.
219 rooms. Restaurant, bar. Business center. Fitness center. Pool. Spa. Pets accepted. $61-150

★★HOLIDAY INN

6500 67th St., Red Deer, 403-342-6567, 888-465-4329; www.ichotelsgroup.com
142 rooms. Restaurant, bar. Complimentary breakfast. Business center. Fitness center. Pool. Spa. Pets accepted. $61-150

★HOLIDAY INN EXPRESS

2803 50th Ave., Red Deer, 403-343-2112,888-465-4329; www.ichotelsgroup.com
91 rooms. Complimentary breakfast. Business center. Fitness center. Pool.
$61-150

BRITISH COLUMBIA

BRITISH COLUMBIANS LIVE IN A CORNER OF CANADA THAT SEES AN EXPLOSION OF daffodils and cherry blossoms while the rest of the country is still shoveling snow. In this western-most province, life is enormous—from 1,000-year-old trees and everyday mountain vistas to towering city sunflowers.

Six diverse regions make up the whole of the province, each pulling tourists a hundred different ways each day: Vancouver Island, the Vancouver Coast and Mountains, Thompson Okanagan, the Kootenay Rockies, the Cariboo Chilcotin Coast and the vast Northern region.

Vancouver Island has one of the world's most diverse ecosystems: Rainforests, marshes, meadows, beaches, mountains, oceans, rivers and lakes create habitats for multitudes of wildlife species. It all adds up to one of the world's premier locations for golf, whale watching, birding and salmon and trout fishing. The island is blanketed in rare, old-growth rainforest and dramatic mountain ranges, picturesque cities and towns, and smaller island groups that invite ferry-bound adventures at an island pace.

Vancouver Coast and Mountains, slated to host the 2010 Olympic Games, is a phenomenal mountainous city—a mecca of peaks, ocean, lakes, rivers and beaches encircling a cosmopolitan gem that rivals the most spectacular cities in the world. Revel in the four-season resort town of Whistler that is famed worldwide for skiing, great shopping and fine restaurants. Visitors and residents cycle, hike, camp, kayak, golf, ski and snowboard year-round—in fact, the mild climate is such that a "West Coast Special" is an everyday option: ski in the morning, then golf or sail in the afternoon.

The Thompson Okanagan region is as famous for its pastoral orchards and vineyards as it is for its wildly varied landscape—the highest mountain in the Canadian Rockies is here, as well as a waterfall twice the height of Niagara Falls and Canada's only true desert. The heart of British Columbia's wine-growing region is located just a four-hour drive east of Vancouver, where more than 40 wineries are within a 150-mile range.

The Kootenay Rockies region is a vast wilderness of rivers, lakes, waterfalls, beaches, mineral hot springs, alpine meadows and snow-capped mountains. Adventure connoisseurs tackle some of the world's most intense mountain biking, fishing, windsurfing, whitewater rafting and kayaking. Golfers come here for world-class courses with unbeatable scenery, and city slickers turn cowboy at dude and guest ranches that offer authentic cattle rides. You can visit restored heritage towns, thriving art communities and gold rush boomtowns, and in the winter, take in the continent's finest powder skiing and snowboarding.

Thousands of lakes and rivers, plus a magnificent stretch of Pacific Ocean coastline, make the Cariboo Chilcotin Coast, which harkens back to the adrenaline-pumping gold rush era, a top destination for fishing, boating, camping, swimming and kayaking. This is a region whose rich, fascinating history is perhaps only rivaled by its captivating present day—complete with cowboys riding off into the sunset. Roam endless gentle trails or hike, ride and canter strenuous backcountry routes. Tramp through the volcanic mountains of Tweedsmuir Provincial Park, stand at the ancient hoodoos and shifting sand dune of Farwell Canyon, and drive the original Cariboo Waggon Road on the historic Gold Rush Trail, taking in famed local rodeos and stampedes.

Northern British Columbia's vast wilderness comprises more than half the province, a land of jagged mountain peaks, roaring rivers, serene lakes, green valleys, rugged coastlines and ancient island archipelagos. The region is known for its magnificent freshwater and saltwater fishing, canoeing, kayaking, whitewater rafting, and in the winter, powder skiing. A wondrous system of national and provincial parks provides habitats and sanctuary for wildlife. The Queen Charlotte Islands are a living mystery within this region: An untamed, old-growth land rich in Haida culture and with distinct island flora and fauna that have evolved over thousands of years.

KAMLOOPS
See also Vancouver
With more than 2,000 hours of annual sunshine, Kamloop is a top destination for fishing, and its trout are world famous and bountiful in more than 200 lakes within an hour's drive of the city. Balmy summers encourage rapid plant and fish growth, making the area widely recognized as a freshwater fishing hotspot. In addition to hundreds of lakes, there are many areas of dry forest, hilly areas that are largely treeless and grasslands that support several endangered species.

WHAT TO SEE
BRITISH COLUMBIA WILDLIFE PARK
9077 Dallas Drive, Kamloops, 250-573-3242, 866-872-2066; www.bczoo.org
More than 300 animals, both native and imported are found in this park. There is also a nature trail and miniature railroad.
Admission: adults $10, seniors and children 13-16 $9, children 3-12 $7. March-May, daily 9:30 a.m.-4 p.m.

KAMLOOPS MUSEUM AND ARCHIVES
207 Seymour St., Kamloops, 250-828-3576; www.kamloops.ca/museum
This museum features exhibits depicting the frontier history of Kamloops. There are self-guided walking tours, bicycle tours and cemetery tours.
Admission: donation. Tuesday-Saturday 9:30 a.m.-4:30 p.m., Thursday until 7:30 p.m.

SECWEPEMC NATIVE HERITAGE PARK
355 Yellowhead Highway, Kamloops, 250-828-9749; www.secwepemc.org/museum
Located on the Kamloops Reserve, this park interprets culture and heritage of the Secwepemc people. Includes archaeological site, full-scale winter village model, indoor museum exhibits and native arts and crafts.
Admission: adults $6, seniors and students $4, children 7-17 $3. Daily 8 a.m.-4 p.m. Closed Saturday-Sunday early September-mid-June.

WHERE TO STAY
★★ACCENT INN KAMLOOPS
1325 Columbia St. W., Kamloops, 250-374-8877, 800-663-0298; www.accentinns.com
83 rooms. Restaurant. Fitness center. Pool. Pets accepted. $61-150

★★★THE COAST CANADIAN INN
339 St. Paul St., Kamloops, 250-372-5201, 800-716-6199; www.coasthotels.com
This hotel is located in downtown Kamloops, the center of the Thompson Valley recreation area. The hotel is ideal for business travelers with complimentary high-speed Internet connection in each room. Enjoy a pint or two at Seargent O'Flaherty's Pub or a light dinner at Pronto Grill.
98 rooms. Restaurant, bar. Business center. Fitness center. Pool. Pets accepted. $61-150

★★RAMADA INN
555 W. Columbia St., Kamloops, 250-374-0358, 800-272-6232; www.ramada.com
88 Rooms. Restaurant, bar. Business center. Fitness center. $61-150

NANAIMO
See also Vancouver, Vancouver Island, Victoria
Nanaimo is located on Vancouver Island across the Strait of Georgia from Vancouver, a main entry port for ferries from Vancouver and Horseshoe Bay. Because of its location, it serves as a fine starting point to visit other attractions on the island, as well as being a vacation highlight in itself. A thriving art, culture and sports scene kicks off your island adventure, a perfect mix of big city amenities with small-town charm.

WHAT TO SEE
BASTION
Front and Bastion streets, Nanaimo; www.nanaimomuseum.ca/bastionpage.htm
Built in 1853 as a Hudson's Bay Company fort, it has been restored as a museum and features a cannon firing ceremony (summer months at noon).

NANAIMO ART GALLERY
900 Fifth St. and 150 Commercial St., Nanaimo, 250-754-1750; www.nanaimoartgallery.com
This gallery has changing exhibits of art, science and history pieces.

NANAIMO DISTRICT MUSEUM
100 Museum Way, Nanaimo, 250-753-1821; www.nanaimomuseum.ca
This museum features a walk-in replica of a coal mine; turn-of-the-century shops; a restored miner's cottage; dioramas; a Chinatown display; and other changing exhibits.
Admission: adults $2, seniors and students $1.75, children 5-12 $0.75.
Daily 10 a.m.-5 p.m. Closed Sunday-Monday December-March.

PETROGLYPH PARK
990 Island Highway S., Nanaimo, 250-474-1336; www.env.gov.bc.ca/bcparks/
This park contains ancient indigenous rock carvings.

SPECIAL EVENTS
BOXING DAY POLAR BEAR SWIM
Departure Bay Road, Nanaimo, 250-756-5200; www.nanaimo.ca
Each Boxing Day, hardy souls take a dip in the frigid waters at Departure Bay Beach. All participants receive prizes as well as free ice cream, bananas and suntan lotion.
December 26.

NANAIMO MARINE FESTIVAL & INTERNATIONAL BATHTUB RACE
Nanaimo Harbor, Nanaimo, 250-753-7223; www.bathtubbing.com
This festival is highlighted by a 36-mile bathtub race. The festival begins a few days prior to the race.
Late July.

VANCOUVER ISLAND EXHIBITION
2300 Bowen Road, Nanaimo, 250-758-3247; www.viex.ca
For more than 100 years, this annual fair has attracted tens of thousands of visitors each year for beautiful artwork, baked goodies and prize-winning livestock.
August.

WHERE TO STAY
★★★COAST BASTION INN
11 Bastion St., Nanaimo, 250-753-6601, 800-716-6199; www.coasthotels.com
This downtown high-rise hotel offers views of Nanaimo Harbor and nearby islands from every guest room. Its location is convenient to harbor-front shops, galleries, restaurants and the B.C. Ferry terminal. After a busy day, Minnoz Restaurant is a great place for a delicious meal, and the menu offers traditional West Coast cuisine. The bar also offers a light tapas menu.
179 rooms. Restaurant, bar. Business center. Fitness center. Pets accepted.
$151-250

★★★CROWN ISLE RESORT
399 Clubhouse Drive, Courtenay, 250-703-5050, 888-338-8439; www.crownisle.com
The Crown Isle course meets the needs and playing levels of both novice and seasoned golfers. Accommodations include fairway rooms, one- and two-bedroom villas and loft villas. The resort is close to the nearby Aquatics Centre and Fifth Street shopping district as well as beaches and hiking.
56 rooms. Restaurant, bar. Fitness center. Golf. $151-250

★★★KINGFISHER OCEANSIDE RESORT & SPA
4330 S. Island Highway, Courtenay, 250-338-1323, 800-663-7929; www.kingfisherspa.com
Located on wooded grounds in Comox Valley, the Kingfisher has a heated outdoor pool, a sauna, canoe and kayak rentals, and nearby golf. The spa offers many services. For a quiet dinner, guests can head to the resort's dining room, the Kingfisher Restaurant, where West Coast cuisine is served and accented by views of Hartley Bay.
64 rooms. Restaurant, bar. Business center. Fitness center. Pool. Spa. Pets accepted. $61-150

WHERE TO EAT
★★THE MAHLE HOUSE RESTAURANT
2104 Hemer Road, Nanaimo, 250-722-3621; www.mahlehouse.ca
International. Dinner. Closed Monday-Tuesday. Reservations recommended.
$36-85

PENTICTON
See also Kamloops
Situated between the beautiful Okanagan and Skaha Lakes on fertile orchard land and rolling hills, this valley town is famous for summer heat, beaches, lakes, spectacular natural scenery, Canada's beast of legend Ogopogo, and the Ironman Canada Triathlon.

WHAT TO SEE
PENTICTON MUSEUM
785 Main St., Penticton, 250-490-2451; www.penticton.ca
Collection of Salish artifacts; taxidermy, ghost town and pioneer exhibits. Changing exhibits. At 1099 Lakeshore Drive West are two historic 1914 steamships: *SS Sicamous*, a 200-foot sternwheeler, and *SS Naramata*, a 90-foot steam tug.
Admission: donation. September-June, Tuesday-Saturday 10 a.m.-5 p.m.; July-August, Monday-Saturday 10 a.m.-5 p.m.

SUMMERLAND RESEARCH STATION ORNAMENTAL GARDENS
4200 Highway 97, Summerland, 250-494-7711; www.summerlandornamentalgardens.org
Enjoy the beautiful display of ornamental gardens, a great canyon view and picnicking at this station.
Daily 8 a.m.-sunset.

SPECIAL EVENTS
IRONMAN CANADA CHAMPIONSHIP TRIATHLON
416 Westminster Ave., Penticton; www.ironman.ca
This triathalon is the qualifier for the Hawaiian Ironman.
Late August.

OKANAGAN WINE FESTIVALS
1304 Ella St., Penticton, 250-861-6654; www.owfs.com
These wine fstivals feature wine tastings, grape stomping, seminars and dinners. They take place at various locations around the Okanagan Valley. August.

PACIFIC NORTHWEST ELVIS FESTIVAL
Okanagan Lake Park, Penticton, 800-663-5052; www.pentictonelvisfestival.com
If you love Elvis, this is the fest for you. There are tribute shows, judged performances, impromptu entertainment, souvenir booths and more.
Late June.

PEACH FESTIVAL

Okanagan Park, Penticton, 250-487-9709, 800-663-5052; www.peachfest.com

This five-day event celebrating the peach harvest has been taking place since 1947. Festivities include a parade, live entertainment, square dancing, a fireworks display, and arts and crafts exhibits. Families especially love Kiddies Day, which features events and activities created with youngsters in mind. Mid-August.

WHERE TO STAY

★★★PENTICTON LAKESIDE RESORT AND CONFERENCE CENTER

21 Lakeshore Drive W., Penticton, 250-493-8221, 800-663-9400;
www.pentictonlakesideresort.com

This resort and conference center is located on the southern shore of Lake Okanagan. The hotel is close to local attractions and offers outdoor packages. Enjoy a meal at the onsite Barking Parrot, a waterfront bar and club. 203 rooms. Restaurant, bar. Fitness center. Pool. Pets accepted. Casino. $151-250

VANCOUVER

See also Vancouver, Vancouver Island, Victoria

Surrounded by the blue waters of the Strait of Georgia and backed by the mile-high peaks of the Coast Range, the most mundane of Vancouver moments elicits a gasp at the view—on public transit crossing one of many bridges or from the window of a hotel room, snow-capped peaks tower over the skyline with rainforest adventure and urban escape a short drive away. Aside from having a natural setting unsurpassed on this continent, Vancouver is one of Canada's largest cities—a major seaport, cultural center, tourist spot and gateway to Asia. Vancouver's downtown area is a peninsula on a peninsula that juts out from the rest of the city into Burrard Inlet, making for plentiful urban beaches and marinas.

WHAT TO SEE

ARTS CLUB THEATRE COMPANY

1585 Johnston St., Vancouver, 604-687-1644; www.artsclub.com

Having helped launch the careers of actors Michael J. Fox and Brent Carver, the Arts Club Theatre steals the Vancouver stage spotlight. In addition to its four annual main stage productions at Stanley Theatre *(2750 Granville St.)*, the company mounts four productions at the Granville Island Stage.

BALLET BRITISH COLUMBIA

677 Davie St., Vancouver, 604-732-5003; www.balletbc.com

With a strong company of 15 dancers, this reigns as Vancouver's top dance troupe. Directed by John Alleyne, former dancer with the Stuttgart Ballet and the National Ballet of Canada, the company's repertoire includes dances by famed choreographers such as William Forsythe and John Cranko and commissioned works by Canadian talents. Ballet BC's home stage is the Queen Elizabeth Theatre. November-May.

BC FERRIES

1112 Fort St., Victoria, 250-386-3431, 888-223-3779; www.bcferries.bc.ca

Destinations include Queen Charlotte Islands, Vancouver Island and various spots along the British Columbia coast. Terminals at Horseshoe Bay, north of Vancouver via Trans-Canada Highway 1 and Tsawwassen near U.S. border, south of Vancouver via Highway 99.

BITES-ON SALMON CHARTERS

Bayshore West Marina, 450 Denman St., Vancouver, 604-688-2483, 877-688-2483; www.bites-on.com

Coho, sockeye and chinook salmon school in the waters around Vancouver, which is convenient for urban-bound fishing fans. Granville Island-based Bites-On offers day trips of five or eight hours, during which you can sink a line into the Strait of Georgia on a yacht up to 40 feet long. The charters serve parties of up to 10 people. Other options include day-long or two-day excursions. Peak fishing months are April-October, although charters operate year-round. Boat trips also allow fishermen to spot sea lion, porpoise and whale populations.

BURNABY ART GALLERY

6344 Deer Lake Ave., Burnaby, 604-297-4422; www.burnabyartgallery.ca

This gallery has monthly exhibitions of local, national and international artists. They have a collection of contemporary Canadian works on paper. It is housed in Ceperley Mansion, overlooking Deer Lake and the surrounding gardens.

Admission: free. Tuesday-Friday 10 a.m.-4:30 p.m., Saturday-Sunday noon-5 p.m.

BURNABY VILLAGE MUSEUM

6501 Deer Lake Ave., Burnaby, 604-293-6501; www.burnabyvillagemuseum.ca

This living museum of the 1920s has costumed attendants and more than 30 full-scale buildings with displays and demonstrations.

Admission: adults $12, seniors and children 13-18 $9, children 6-12 $6. May-September, Tuesday-Sunday 11 a.m.-4:30 p.m. Half-price admission on Tuesday.

CAPILANO SUSPENSION BRIDGE

3735 Capilano Road, Vancouver, 604-985-7474; www.capbridge.com

The 136-meter Capilano Suspension Bridge towers precariously 230 feet above the Capilano River gorge. Originally constructed in 1889 and rebuilt in 1956, the wooden bridge is engineered of wire rope cemented at both ends. In addition to the bridge, the surrounding park provides walking trails, gardens, a totem pole collection and audiences with First Nations carvers at work. Arrive early in high season.

Admission: adults $27.95, seniors $25.95, students $21.75, children 6-12 $8.75, children 13-16 $16.65. Year-round; hours vary by season.

THE CENTRE IN VANCOUVER FOR PERFORMING ARTS

777 Homer St., Vancouver, 604-602-0616; www.centreinvancouver.com

Acclaimed Canadian architect Moshe Safdie designed the dramatic Centre in Vancouver with an arched glass façade and, punctuating the entry, a spiraling glass cone. The auditorium seats 1,800 and features major Broadway tours.

CHAN CENTRE FOR THE PERFORMING ARTS

University of British Columbia, 6265 Crescent Road, Vancouver, 604-822-9197; www.chancentre.com

Located in the University of British Columbia district, the Chan houses three venues for theater and music, all of which share the same light-flooded lobby. Built in 1997, the distinctive zinc-clad cylindrical building stands out amid the verdant campus. With superior acoustics, this is one of the best spots in town to hear concerts by touring soloists, UBC musicians and the Vancouver Symphony.

CHINATOWN

Bordered by Hastings, Keefer, Gore and Taylor streets, Vancouver

This downtown area is the nucleus of the third-largest Chinese community in North America (behind San Francisco and New York). At the heart lies the Chinese Market where 100-year-old duck eggs may be purchased andherbalists promise cures with roots and powdered bones. The Dr. Sun Yat-Sen Classical Chinese Garden provides a beautiful centerpiece. Chinese shops display a variety of items ranging from cricket cages to cloisonné vases. Offices of three Chinese newspapers and one of the world's narrowest buildings are located within the community's borders. Resplendent Asian atmosphere offers fine examples of Chinese architecture, restaurants and nightclubs.

CN IMAX THEATRE

201-999 Canada Place, Vancouver, 604-682-4629; www.imax.com/vancouver

Under the white sails that distinguish waterfront Canada Place, CN IMAX screens wide-format documentary films on subjects ranging from space travel to wildlife conservation.
Show times vary; see Web site for information.

THE COMMODORE BALLROOM

868 Granville St., Vancouver, 604-739-4550; www.livenation.com

It's been swinging since the big band era, and the Commodore flaunts its age with brass chandeliers and polished wood stairs. A renovation in 1999 restored its elegance (and kept the spring-loaded dance floor) while modernizing its stage wizardry. U.S. based LiveNation now programs the acts that come through the ballroom, ranging primarily from rock to blues with a smattering of world talent.

CYPRESS MOUNTAIN

Cypress Bowl and Highway 1, Vancouver, 604-419-7669; www.cypressmountain.com

With 52 runs and nine lifts, Cypress Mountain claims the region's highest vertical rise at 2,010 feet. But the ski area's bigger claim to fame are its cross-country skiing facilities, which span 12 miles of groomed trails, nearly five

of which are lit for night gliding. The region's most popular Nordic destination also offers private and group lessons as well as rental equipment. Snowshoers can tramp on designated trails solo or take a guided tour.
December-mid-April; hours vary by season and weather conditions.

DR. SUN-YAT-SEN CLASSICAL CHINESE GARDEN

578 Carrall St., Vancouver, 604-662-3207; www.vancouverchinesegarden.com
Unique to the Western Hemisphere, this garden was originally built in China circa 1492 and transplanted to Vancouver for Expo '86. Guided tours are available daily.
Admission: adults $10, seniors $9, students $8. Year-round; hours vary by season,

ECOMARINE OCEAN KAYAK CENTRE

1668 Duranleau St., Vancouver, Granville Island, 604-689-7575, 888-425-2925;
www.ecomarine.com
To get the full impact of Vancouver's magnificent setting on the coast, troll the waterways under paddle power with a kayak from Ecomarine. The outfitter rents both single and double kayaks at its Granville Island headquarters and at two other outposts at Jericho Beach and English Bay. Tours are available, and first-timers can take a three-hour lesson before getting started. Navigate from placid False Creek to more rugged inlets up the shore.

FORT LANGLEY NATIONAL HISTORIC SITE

23433 Mavis Ave., Fort Langley, 604-513-4777; www.pc.gc.ca
Originally one of a string of the Hudson's Bay Company trading posts across Canada, the Fraser Valley's Fort Langley became the birthplace of modern-day British Columbia with the Crown Colony Proclamation, an act of protection by the British against an American gold rush influx, which was read there in 1858. In addition to preserving the restored buildings, Fort Langley is garrisoned by costumed re-enactors who demonstrate pioneer activities such as blacksmithing and open-fire cooking.
Admission: adults $7.80, seniors $6.55, children 6-16 $3.90. September-late June 10 a.m.-5 p.m.; late June-August 9 a.m.-8 p.m.

GASTOWN

Vancouver, 604-683-5650; www.gastown.org
Vancouver's historic nucleus consists of a series of Victorian buildings rehabbed to shelter an array of shops, clubs and eateries. Among the highlights, the Gastown Steam Clock pipes up every 15 minutes and the Vancouver Police Centennial Museum covers the most notorious local crimes. To fully appreciate the neighborhood, show up for a free tour sponsored by the Gastown Business Improvement Society in Maple Tree Square (2 p.m. daily mid-June-August).

GRANVILLE ISLAND

Beneath the south end of the Granville Street Bridge, Vancouver, 604-666-5784;
www.granvilleisland.bc.ca
A former industrial isle, Granville Island is an urban renewal case study with

markets, shops, homes and entertainment fashioned out of decaying wharf warehouses beginning in the 1970s. Its hub is the Public Market, a prime picnic provisioner teeming with fishmongers, produce-vendors, butchers, cheese shops, bakeries and chef demonstrations. A specialized kids' market and a free outdoor water park (Late May-early September) appeal to children. The Maritime Market on the southwest shore serves as a dock for boat owners as well as those looking to hire a fishing charter, hop on a ferry or rent a kayak. Three Granville Island museums showcase miniature trains, ship models and sport fishing. Dozens of bars and restaurants, many with views back across the water to the downtown skyline, drive the after-dark trade. An art school, artists' studios and several galleries lend bohemian flare to Granville, abetted by several theaters and street musicians.

GRANVILLE ISLAND KIDS' MARKET
1496 Cartwright St., Vancouver, 604-689-8447; www.kidsmarket.ca
Vancouver's open food market turns its third floor into something kids can enjoy. More than 20 children's shops, including eight selling toys and another seven selling clothes, take aim at junior consumers, many of whom, of course, prefer Kids' Market's indoor play area. Strolling clowns and facepainters amplify the carnival-like setting.
Daily 10 a.m.-6 p.m.

GREATER VANCOUVER ZOO
5048 264th St., Aldergrove, 604-856-6825; www.gvzoo.com
Explore 120 acres housing more than 700 animals. Take a miniature train ride or bus tour of the North American Wilds exhibit.
Admission: adults $18, seniors and children 4-15 $14. May-September, daily 9 a.m.-7 p.m.; October-April, daily 9 a.m.-4 p.m.

GROUSE MOUNTAIN
6400 Nancy Greene Way, North Vancouver, 604-986-6262; www.grousemountain.com
For skiing in winter, hiking in summer and sightseeing year-round, Grouse Mountain draws legions of visitors to Vancouver's North Shore. The area's first ski mountain is still its most convenient, with ski and snowboard runs that overlook the metropolis, as well as a skating rink and sleigh rides available. Hikers have loads of trails to choose from, but the one to boast about is the Grouse Grind, a 1.8-mile hike straight up the 3,700-foot peak. The Skyride Gondola takes the easy route up in an eight-minute ride. At the top, all-season attractions include Theater in the Sky, a high-definition aerial film, and several panoramic-view restaurants starring the Strait of Georgia and the twinkling lights of Vancouver.

HASTINGS PARK RACECOURSE
Renfrew and McGill streets, Vancouver, 604-254-1631, 800-677-7702;
www.hastingsracecourse.com
Thoroughbreds run in Vancouver at Hastings Park on the city's east side. Although the lengthy racing season runs late April-early November, most races are held on Saturday and Sunday, with extra meets scheduled for major holidays like Canada Day and Labor Day. Two-dollar bet minimums are

encouraged, while self-service betting terminals patiently acquaint you with the track lingo.

H.R. MACMILLAN SPACE CENTRE

1100 Chestnut St., Vancouver, 604-738-7827; www.hrmacmillanspacecentre.com
One of several museums in Vanier Park tucked between Kitsilano Beach and Granville Island, the MacMillan Space Centre appeals to would-be astronauts with a space flight simulator, planetarium and interactive games. After hours, laser light shows integrate music from the likes of Pink Floyd and Led Zeppelin.
Admission: adults $15, seniors, students, children 5-18 $10.75. Hours vary by season. Closed Monday.

INUIT GALLERY OF VANCOUVER

206 Cambie St., Vancouver, 604-688-7323; www.inuit.com
Immerse yourself in the rich artistic tradition of coastal natives with soapstone sculptures, native prints, ceremonial masks and bentwood boxes. One of Vancouver's best sources for First Nations art, Inuit represents tribes up and down the Pacific Northwest. In the Gastown district, Inuit is a short walk from the convention center and cruise ship terminal.
Monday-Saturday 10 a.m.-6 p.m.

THE LOOKOUT AT HARBOR CENTRE

555 W. Hastings St., Vancouver, 604-689-0421; www.vancouverlookout.com
Glass elevators take you to a 360-degree viewing deck 430 feet above street level where you can also catch a multimedia presentation, historical displays and tours.
Admission: adults $13, seniors $11, students and children 13-18 $9, children 6-12 $6. May-mid-October, daily 8:30 a.m.-10:30 p.m.; Mid-October-April, daily 9 a.m.-9 p.m.

MUSEUM OF ANTHROPOLOGY AT THE UNIVERSITY OF BRITISH COLUMBIA

6393 N.W. Marine Drive, Vancouver, 604-822-5087; www.moa.ubc.ca
Built to reference a First Nations longhouse, the glass and concrete Museum of Anthropology makes a fitting shrine for the art and artifacts of West Coast natives. The Great Hall surrounds visitors with immense totem poles, canoes and feast dishes of the Nisgaa, Gitksan and Haida people, among others. An outdoor sculpture garden sets tribal houses and totem poles, many carved by the best-known contemporary artists, against a backdrop of sea and mountain views. In its mission to explore all the cultures of the world, the MOA also catalogs 600 ceramics works from 15th- to 19th-century Europe.
Admission: adults $12, seniors and students $10. Mid-May-mid-October, daily 10 a.m.-5 p.m., Tuesday until 9 p.m.; early March-mid-May, Wednesday-Sunday 10 a.m.-5 p.m., Tuesday 10 a.m.-9 p.m.

OLD HASTINGS MILL

1575 Alma Road, Vancouver, 604-734-1212
One of the few buildings remaining after the fire of 1886, the structure now

houses indigenous artifacts and memorabilia of Vancouver's first settlers. Mid-June-mid-September, Tuesday-Sunday 11 a.m.- 4 p.m.; Mid-September-November, Saturday-Sunday 1 p.m.-4 p.m.; February-mid-June, Saturday-Sunday 1 p.m.-4 p.m.

ROBSON STREET

The epicenter of Vancouver's street chic, Robson makes a nice window-shopping stroll. A string of shops and sidewalk cafés runs several blocks in either direction from the intersection of Robson and Thurlow streets. Retailers range from the posh Giorgio Armani and Salvatore Ferragamo to the playful Benetton on down to the divine ice cream at Cows. Jewelry stores, chocolatiers and craft galleries round out the offerings.

ROYAL CITY STAR RIVERBOAT CASINO

788 Quayside Drive, New Westminster, 604-519-3660
The late-model paddle wheeler Queen of New Orleans, once stationed on the Mississippi, is now docked on the Fraser River as the Royal City Star. Games of chance include Pai Gow poker, mini baccarat, blackjack, roulette and Caribbean stud poker. Several bars, a deli and a restaurant feed and water patrons.

SAMSON V MARITIME MUSEUM

Westminster Quay, New Westminster 604-522-6891; www.samsonmuseum.org
The last steam-powered paddle wheeler to operate on the Fraser River now functions as a floating museum. Displays focus on the various paddle wheelers and paddle wheeler captains that have worked the river and on river-related activities.
May-June, Saturday-Sunday noon-5 p.m.; July-early September, daily noon-5 p.m.; Early September-mid-October, Saturday-Sunday noon-5 p.m.

SCIENCE WORLD BRITISH COLUMBIA

1455 Quebec St., Vancouver, 604-443-7443; www.scienceworld.bc.ca
The massive, golf ball-shaped Science World attracts both architecture and museum fans. Modeled on the geodesic domes of F. Buckminster Fuller, the aluminum ball was erected for Expo '86 and now houses a science center devoted to interactive exhibits on nature, invention, ecology and optical illusions. A play space with a water table and giant building blocks engages the 3-to-6 set, while the dome-projection Omnimax theater entertains the whole brood.
Admission: adults $18.75, seniors, students and children 13-18 $15.25, children 4-12 $12.75. Monday-Friday 10 a.m.-5 p.m., Saturday-Sunday 10 a.m.-6 p.m.

SPOKES BICYCLE RENTALS

1789 W. Georgia St., Vancouver, 604-688-5141; www.vancouverbikerental.com
Located just across from the Stanley Park entrance on Georgia Street, this cycle shop rents from a vast fleet that includes cruisers, tandems, mountain bikes and hybrid models. Complimentary helmets and locks; hourly, half-day, daily and weekly rental rates.
Daily 9 a.m.-8 p.m.

STANLEY PARK

West end of Georgia Street, Vancouver, 604-681-6728; www.vancouver.ca/parks

One thousand acres of unspoiled British Columbia in the heart of the city, Stanley Park, the largest city park in Canada, is a green haven with few peers. Towering forests of cedar, hemlock and fir spill onto sand beaches, immersing visitors and residents alike in the wild just minutes from the civilized. Park-goers recreate along forest hiking trails, on three beaches and along the 5-mile 1920s vintage seawall, where in-line skaters, runners and cyclists admire skyline and ocean views. Man's hand distinguishes the park in gardens devoted to roses and rhododendrons and in a vivid stand of First Nations totem poles. Providing an appeal for every interest, Stanley Park also hosts the Vancouver Aquarium, Children's Farmyard, Miniature Railway, Theatre Under the Stars and several restaurants.

UBC BOTANICAL GARDEN

6804 S.W. Marine Drive, Vancouver, 604-822-9666; www.ubcbotanicalgarden.org

There are seven separate areas including Asian, native, alpine and food gardens. Nitobe Memorial Garden, an authentic Japanese tea garden, is located behind Asian Centre.

Admission: adults $8, seniors, students and children 13-17 $6. Monday-Friday 9 a.m.-5 p.m., Saturday-Sunday 9:30 a.m.-5:30 p.m.

VANCOUVER AQUARIUM MARINE SCIENCE CENTRE

845 Avison Way, Stanley Park, Vancouver, 604-659-3474; www.vanaqua.org

With inviting, hands-on exhibits, Vancouver Aquarium in sylvan Stanley Park explores the undersea world from the Amazon to Arctic, assembling 300 species of fish. For all its globetrotting interests, the aquarium is a top spot to study the local environment as well. In outdoor pools, graceful beluga whales, frisky sea lions and playful otters prove comfortable with the changeable Pacific Northwest climate. Progeny of salmon released by the aquarium in 1998 from a park river return each winter, roughly November to February, illustrating B.C.'s rich salmon-spawning waterways. Behind-the-scenes tours with trainers provide visitors a glimpse of the marine mammal rescue and rehab program for which the aquarium is lauded.

Admission: adults $28, seniors $22, children 13-18 $22, children 4-12 $18, children 3 and under free. Daily 9:30 a.m.-7 p.m.

VANCOUVER ART GALLERY

750 Hornby St., Vancouver, 604-662-4719; www.vanartgallery.bc.ca

Most visitors bound up to the Vancouver Art Gallery's fourth floor for a look at the largest collection of works by British Columbia's best-known painter Emily Carr. The other galleries in Western Canada's largest art museum, housed in an early 20th-century courthouse, are fantastic—subjects range from Group of Seven landscapes to photo conceptual art.

Admission: adults $20.50, seniors $16, students $15, children 5-12 $7, children 4 and under free. Daily 10 a.m.-5:30 p.m., Tuesday and Thursday until 9 p.m.

VANCOUVER CIVIC THEATRES

649 Cambie St., Vancouver, 604-665-3050; www.city.vancouver.bc.ca/theatres

A symphony orchestra, opera company and many theater groups present productions at this group of three theaters: Queen Elizabeth Theatre, Vancouver Playhouse and Orpheum.

VANCOUVER MARITIME MUSEUM

1905 Ogden Ave., Vancouver, 604-257-8300; www.vancouvermaritimemuseum.com

Built around the St. Roch, the first ship to navigate Canada's Inside Passage from west to east, Vanier Park's Maritime Museum lets seafaring fans explore the 1928 supply ship from the wheelhouse to the captain's quarters. In addition to the series of historic model ships housed inside the museum, several historic crafts are tethered outside its waterfront Heritage Harbour, including two tugs, a rescue boat and the 1927 seiner once featured on Canada's $5 bill.

Admission: adults $10, seniors and children 6-18 $7.50. Mid-May-early September, Tuesday-Saturday 10 a.m.-5 p.m. Sunday noon-5 p.m.; early September-mid-May, daily 10 a.m.-5 p.m.

VANCOUVER MUSEUM

1100 Chestnut St., Vancouver, 604-736-4431; www.vanmuseum.bc.ca

The keeper of city history and another Vanier Park attraction, Vancouver Museum takes a sweeping view of civilization, collecting everything from Egyptian mummies to local vintage swimming togs. In addition to the urban story told in lifelike recreations of an Edwardian parlor, ship's berth and trading post, the museum also examines First Nations artifacts, the contributions of Asian Rim cultures and world history.

Admission: adults $11, seniors and students $9, children 5-17 $7. Daily 10 a.m.-5 p.m., Thursday until 7 p.m. Closed Monday September-June.

VANCOUVER OPERA

835 Cambie St., Vancouver, 604-683-0222; www.vancouveropera.ca

Vancouver Opera stages four productions annually. Established in 1958, the company has hosted a roster of greats, including guest singers Placido Domingo, Joan Sutherland and Marilyn Horne. Performances take place at the Queen Elizabeth Theatre.

VANCOUVER POLICE MUSEUM

240 E. Cordova St., Vancouver, 604-665-3346; www.vancouverpolicemuseum.ca

For fans of the macabre, the Vancouver Police Centennial Museum not only supplies the gruesome details of the city's most lurid crimes but also dramatizes them, crime-scene style. Run by the city's police department, the museum tells the history of local law-keeping and ushers visitors into an eerie mock-forensics laboratory in the former city morgue.

Admission: adults $7, seniors and students $5. Monday-Saturday 9 a.m.-5 p.m.

VANCOUVER SYMPHONY ORCHESTRA

601 Smithe St., Vancouver, 604-876-3434; www.vancouversymphony.ca

Canada's third-largest orchestra, the Vancouver Symphony presents more

than 150 concerts annually, most of them at the ornate Orpheum Theatre. The symphony's featured programs broadly encompass classical, light classical, pops and children's works. Most concerts are on weekends with family-oriented matinees.
September-June.

VANCOUVER TROLLEY COMPANY LTD

875 Terminal Ave., Vancouver, 604-801-5515, 888-451-5581; www.vancouvertrolley.com
Narrated trolley tours to top attractions and neighborhoods throughout the city. Get on and off at designated stops throughout the day.
Price varies by tour; see Web site for information.

VANDUSEN BOTANICAL GARDEN

5251 Oak St., Vancouver, 604-878-9274; www.vandusengarden.org
Approximately 55 acres of flowers and exotic plants. Seasonal displays, mountain views, restaurant.
Prices and schedule varies; see Web site for information.

WINDSURE WINDSURFING SCHOOL

1300 Discovery St., Vancouver, 604-224-0615; www.windsure.com
Head to Jericho Beach to catch the offshore drafts in English Bay aboard a windsurfer. Operating out of the Jericho Sailing Center, this school rents both boards and wetsuits, including rigs suitable for children.
April-October, daily 9 a.m.-8 p.m.

THE YALE HOTEL

1300 Granville St., Vancouver, 604-681-9253; www.theyale.ca
Built in the mid 1880s as a hotel for rough-and-tumble miners, fishermen and loggers, The Yale, prizes its working-class roots and makes a fitting home for the city's best blues club. Past headliners include John Lee Hooker, Clarence "Gatemouth" Brown, Jeff Healey and Jim Byrnes.

YALETOWN

Bounded by Georgia Street, Richards Street, False Creek and Cambie Street.
A former rail yard, Yaletown once held the world record for the most bars per acre. With time and prosperity the redevelopment grew, and the warehouse district is now one of Vancouver's hippest, drawing urban dwellers with an arty bent. The former loading docks along Hamilton and Mainland teem with cafés with umbrella-shaded tables on concrete terraces. Tucked in between are a slew of shops, galleries and clothiers.

SPECIAL EVENTS
ALCAN INTERNATIONAL DRAGON BOAT FESTIVAL

110 Keefer St., Vancouver, 604-688-2382; www.dragonboatbc.ca
Vancouver's considerable Asian community imports an eastern rite in dragon boat racing, the traditional Chinese rain ceremony that is equal parts pageant and competition. But don't tell that to the 100 or so crews that enter the False Creek event paddling boats with dragon figureheads representing the Asian water deity. Bring loads of film to the colorful event, which also features a

Taoist blessing of the fleet, Asian entertainment, crafts and food. Mid-June.

BARD ON THE BEACH SHAKESPEARE FESTIVAL

Vanier Park, Vancouver, 604-739-0559, 877-739-0559; www.bardonthebeach.org
The works of Shakespeare take the outdoor stage at Vanier Park's permanent seasonal theater, Bard on the Beach. Elizabethan-style tents cover the audience and actors, who play against an open backdrop of coastal landscape. The company mounts approximately three plays each summer, performed in repertory with several shows slated daily on two stages.
Late May-September.

CARIBBEAN DAYS FESTIVAL

Waterfront Park, North Vancouver, 604-515-2400; www.caribbeandays.ca
The Trinidad and Tobago Cultural Society of British Columbia throws the province's biggest island jump-up at this North Vancouver park. Its highlight parade kicks off Saturday morning with a slow, carnival-like promenade of bands and costumes, drawing crowds of pan-Caribbean expats. Head to the park festival grounds for calypso, steel drum, soca and reggae music, as well as island food and crafts.
Late July.

HSBC CELEBRATION OF LIGHT

English Bay, Vancouver, 604-642-6835; www.celebration-of-light.com
On four nights spread over two weeks, pyrotechnic fans gasp as the world's best fireworks designers compete for bragging rights in Vancouver's Celebration of Light. Teams from China, Canada and Spain have competed on the basis of originality, rhythm, musical synchronization and color, leading up to the grand finale night on which all competitors restage their shows. For best viewing, park your beach towel along English Bay at Stanley or Vanier Parks, Kitsilano or Jericho Beaches. Come prepared for very large crowds, especially for the finale.
Late July-early August.

HYACK FESTIVAL

First and Third Avenues, New Westminster, 604-522-6894; www.hyack.bc.ca
This festival commemorates the birthday of Queen Victoria. Held yearly since 1971, it features a 21-gun salute, band concerts, a parade, carnival and sports events.
Ten days in mid-May.

PACIFIC NATIONAL EXHIBITION ANNUAL FAIR

Hastings Park, 2901 E. Hastings St., Vancouver, 604-253-2311; www.pne.bc.ca
The second-largest fair in Canada, there are hundreds of free exhibits, major theme events, concerts, thrill shows, a world championship timber show, a petting zoo, thoroughbred horse racing, commercial exhibits, a roller coaster, agricultural shows, livestock competitions and horticultural exhibits.
Mid-August-early September.

THEATRE UNDER THE STARS

Stanley Park, Malkin Bowl, Vancouver, 604-684-2787; www.tuts.ca

Towering forests of Douglas firs surround the 1,200-seat open-air Malkin Bowl Theater in Stanley Park, binding art and nature in nightly performances. The short summer season generally presents two shows on alternating nights, an annual repertory that hews to comedies and musicals. July-August.

VANCOUVER FRINGE FESTIVAL

1398 Cartwright St., Vancouver, 604-257-0350; www.vancouverfringe.com

From comedies to musical acts to full-on drama, Vancouver Fringe trains the spotlight on fledgling theater troupes who come from around the globe to participate in the 11-day annual arts festival. Modeled on the oft-copied fringe festival in Edinburgh, Scotland, the Canadian organization mounts about 100 productions in a variety of venues including theaters, garages and even an Aquabus.

Early-mid-September.

VANCOUVER INTERNATIONAL CHILDREN'S FESTIVAL

Vanier Park, Vancouver, 604-708-5655; www.childrensfestival.ca

Though the seven-day slate of events programmed by the annual Children's Festival aims at school group audiences, its talent warrants broader attention. In a program ranging from music to theater, the performance lineup for young audiences may include Japanese dancers, Australia's teen troupe Flying Fruit Fly Circus, Aboriginal storytellers and clown companies. Aside from shows, the festival engages kids with more than two-dozen hands-on art activities.

Mid-May.

VANCOUVER INTERNATIONAL JAZZ FESTIVAL

316 W. Sixth Ave., Vancouver, 604-872-5200, 888-438-5299; www.coastaljazz.ca

The Coastal Jazz and Blues Society runs this annual jazz festival over a 10-day span in several venues, both indoors and outdoors. Past performers range from greats such as the late Dizzy Gillespie to New Age interpreters such as Pat Metheny to crooners such as Diana Krall. In addition to the main event, CJBS also sponsors 40 concerts between September and May each year (its 24-hour jazz hotline delivers a useful "what's-on-now" club report year-round).

Late June-early July.

WHERE TO STAY

★★★COAST PLAZA HOTEL AND SUITES

1763 Comox St., Vancouver, 604-688-7711, 800-716-6199; www.coasthotels.com

This tower hotel is located just blocks from Stanley Park in Vancouver's West End, overlooking English Bay. Because of the range of amenities offered here, this hotel is a nice choice for the business or leisure traveler. Many suites have kitchenettes, and there's a mall on the lower floors of the hotel. 269 rooms. Restaurant, bar. Business center. Fitness center. Pool. Pets accepted. $251-350

★★★DELTA VANCOUVER SUITES

550 W. Hastings St., Vancouver, 604-689-8188, 888-890-3222;
www.deltavancouversuites.ca

This high-rise, all-suite hotel is located in the middle of downtown Vancouver and just minutes from Gastown, Yaletown, Chinatown, Robson Square, Canada Place, Stanley Park and Kitsilano Beach.
225 rooms. Restaurant, bar. Business center. Fitness center. Spa. Pets accepted. $251-350

★★★ENGLISH BAY INN

1968 Comox St., Vancouver, 604-683-8002, 866-683-8002; www.englishbayinn.com

This relaxing, 20th-century Tudor-style escape is a short walk from the West End's Stanley Park and shops and restaurants on Denman Street. All guest rooms feature Ralph Lauren linens, featherbeds, antiques, reproductions and some rooms have fireplaces. Take some time to lounge in the back garden.
6 rooms. Complimentary breakfast. $151-250

★★★THE FAIRMONT HOTEL VANCOUVER

900 W. Georgia St., Vancouver, 604-684-3131, 866-540-4452; www.fairmont.com

The Fairmont Hotel echoes the vibrancy of its home city. Grand and inviting, it has been a local favorite since 1939, when it opened to celebrate the royal visit of King George VI and Queen Elizabeth. The décor gives a nod to the past, but the dining and entertainment venues are cutting edge. The building is also home to high-end boutiques such as Louis Vuitton and St. John.
556 rooms. Restaurant, bar. Business center. Fitness center. Pool. Spa. Pets accepted. $151-250

★★★THE FAIRMONT VANCOUVER AIRPORT

3111 Grant McConachie Way, Vancouver, 604-207-5200, 866-540-4441;
www.fairmont.com

This stylish hotel is located inside the airport and features contemporary rooms and suites. Airport dining is elevated to new levels at the Globe@ YVR, where you can watch approaching and departing jets while enjoying cosmopolitan cuisine.
392 rooms. Restaurant, bar. Business center. Fitness center. Pool. Spa. Pets accepted. $151-250

★★★THE FAIRMONT WATERFRONT

900 Canada Place Way, Vancouver, 604-691-1991, 866-540-4509; www.fairmont.com

With state-of-the-art conference facilities, a comprehensive health club and fine dining, this hotel offers just about everything a business or leisure traveler would need. It is located beside an enclosed walkway to the Vancouver Convention and Exhibition Center, the Cruise Ship Terminal, and is within walking distance to Stanley Park and Gastown.
489 rooms. Restaurant, bar. Business center. Fitness center. Pool. Pets accepted. $251-350

★★★★FOUR SEASONS HOTEL VANCOUVER

791 W Georgia St., Vancouver, 604-689-9333; www.fourseasons.com/vancouver

Located downtown in the commercial and cultural hub of the city, the Four Seasons Hotel Vancouver is a home-away-from-home for both business and leisure travelers. Families are welcome—children will love the indoor/outdoor pool. In addition to 24-hour room service, the hotel houses YEW restaurant + bar, headed by Executive Chef Oliver Beckert and featuring a contemporary raw bar, more than 150 choices of wine and a Latin-inspired Sunday brunch.

372 rooms. Restaurant, bar. Business center. Fitness center. Pool. Spa. $251-350

★★GEORGIAN COURT HOTEL

773 Beatty St., Vancouver, 604-682-5555, 800-663-1155; www.georgiancourt.com

180 rooms. Restaurant, bar. Business center. Fitness center. Spa. Pets accepted. $151-250

★★HAMPTON INN & SUITES

111 Robson St., Vancouver, 604-602-1008, 877-602-1008; www.hamptoninnvancouver.com

132 rooms. Restaurant, bar. Complimentary breakfast. Business center. Fitness center. $151-250

★★★HILTON VANCOUVER METROTOWN

6083 McKay Ave., Burnaby, 604-438-1200, 800-445-8667; www.hiltonvancouver.com

The Hilton Vancouver Metrotown is located in suburban Burnaby, a 20-minute drive from downtown and the airport, in the Metrotown Shopping Mall complex. The SkyTrain light rail station is across the street and offers high-speed travel to downtown. After a busy day, head to the hotel's small outdoor area with a lap pool, children's pool, whirlpool and sundeck for some relaxation.

283 rooms. Restaurant, bar. Business center. Fitness center. Pets accepted. $151-250

★★★HYATT REGENCY VANCOUVER

655 Burrard St., Vancouver, 604-683-1234, 800-233-1234; www.vancouver.hyatt.com

This hotel is located within the Royal Centre shopping complex, which also includes two levels of shops, restaurants and a SkyTrain station. After checking in, take a dip in the pool, or get a bite to eat in one of the three restaurants. Then, relax in the guest rooms which all feature pillow-top mattresses and flat-screen televisions.

644 rooms. Restaurant, bar. Business center. Fitness center. Pool. $151-250

★★★LE SOLEIL HOTEL

567 Hornby St., Vancouver, 604-632-3000, 877-632-3030; www.lesoleilhotel.com

In the heart of the city's financial and business districts sits this charming boutique hotel. The lobby boasts 30-foot gilded ceilings and a Louis XVI-style collection of imported Italian furniture. Complimentary bottled water and fruit upon arrival are welcome surprises, and the property's restaurant offers a variety of luxury comfort food.

119 rooms. Restaurant, bar. Business center. Pets accepted. $151-250

★★★METROPOLITAN HOTEL

645 Howe St., Vancouver, 604-687-1122, 800-667-2300; www.metropolitan.com/vanc

Located in the heart of Vancouver's downtown, the hotel is convenient to local sightseeing. The guest rooms are modern and spacious, with marble washrooms, down duvets and Frette linens, and some have Juliet balconies. Enjoy a dinner at the Diva at the Met, with its international and Pacific Northwest-influenced cuisine.

197 rooms. Restaurant, bar. Business center. Fitness center. Pool. $61-150

★★★OPUS HOTEL

322 Davie St., Vancouver, 604-642-6787, 866-642-6787; www.opushotel.com

This hip boutique hotel blends contemporary design with great service. Located in the Yaletown area, it is close to all local attractions. Guest rooms feature unique décor that's modern and minimalist without losing warmth and comfort. The hotel is home to modern bistro, Elixir, and hot spot, Opus Bar.

96 rooms. Restaurant, bar. Business center. Fitness center. Spa. Pets accepted. $61-150

★★★PACIFIC PALISADES HOTEL

1277 Robson St., Vancouver, 604-688-0461, 800-663-1815;
www.pacificpalisadeshotel.com

This hotel underwent a total makeover in 2001 and now earns its reputation as one of the trendiest home bases on the legendary Robson Street. Fitness-minded guests can take advantage of complimentary yoga kits and a designated yoga channel, with personal trainers available for private yoga and Pilates sessions.

232 rooms. Restaurant, bar. Business center. Fitness center. Pool. Spa. Pets accepted. $$$

★★★PAN PACIFIC VANCOUVER

300-999 Canada Place, Vancouver, 604-662-8111, 800-937-1515; www.panpacific.com

Awe-inspiring waterfront views take center stage at Vancouver's Pan Pacific Hotel, located minutes from some of the city's best shopping. Luxurious guest rooms overlook unobstructed mountains and ocean, and some feature private balconies. Three distinctive restaurants offer international cuisine.

504 rooms. Restaurant, bar. Business center. Fitness center. Pool. Spa. Pets accepted. $251-350

★★★RENAISSANCE VANCOUVER HARBORSIDE HOTEL

1133 W. Hastings, Vancouver, 604-689-9211, 800-905-8582;
www.renaissancevancouver.com

Located on the waterfront and close to local attractions, this is a great spot for both leisure and business travelers. Some rooms offer a balcony and all rooms have duvets and feather pillows. Enjoy a meal and the views at Patina Restaurant, or dinner and a drink at the Coal Harbour Bar.

442 rooms. Restaurant, bar. Business center. Fitness center. Pool. Pets accepted. $151-250

★★★★SHANGRI-LA HOTEL

1128 West Georgia St., Vancouver, 604-689-1120; www.shangri-la.com

The Shangri-La Hotel makes its North American debut in a grandiose way by occupying fifteen floors of the tallest building in downtown Vancouver. The hotel oozes sleek sophistication. The spacious rooms and suites are decadently decorated with warm beige and golden tones as well as contain contemporary Asian-influenced furniture. All guestrooms feature a 42-inch flat-screen TV, CD/DVD player with surround sound, and Nespresso coffee machine. Most suites have a private balcony in which to absorb stunning views of the city. MARKET by Chef Jean-Georges offers an unforgettable fine dining experience by offering four unique "destinations" for diners to choose a table.

119 rooms. Restaurant, bar. Business center. Fitness center. Spa. $350 and up

★★SHERATON VANCOUVER GUILDFORD HOTEL

15269 104th Ave., Surrey, 604-582-9288; www.sheratonguildford.com

279 rooms. Restaurant, bar. Business center. Fitness center. Pool. Pets accepted. $61-150

★★★★THE SUTTON PLACE HOTEL VANCOUVER

845 Burrard St, Vancouver, 604-682-5511, 866-378-8866;
www.vancouver.suttonplace.com

Located in the business and shopping core of downtown Vancouver, the hotel offers guest rooms that exude a European flavor, while the dining and lounge areas feature comforting old-world décor. Business travelers are pampered with the business center providing state-of-the-art technology. The hotel offers a serene spa, an indoor swimming pool under a big sunroof and a fitness center.

396 rooms. Restaurant, bar. Business center. Fitness center. Pool. Spa. Pets accepted. $251-350

★★★WEDGEWOOD HOTEL

845 Hornby St., Vancouver, 604-689-7777, 800-663-0666;
www.wedgewoodhotel.com

Tradition abounds at this independent boutique hotel, which features rooms decorated with classic furnishings and luxurious fabrics. Bacchus, the onsite restaurant, offers a full menu plus sumptuous weekend brunch menus and traditional high tea is served from 2 to 4 p.m. daily.

83 rooms. Restaurant, bar. Business center. Fitness center. Spa. $251-350

★★★THE WESTIN GRAND

433 Robson St., Vancouver, 604-602-1999, 888-680-9393;
www.westingrandvancouver.com

All of Vancouver is within reach of the Westin Grand. Sleek and stylish, this property introduces visitors to the hip side of this western Canadian city. Guests never leave behind the comforts of home here, where all rooms feature well-stocked kitchenettes. The hotel caters to the sophisticated, and many services are offered 24 hours daily. Guests can dine on Pacific Rim dishes at the Aria Restaurant & Lounge.

207 rooms. Restaurant, bar. Business center. Fitness center. Pool. Spa. $151-250

WHERE TO EAT
★★AQUA RIVA
200 Granville St., Vancouver, 604-683-5599; www.aquariva.com
Pacific Northwest. Lunch (Monday-Friday), dinner. Reservations recommended. $36-85

★★★BACCHUS
845 Hornby St., Vancouver, 604-608-5319, 800-663-0666; www.wedgewoodhotel.com
This luxurious restaurant is adorned with richly upholstered furniture, décor from Venice and of course, a large canvas depicting Bacchus, Greek god of wine and revelry. The menu spotlights local ingredients, including seafood, organic chicken and Alberta beef.
French. Breakfast, lunch, dinner, late-night, brunch. Reservations recommended. $36-85

★★★BEACH HOUSE
Dundarave Pier, 150 25th St., West Vancouver, 604-922-1414;
www.atthebeachhouse.com
Originally built in 1912, this waterfront restaurant affords diners beautiful views of Burrard Inlet. The rustic wood shingled building provides a cozy setting where diners can sample dishes such as seared trout with almondine sauce and pan roasted sablefish with maple syrup and soy glaze.
Seafood, steak. Lunch, dinner, Sunday brunch. Reservations recommended. Outdoor seating. $36-85

★★★★BISHOP'S
2183 W. Fourth Ave., Vancouver, 604-738-2025; www.bishopsonline.com
Intimate, modern and airy, with a loft-like yet upscale feel, this chic duplex restaurant is known for West Coast continental cuisine and has a menu that emphasizes seasonal, organic produce and locally sourced seafood. It isn't uncommon to spy celebrities nibbling on these delicious culinary gems. For those who like to sample lots of different wines with dinner, Bishop's offers a nice selection of wines by the glass and an outstanding range of wines by the half-bottle. In addition to being a visionary chef, owner John Bishop is a gracious host.
Seafood. Lunch, dinner. Reservations recommended. Outdoor seating. Bar. $36-85

★★★C RESTAURANT
2-1600 Howe St., Vancouver, 604-681-1164; www.crestaurant.com
Located along the boardwalk running under the Granville Building and overlooking the marina, this contemporary seafood house offers a raw bar, an enclosed patio area and more than 900 wines. The sleek, modern décor is a nice complement to the inventive presentations of the fresh, inventive cuisine. Sample dishes such as bacon glazed scallops with spinach and tarragon puree, and seared Albacore tuna with red wine gastrique.
Seafood. Lunch (Monday-Friday), dinner. Reservations recommended. Outdoor seating. $36-85$

★★CAFE DE PARIS
751 Denman St., Vancouver, 604-687-1418
French. Dinner. Closed Sunday. Reservations recommended. $36-85

★★THE CANNERY
2205 Commissioner St., Vancouver, 604-254-9606, 877-254-9606;
www.canneryseafood.com
Seafood. Lunch (Tuesday-Friday), dinner, Saturday-Sunday brunch. Reservations recommended. $36-85

★★★CINCIN RISTORANTE
1154 Robson St., Vancouver, 604-688-7338; www.cincin.net
Located upstairs in a two-story building on trendy Robson Street, this Italian dining room has a mellow Tuscan atmosphere. A wood-fired brick oven emits a wonderful aroma throughout the restaurant and the extensive wine list offers the perfect complement to any meal.
Italian. Dinner, late-night. Reservations recommended. Outdoor seating. Bar. $36-85

★★CLOUD 9
1400 Robson St., Vancouver, 604-687-0511; www.cloud9restaurant.ca
Seafood, steak. Breakfast, dinner, late-night. Reservations recommended. Bar. $36-85

★★DELILAH'S
1789 Comox St., Vancouver, 604-687-3424; www.delilahs.ca
Continental, seafood.Dinner. Closed Monday. Reservations recommended. $36-85

★★DOCKSIDE BREWING COMPANY
1253 Johnston St., Granville Island, Vancouver, 604-685-7070;
www.docksidebrewing.com
Seafood. Breakfast, lunch, dinner, Sunday brunch. Reservations recommended. Outdoor seating. $36-85

★★★FISH HOUSE IN STANLEY PARK
8901 Stanley Park Drive, Vancouver, 604-681-7275, 877-681-7275;
www.fishhousestanleypark.com
This Vancouver landmark seafood restaurant favored by both locals and tourists is located in Vancouver's West End at the south entrance to beautiful Stanley Park. The leafy setting is a relaxing spot to tuck into steamed mussels, maple-glazed salmon or cedar-planked arctic char.
Seafood. Lunch, dinner, Saturday-Sunday brunch. Reservations recommended. Outdoor seating. $36-85

★★★FIVE SAILS
410-999 Canada Place, Vancouver, 604-844-2855, 800-937-1515;
www.fivesails.ca
Exceptional views of the harbor and neighboring mountains, a talented kitchen that produces creative Northwest/Asian fusion food and good service make this restaurant a favorite destination among locals. The affable staff can

make recommendations for local or international wines to pair with the fresh seafood on the menu.

Seafood, steak. Dinner. Reservations recommended. $86 and up

★★★GOTHAM STEAKHOUSE AND COCKTAIL BAR
615 Seymour St., Vancouver, 604-605-8282; www.gothamsteakhouse.com

It's worth the splurge for truly excellent steaks, smooth, friendly service and a sleek crowd at this downtown destination. The dining room, a converted bank, is modern and opulent with main floor and balcony dining.

Steak, seafood. Dinner. Reservations recommended. Outdoor seating. Bar. $36-85

★★★HART HOUSE RESTAURANT
6664 Deer Lake Ave., Burnaby, 604-298-4278; www.harthouserestaurant.com

Known as having some of the best steaks in the Vancouver area, the Hart House Restaurant also offers one of the most charming dining atmospheres. The imaginative menu takes its inspiration from the flavors native to countries around the globe. In pleasant weather, the outdoor patio opens up to let diners enjoy the fresh air and views of Deer Lake.

Steak, seafood. Lunch (Tuesday-Friday), dinner, Sunday brunch. Closed Monday. Reservations recommended. Outdoor seating. $16-35

★★★IL GIARDINO DI UMBERTO RISTORANTE
1382 Hornby St., Vancouver, 604-669-2422; www.umberto.com

This rustic room, housed in a historic Victorian building, transports its young, established fans to a Tuscan villa. Come for the fresh pastas, grilled steaks and transcendent desserts, but linger over the elegant atmosphere and attention of the staff.

Italian. Lunch (Monday-Friday), dinner. Closed Sunday. Reservations recommended. Outdoor seating. $36-85

★★IMPERIAL CHINESE SEAFOOD RESTAURANT
355 Burrard St., Vancouver, 604-688-8191; www.imperialrest.com

Cantonese, Chinese. Lunch, dinner. Reservations recommended. Bar. $36-85

★★★★LA BELLE AUBERGE
4856 48th Ave., Ladner, 604-946-7717; www.labelleauberge.com

If you crave the glorious food of France's best kitchens, opt for a 30-minute drive from Vancouver to Ladner and enjoy dinner at La Belle Auberge. Set in a charming 1902 country inn, the restaurant comprises five intimate, antique-filled salon-style dining rooms. The kitchen, led by chef and owner Bruno Marti, a masterful culinary technician, offers spectacular, authentic French cuisine.

French. Dinner. Closed Sunday-Monday. Reservations recommended. Outdoor seating. $36-85

★★★LA TERRAZZA
1088 Cambie St., Vancouver, 604-899-4449; www.laterrazza.ca

This Italian restaurant feels like a classic villa with burnt-sienna walls, murals, massive windows and vaulted ceilings, as well as an impressive wine cellar. The menu features classic Italian dishes, from taglierini with sautéed prawns to pan-seared Canadian duck.

Italian. Dinner. Reservations recommended. Outdoor seating. $36-85

★★★LE CROCODILE

100-909 Burrard St., Vancouver, 604-669-4298; www.lecrocodilerestaurant.com

A wonderful dress-up place, this downtown French bistro is worth a trip for the food alone. Classically trained chef Michel Jacob creates classic dishes such as Dover sole with beurre blanc, and pan-seared veal sweetbreads with black truffle foie gras cream sauce. The extensive wine list spotlights French bottles that pair perfectly with the menu.

French. Lunch (Monday-Friday), dinner. Closed Sunday. Reservations recommended. Outdoor seating. $36-85

★★★★LUMIÈRE

2551 W. Broadway, Vancouver, 604-739-8185; www.lumiere.ca

Lumière has made a name for itself for being a stunning and elegant restaurant that offers European-style dining of the most divine order. After an extensive renovation, Lumiere is now open and even better than before. Executive Chef Dale MacKay recently partnered with New York-based chef Daniel Boulud to provide a menu filled with innovative dishes to please your palette. Choose from a five-course tasting menu ($115), a five-course vegetarian tasting menu ($115) or the seven-course chef's menu ($155), all of which offer wine pairings. Besides the menu, the dining room has been revamped with warm neutral tones of browns and greens throughout and a sophisticated retro style.

French. Dinner. Reservations recommended. Bar. $86 and up

★★MONK MCQUEENS

601 Stamps Landing, Vancouver, 604-877-1351; www.monkmcqueens.com

Seafood. Lunch, dinner, Saturday-Sunday brunch. Outdoor seating. $36-85

★★PROVENCE MEDITERRANEAN GRILL

4473 W. 10th Ave., Vancouver, 604-222-1980; www.provencevancouver.com

Mediterranean. Lunch (Monday-Friday), dinner, Saturday-Sunday brunch. Reservations recommended. Outdoor seating. $16-35

★★★QUATTRO ON FOURTH

2611 W. Fourth Ave., Vancouver, 604-734-4444; www.quattroonfourth.com

This popular Italian restaurant, located in the heart of Kitsilano near downtown, has an excellent selection of Italian entrées paired with fantastic wines. Sample fresh-made pastas and traditional grilled meats in an elegant setting.

Italian, Mediterranean. Dinner. Reservations recommended. Outdoor seating. $36-85

★★★RAINCITY GRILL

1193 Denman St., Vancouver, 604-685-7337; www.raincitygrill.com

Located in Vancouver's West End, this eclectic, fine dining restaurant has views across a small park to English Bay. The delicious à la carte and chef's tasting menus draw almost exclusively on organic, regional sources. Don't miss brunch on Saturday and Sunday.

Seafood, steak. Lunch (Monday-Friday), dinner, Saturday-Sunday brunch. Reservations recommended. Outdoor seating. $36-85

★★★SAVEUR
850 Thurlow St., Vancouver, 604-688-1633; www.saveurrestaurant.com
Located a block off Robson in downtown Vancouver, this warm and intimate French restaurant is the perfect spot for a special occasion celebration.
French. Lunch (Monday-Friday), dinner. Closed Sunday. Reservations recommended. $36-85

★★★SEASONS IN THE PARK
W. 33rd Avenue and Main Street, Queen Elizabeth Park, Vancouver, 604-874-8008, 800-632-9422; www.vancouverdine.com/seasons/home.html
This restaurant was the site of a Clinton-Yeltsin summit in 1993—come for the history and stay for the incredible international menu (and the view). Located on top of a hill in beautiful Queen Elizabeth Park in suburban Vancouver, there are magnificent views from the tiered dining room and attractive heated terrace.
International. Lunch (Monday-Friday), dinner, Saturday-Sunday brunch. Reservations recommended. Outdoor seating. $36-85

★★TEAHOUSE AT STANLEY PARK
Fergson Point, Stanley Park Drive, Vancouver, 604-669-3281, 800-280-9893; www.sequoiarestaurants.com
International. Lunch, dinner, Saturday-Sunday brunch. Reservations recommended. Outdoor seating. $36-85

★★SUN SUI WAH SEAFOOD RESTAURANT
3888 Main St., Vancouver, 604-872-8822, 866-872-8822; www.sunsuiwah.com
Chinese. Lunch, dinner. Reservations recommended. $16-35

★★TOJO'S
1133 W. Broadway, Vancouver, 604-872-8050; www.tojos.com
Japanese. Dinner. Closed Sunday. Reservations recommended. Outdoor seating. $16-35

★★TOP OF VANCOUVER
555 W. Hastings St., Vancouver, 604-669-2220; www.topofvancouver.com
International. Lunch (Monday-Saturday), dinner, Sunday brunch. Reservations recommended. $36-85

★TRUE CONFECTIONS
866 Denman St., Vancouver, 604-682-1292; www.trueconfections.ca
Desserts. Lunch, dinner, late-night. $16-35

★★★VILLA DEL LUPO
869 Hamilton St., Vancouver, 604-688-7436
Tiny white lights and sparkling bay windows attract attention at this classic

Italian restaurant housed in a charming, turn-of-the-century home. The menu highlights different regions of Italy, using fresh, local ingredients in dishes such as osso bucco with risotto Milanese.

Italian. Dinner. Reservations recommended. $36-85

★★★★WEST

2881 Granville St., Vancouver, 604-738-8938;
www.westrestaurant.com

West is one of those sleek, heavenly spots that make sipping cocktails for hours on end an easy task. It is an ideal choice for gourmets in search of an inventive, eclectic meal, as well as those who crave local flavor and seasonal ingredients. Located in Vancouver's chic South Granville neighborhood, West offers diners the chance to sample the vibrant cuisine of the Pacific Northwest region. Stunning, locally sourced ingredients are on display here thanks to the masterful kitchen.

Seafood, steak. Dinner. Reservations recommended. Bar. $36-85

SPA

★★★★CHI SPA AT SHANGRI-LA HOTEL

1128 West Georgia St., Vancouver, 604-689-1120; www.shangri-la.com

Relaxation is key at CHI. A self-proclaimed "spa within a spa," the concept is based on the five Chinese elements: metal, water, wood, fire and earth. There are five individual suites representing each element of tailored treatments. A consultation is performed upon arrival to determine which element best suites your needs. If rejuvenation is what you seek, try the Vitality Ritual, which is a 4-hour Himalayan experience that includes a bath therapy, mud wrap, healing stone massage and mountain Tsampa rub. The CHI skin polish is also a must-have treatment. The mineral salt and citrus oil scrub will leave your skin glowing and silky smooth.

VANCOUVER ISLAND

See also Vancouver, Victoria

The largest of the Canadian Pacific Coast Islands, Vancouver Island stretches almost 300 miles along the shores of Western British Columbia. It is easily accessible by ferry from the city of Vancouver as well as from other parts of the province and the state of Washington. With most of its population located in the larger cities on the eastern coast, much of the island remains a wilderness and is very popular with outdoor enthusiasts.

The Vancouver Island Mountain Range cuts down the middle of the island, providing spectacular snowcapped scenery, fjords and rocky coastal cliffs. The southern portion of the island contains more than half the island's total population and includes Victoria, British Columbia's capital. Here, the countryside resembles rural Britain with its rolling farmland, rows of hedges and colorful flower gardens. Travelers go island-hopping among the Gulf Islands, located in the sheltered waters of the Strait of Georgia between the big island and the mainland. These beautiful, isolated islands are a mecca for artists, cottagers and tourists alike.

Nanaimo is the dominant town, an area known for excellent sandy beaches and beautiful parks. In the center of the island is the Alberni Valley, which includes several parks with excellent swimming and fishing and one of the tallest waterfalls in North America (Della Falls). From Port Alberni, the mountain highway winds its way to the peaceful fishing village of Tofino, the rugged northern boundary of the Long Beach section of the Pacific Rim National Park.

WHAT TO SEE
BC FOREST DISCOVERY CENTRE
North of Victoria, Highway 1, near Duncan, 250-715-1113; www.bcforestmuseum.com
This centre fatures a logging museum with old logging machines and tools as well as hands-on exhibits, a logging camp, a 1 mile (2.4 kilometers) steam railway ride, sawmill, films, and a nature walk.
Admission: adults $14, seniors and students $12, children $9. Hours vary by season.

WHALE WATCHING
Vancouver Island is known as one of the best places to view migrating and resident whales. Whale-watching tours leave from Victoria and other large city centers on the island. View migrating gray whales during March and April, while Orca (killer) whales are best observed between May and October, with July and August as the key months for sightings. Three Orca pods totaling more than 80 whales make their home in the waters off of Victoria. North of Vancouver Island, a resident community of 217 whales, patrol the Johnstone Strait in 16 pods. Other whales and marine mammals that can be seen off of Vancouver Island include humpback whales, minke whales, otters, seals, sea lions and dolphins.

WHERE TO STAY
★★★★THE AERIE RESORT AND SPA
600 Ebedora Lane, Malahat, 250-743-7115, 800-518-1933; www.aerie.bc.ca
Built into the mountains on 85 acres above the southern part of Vancouver Island, the Aerie Resort attracts travelers with its casual sophistication and incredible views. Persian and Chinese carpets, goose-down comforters and wood-burning fireplaces make the rooms cozy and comfortable. A multitude of activities, from biking and sailing to hiking and fishing are available. The fantastic Aerie Spa and Wellness Centre offers everything from facials to massages and body wraps. The resort's dining room is a sophisticated spot bathed in tones of cream and white with views of the mountains, and the Asian-influenced cuisine is equally alluring.
29 rooms. Restaurant, bar. Fitness center. Spa. Pets accepted. $36-85

★★★MALAHAT MOUNTAIN INN
265 Trans-Canada Highway, Malahat, 250-478-1979, 800-913-1944;
www.malahatmountaininn.com
Just a short drive from Victoria brings guests to this inn's ocean-view rooms and lofts. Take in dramatic ocean landscapes and views of Saanich Inlet while dining on the outdoor patio.
10 rooms. Restaurant, bar. $16-35

★★★★WICKANINNISH INN

500 Osprey Lane, Tofino, 250-725-3100, 800-333-4604; www.wickinn.com

Famous for its storm-watching events (the luxurious resort is perched on the edge of a particularly volatile stretch of Pacific Ocean), this three-story cedar inn is a rustic retreat on a remote stretch of Vancouver Island. Floor-to-ceiling windows frame dazzling views of the crashing surf. Furnishings crafted from recycled fir, cedar, and driftwood add a unique touch in the comfortable accommodations, as do fireplaces, oversized tubs and private balconies. Beach comb with your pet in tow on Chesterman Beach, and then stop by the pet shower station to freshen up. The superb onsite spa takes its cues from botanicals from the nearby ancient rainforest. The sea is the focus at the Pointe Restaurant, where the ocean's bounty is highlighted.

75 rooms. Restaurant, bar. Business center. Fitness center. Spa. Pets accepted. $86 and up

WHERE TO EAT

★★★★THE AERIE DINING ROOM

Aerie Resort & Spa, 600 Ebedora Lane, Malahat, 250-743-0141, 800-518-1933; www.aerie.bc.ca

Spectacular views of snowy mountaintops are among the many highlights of an evening at The Aerie Dining Room. The Aerie's kitchen is known for its use of superb local produce, sourcing its ingredients from a network of 60 small farms. The kitchen is loyal to classic French technique but brings plates to modern life with Pacific accents. The result is straightforward yet innovative and sophisticated fare. A lengthy wine list features Vancouver's own, in addition to wines of the Pacific Coast.

French. Breakfast, lunch, dinner. Reservations recommended. Outdoor seating. Bar. $36-85

★★★THE POINTE RESTAURANT

Wickaninnish Inn, 500 Osprey Lane, Tofino, 250-725-3106, 800-333-4604; www.wickinn.com/restaurant.html

Perched above the crashing waves of Vancouver Island's west shore is the Pointe Restaurant at the Wickaninnish Inn. The cedar-beamed, circular dining room features a breathtaking 240-degree view of the Pacific Ocean. The adjoining On the Rocks Bar & Lounge is a perfect spot for a pre- or post-dinner cocktail, with a variety of wines by the glass and an extensive selection of single-malt scotches.

Seafood. Breakfast, lunch, dinner, Sunday brunch. Reservations recommended. $36-85

SPA

★★★★ANCIENT CEDARS SPA

Wickaninnish Inn, 500 Osprey Lane, Tofino, 250-725-3100; www.wickinn.com

Resting on a rocky promontory jutting into the Pacific Ocean with an old-growth rainforest in the background, this is truly a one-of-a-kind hideaway. The interiors have been designed to bring the outdoors in, with slate tiles, dark colors and cedar decorating this serene space. The treatment menu focuses on relaxation and renewal. Thai, lomi lomi and hot stone massage are among the bodywork therapies available, or try the signature sacred sea treatment, which uses the renowned Bouvier Hydrotherapy tub.

VICTORIA

See also Vancouver, Vancouver Island

One of Canada's most temperate and eminently walkable cities, British Columbia's capital has a distinctly British flavor, yet is a heartland of Pacific Northwest indigenous culture. This city of lush parks and gardens literally bursts with beauty in early spring, when even the five-globed Victorian lamp-posts are decorated with baskets of flowers. Take a horse-drawn carriage or double-decker bus tour through many historic and scenic landmarks and wander through the bistros, boutiques and colorful alleys of a delightfully compact downtown and Chinatown district that sparkles with history.

WHAT TO SEE

ART GALLERY OF GREATER VICTORIA

1040 Moss St., Victoria, 250-384-4101; www.aggv.bc.ca

This gallery is said to have the finest collection of Japanese art in Canada and it includes major holdings of Asian ceramics and paintings. Also housed here are collections of Canadian and European art, with a focus on prints, drawings and decorative arts. The gallery is home to the only Shinto shrine outside of Japan and is the site of many lectures, film screenings and concerts. Admission: adults $12, seniors and students $10, children 6-17 $2. By donation first Tuesday of the month. Monday-Saturday 10 a.m.-5 p.m., Thursday 10 a.m.-9 p.m., Sunday noon-5 p.m. Closed Monday September-mid-May.

BUTCHART GARDENS

800 Benvenuto Ave., Victoria, 250-652-5256, 866-652-4422; www.butchartgardens.com

At approximately 55 acres (22 hectares), the Sunken Garden was created in the early 1900s by the Butcharts on the site of their depleted limestone quarry with topsoil brought in by horse-drawn cart. Already a tourist attraction by the 1920s, Butchart now includes rose, Japanese and Italian gardens; also Star Pond, Concert Lawn, Fireworks Basin, Ross Fountain and Show Greenhouse. The gardens are subtly illuminated at night (mid-June-mid-September) and on Saturday evenings in July and August, visitors enjoy firework displays. Daily; hours vary.

CARR HOUSE

207 Government St., Victoria, 250-383-5843; www.emilycarr.com

Built in 1863, this is the birthplace of famous Canadian painter and author Emily Carr. The ground floor was restored to represent that time period. May-September, Tuesday-Saturday 11 a.m.- 4 p.m.; rest of year, by appointment.

CHINATOWN

Fisgard and Government streets, Victoria

Chinese immigrants, employed for railroad labor, established Canada's oldest Chinatown in 1858. Two key attractions are Fan Tan Alley, the narrowest street in Canada, and the Gate of Harmonious Interest, guarded by hand-carved stone lions from Suzhou, China. Visit shops with exotic merchandise and restaurants.

CRAIGDARROCH CASTLE

1050 Joan Crescent, Victoria, 250-592-5323; www.craigdarrochcastle.com
This historic house museum was constructed in 1890 with beautifully crafted wood, and stained glass and is furnished with period furniture and artifacts. Admission: adults $12, seniors $11, students $8, children 6-18 $4. Mid-June-mid-September 9 a.m.-7 p.m.; Mid-September-mid-June 10 a.m.-4 p.m.

CRAIGFLOWER FARMHOUSE & SCHOOLHOUSE HISTORIC SITE

Admirals and Craigflower roads, Victoria, 250-383-4627, 877-485-2422;
www.conservancy.bc.ca
This farmhouse was built in 1856 in simple Georgian style. The adjoining 1854 schoolhouse is the oldest in Western Canada. The house has some original furnishings.
Admission: adults $6, students and seniors $4. May-September 11 a.m.-5 p.m.; rest of year, by appointment.

DOMINION ASTROPHYSICAL OBSERVATORY

5071 W. Saanich Road, Victoria, 250-363-0001; www.hia-iha.nrc-cnrc.gc.ca
The observatory contains three telescopes, two of which are used for research by professional astronomers. The 72-inch Plaskett Telescope is used for public viewings during "Star Parties" (late July-September). Interactive exhibits, film presentations and other special programs are designed to entertain visitors while educating them about the universe.
Admission: adults $9, students and seniors $8, children 4-12 $5. May-early September, hours vary; rest of year, by appointment.

FORT RODD HILL & FISGARD LIGHTHOUSE NATIONAL HISTORIC SITE

603 Fort Rodd Hill Road, Victoria, 250-478-5849; www.fortroddhill.com
A coastal artillery fort from 1895 to 1956 has casemated barracks, gun and searchlight positions and a historic lighthouse is adjacent.
Admission: adults $3.90, seniors $3.40, children 6-16 $1.90. Mid-February-October 10 a.m.-5:30 p.m.; November-mid-February 9 a.m.-4:30 p.m.

HATLEY CASTLE

2005 Sooke Road, Colwood, 250-391-2666, 866-241-0674; www.hatleycastle.com
This castle was once the private estate of James Dunsmuir, the former Lieutenant Governor of British Columbia. Buildings are noted for their beauty, as are the grounds, which include Japanese, Italian and rose gardens.

HELMCKEN HOUSE

Elliot Street Square, Victoria, 250-356-7226, 888-447-7977;
www.royalbcmuseum.bc.ca
Second-oldest house in British Columbia, built in 1852; most furnishings are original. Extensive 19th-century medical collection.
Admission: included with Royal B.C. Museum admission or by donation. June-early September noon-4 p.m.

MARITIME MUSEUM OF BRITISH COLUMBIA

28 Bastion Square, Victoria, 250-385-4222; www.mmbc.bc.ca

This museum depicts rich maritime heritage of the Pacific Northwest from early explorers through age of sail and steam as well as Canadian naval wartime history and a large collection of ship models used throughout the history of British Columbia. The Tilikum, a converted dugout that sailed from Victoria to England during the years 1901 to 1904, is here also

Admission: adults $10, seniors and students $8, children 6-11 $5.

PACIFIC UNDERSEA GARDENS

490 Belleville St., Victoria, 250-382-5717; www.pacificunderseagardens.com

Uunderwater windows in a floating vessel allow the viewing of more than 5,000 marine specimens with scuba diver shows at this undersea garden. Admission: adults $9.75, seniors $8.75, children 5-11 $5.75, children 12-17 $7.75. September-April, daily 10 a.m.-5 p.m.; April-June, daily 10 a.m.-6 p.m.; June-September, daily 9 a.m.-8 p.m.

POINT ELLICE HOUSE MUSEUM

2616 Pleasant St., Victoria, 250-380-6506; www.victorialodging.com/pointellice

This museum features an original Victorian setting and furnishings. Afternoon tea served in restored garden (11 a.m.-3 p.m., reservations recommended).

May-September 10 a.m.-4 p.m.

ROYAL BRITISH COLUMBIA MUSEUM

675 Belleville St., Victoria, 250-356-7226, 888-447-7977; www.royalbcmuseum.bc.ca

Three-dimensional exhibits include natural and human history, indigenous history and art. There is also a re-creation of a turn-of-the-century town. In the natural history gallery, the exhibits depict British Columbia from the Ice Age to the present.

Admission: adults $27.50, seniors, students and children 6-18 $18.50. Daily 9 a.m.-5 p.m.

THUNDERBIRD PARK

Belleville and Douglas streets, Victoria

You'll find a collection of authentic totem poles and indigenous carvings, representing the works of the main Pacific Coastal tribes at this park. Indigenous carvers may be seen at work in the Carving Shed.

May-September.

WHALE-WATCHING TOURS

Wharf Street, Victoria

Whale-watching boats line both the Wharf Street waterfront and Inner Harbor. Half-day tours display marine life, including orcas, sea lions, seals and porpoises. Victoria Marine Adventures and Prince of Whales operate tours.

WHERE TO STAY
★★★ABIGAIL'S HOTEL
906 McClure St., Victoria, 250-388-5363, 800-561-6565; www.abigailshotel.com
This colorfully painted inn consists of a historic Tudor mansion and converted carriage house. The quiet setting belies the inn's location just three blocks from Victoria's Inner Harbor and main tourist attractions. A gourmet breakfast is served overlooking the patio and English-style gardens.
23 rooms. Complimentary breakfast. Spa. Pets accepted. $251-350

★★★BEACONSFIELD INN
998 Humboldt St., Victoria, 250-384-4044, 888-884-4044; www.beaconsfieldinn.com
This three-story Edwardian mansion on Victoria's south side is a Registered Heritage Property. The gardens are kept in the English style, and high tea and sherry are served each afternoon. Each guest room boasts unique features such as canopied beds, beamed ceilings, stained-glass windows and wood-burning fireplaces.
9 rooms. Complimentary breakfast. $251-350

★★★BEACON INN AT SIDNEY
9724 Third St., Sidney, 250-655-3288, 877-420-5499; www.beaconinns.com
Located in the center of Book Town, this elegant Edwardian-inspired property is the perfect romantic getaway. A complimentary gourmet breakfast in the breakfast room (or on the front patio) starts each day. For guests who want pure relaxation, the Ocean Palm Spa is just a few minutes from the inn.
9 rooms. Complimentary breakfast. $151-250

★★BEDFORD REGENCY HOTEL
1140 Government St., Victoria, 250-384-6835, 800-665-6500; www.bedfordregency.com
40 rooms. Restaurant, bar. $61-150

★★★COAST HARBORSIDE HOTEL & MARINA
146 Kingston St., Victoria, 250-360-1211, 800-716-6199;
www.coasthotels.com
This location can't be beat. The hotel has an inner harbor spot with a 42-slip private marina and it's close to Victoria International Airport. All rooms have balconies or terraces, some with marina side views, and complimentary high-speed Internet access. Guests can relax in one of the two pools or hot tub and enjoy a seafood dinner at the Blue Crab Bar & Grill.
132 rooms. Restaurant, bar. Business center. Fitness center. Pool. Pets accepted. $151-250

★★CHATEAU VICTORIA HOTEL AND SUITES
740 Burdett Ave., Victoria, 250-382-4221, 800-663-5891; www.chateauvictoria.com
177 rooms Restaurant, bar. Fitness center. Pool. Spa. Pets accepted. $151-250

★★★DELTA VICTORIA OCEAN POINTE RESORT AND SPA
45 Songhees Road, Victoria, 250-360-2999, 800-667-4677; www.deltahotels.com
Located on a point between Victoria's Inner and Upper harbors, this elegant,

modern hotel offers wonderful views of the waterfront, Parliament Buildings and the Royal British Columbia Museum. Take advantage of the resort experience by participating in fitness classes, booking a tee time on a nearby golf course and playing tennis on one of the hotel's two lighted courts.

239 rooms. Restaurant, bar. Business center. Fitness center. Pool. Spa. Pets accepted. Tennis. $151-250

★★★ENGLISH INN & RESORT
429 Lampson St., Victoria, 250-388-4353, 866-388-4353; www.englishinnresort.com
This unique resort was built to echo an English country village, and its buildings are set amidst five acres of beautifully landscaped English-style gardens. Rooms are spacious and streamlined, with contemporary furnishings and some with fireplaces or spa tubs.

30 rooms. Restaurant, bar. Spa. $251-350

★★EXECUTIVE HOUSE HOTEL
777 Douglas St., Victoria, 250-388-5111, 800-663-7001; www.executivehouse.com
181 rooms. Restaurant, bar. Business center. Fitness center. Pets accepted. $151-250

★★★THE FAIRMONT EMPRESS
721 Government St., Victoria, 250-384-8111, 866-540-4429;
www.fairmont.com/empress
The Fairmont Empress is one of Victoria's most cherished landmarks. Nearly a century old, this storybook castle resting on the banks of Victoria's Inner Harbor enjoys a legendary past, sparkling with royals, celebrities and a bygone era. Afternoon tea at The Fairmont Empress is a must for all visitors to Victoria.

477 rooms. Restaurant, bar. Business center. Fitness center. Pool. Spa. Pets accepted.$$$

★★★★HASTINGS HOUSE
160 Upper Ganges Road, Salt Spring Island, 250-537-2362, 800-661-9255;
www.hastingshouse.com
Snuggled on Salt Spring Island, the Tudor-style Hastings House captures the essence of the English countryside. Scattered throughout the lovely grounds, the rooms and suites are housed within ivy-covered garden cottages and the timber-framed barn. High Tea and pre-dinner cocktails are served daily in the lounge. Hastings House boasts one of the most accomplished kitchens in British Colombia. Longtime executive chef Marcel Kauer and his brigade have the great fortune to draw on British Columbia's Pacific Northwest bounty. The wine list, although international in scope, features a slate of reds and white from B.C.'s Okanagan Valley.

18 rooms. Restaurant. Spa. Closed November-March. $351 and up

★★HARBOR TOWERS HOTEL & SUITES
345 Quebec St., Victoria, 250-385-2405, 800-663-5896; www.harbourtowers.com
195 rooms Restaurant, bar. Business center. Fitness center. Pool. Pets accepted. $151-250

★★★HOTEL GRAND PACIFIC

463 Belleville St., Victoria, 250-386-0450, 800-663-7550; www.hotelgrandpacific.com

Located at the southern tip of Vancouver Island, this hotel offers serene water views and easy access to historic Old Town and area businesses. The rooms and suites are light and airy. Fine dining is one of Victoria's hallmarks, and this hotel is no exception. The Pacific Northwest cuisine at the Pacific Restaurant is a standout, while The Mark's regionally influenced dishes are equally delicious.

304 rooms. Restaurant, bar. Business center. Fitness center. Pool. Spa. Pets accepted. $151-250

★★★LAUREL POINT INN

680 Montreal St., Victoria, 250-386-8721, 800-663-7667; www.laurelpoint.com

Every room of this hotel has a balcony and a fabulous view of either the Inner or Upper Harbor. The grounds include a Japanese-style garden, and the Asian influence is felt in the décor. Relax in the cozy piano lounge, the fragrant garden or the outdoor patio.

200 rooms. Restaurant, bar. Business center. Pool. Spa. Pets accepted. $251-350

★★★MAGNOLIA HOTEL AND SPA

623 Courtney St., Victoria, 250-381-0999, 877-624-6654; www.magnoliahotel.com

This luxury boutique hotel one block from the Inner Harbor provides comfort and pampering throughout. The spa offers a full range of beauty and relaxation regimens and prides itself on using natural products from renewable resources.

64 rooms. Restaurant, bar. Complimentary breakfast. Fitness center. Spa. Pets accepted. $251-350

★★★MIRALOMA ON THE COVE

2306 Harbour Road, Sidney, 250-656-6622, 877-956-6622; www.miraloma.ca

This luxurious seaside property is located just 20 minutes from downtown Victoria and five minutes from ferries and the airport. Guests can choose from studios, one-bedroom suites or two-bedroom suites. Each guest room also includes pillow-top mattresses, a balcony or patio, spa tubs and heated towel bars. Guests can enjoy a number of amenities such as hot chocolate, cookies, use of mountain bikes and a complimentary breakfast buffet.

22 rooms. Fitness center. Pets accepted. $151-250

★★ROYAL SCOT SUITE HOTEL

425 Quebec St., Victoria, 250-388-5463, 800-663-7515; www.royalscot.com

178 rooms. Restaurant, bar. Business center. Fitness center. Pool. Pets accepted. $61-150

★★★SOOKE HARBOR HOUSE

1528 Whiffen Spit Road, Sooke, 250-642-3421, 800-889-9688;
www.sookeharbourhouse.com

Located on Vancouver Island by the sea, this bed and breakfast features beautifully designed guest rooms with fireplaces and spectacular ocean views. Guests can enjoy area activities such as hiking, whale watching and cross-country skiing.

28 rooms Restaurant, bar. Complimentary breakfast. Spa. Pets accepted. Closed three weeks in January. $251-350

★★★SWANS SUITE HOTEL

506 Pandora Ave., Victoria, 250-361-3310, 800-668-7926; www.swanshotel.com

Built in 1913, this hotel holds 30 one- and two-bedroom suites. Most of the guest rooms have a loft that contributes a spacious feeling, and some have skylights and private patios. All rooms boast full kitchens, duvets and original artwork. It's a lively place with its own brewery and two popular eating and drinking establishments.

29 rooms. Restaurant, bar. Complimentary breakfast. $151-250

WHERE TO EAT

★★BLUE CRAB BAR AND GRILL

146 Kingston, Victoria, 250-480-1999; www.bluecrab.ca

Seafood. Breakfast (Monday-Saturday), lunch (Monday-Saturday), dinner, Sunday brunch. Reservations recommended. $36-85

★★★CAFE BRIO

944 Fort St., Victoria, 250-383-0009, 866-270-5461; www.cafe-brio.com

This award-winning restaurant is located in downtown Victoria and offers West Coast/Continental cuisine featuring an abundance of fresh wild fish. The daily menu also offers local, seasonal, organic foods. For an exceptional value, come for the early prix fixe menu.

International. Dinner. Closed first two weeks in January. Reservations recommended. Outdoor seating. $36-85

★★CAMILLE'S

45 Bastion Square, Victoria, 250-381-3433; www.camillesrestaurant.com

International. Dinner. Closed Sunday-Monday. Reservations recommended. $36-85

★★CEDAR DINING ROOM AT TIGH-NA-MARA RESORT

1155 Resort Drive, Parksville, 250-248-2072; www.tigh-na-mara.com

International. Breakfast, lunch, dinner. Reservations recommended. $16-35

★★★DEEP COVE CHALET

11190 Chalet Road, Sidney, 250-656-3541; www.deepcovechalet.com

This charming and historic country inn has a great view overlooking the waters of the inside passage. Built in 1914, it was originally a teahouse for a railroad station.

French. Lunch, dinner. Closed Monday-Tuesday. Reservations recommended. Outdoor seating. $36-85

★★★EMPRESS ROOM

721 Government St., Victoria, 250-389-2727; www.fairmont.com/empress

Dine on classic cuisine in this richly appointed room of tapestries, intricately carved ceilings and live harp music. The 100-year-old hotel's waterfront location is full of European style, a great spot for a romantic meal. International. Breakfast, dinner. Reservations recommended. $86 and up

★★GATSBY MANSION RESTAURANT
309 Belleville St., Victoria, 250-388-9191, 800-563-9656; www.gatsbymansion.com
International. Reservations recommended. Outdoor seating. $36-85

★★IL TERRAZZO
555 Johnson St., Victoria, 250-361-0028; www.ilterrazzo.com
Italian. Lunch, dinner. Reservations recommended. Outdoor seating. $36-85

★★JAPANESE VILLAGE STEAK AND SEAFOOD HOUSE
734 Broughton St., Victoria, 250-382-5165; www.japanesevillage.bc.ca
Japanese. Lunch (Monday-Friday), dinner. Reservations recommended. $16-35

★★KINGFISHER RESTAURANT
4330 S. Island Highway, Courtenay, 250-338-1323, 800-663-7929;
www.kingfisherspa.com
International. Breakfast, lunch, dinner, Sunday brunch. Reservations recommended. Outdoor seating. $16-35

★★★LURE
Delta Ocean Pointe Resort, 45 Songhees Road, Victoria, 250-360-5873;
www.lurevictoria.com
This contemporary, sophisticated seafood restaurant is located inside the Delta Ocean Pointe Resort and offers excellent water and downtown views. Seafood. Breakfast, lunch, dinner. Reservations recommended. Outdoor seating. $36-85

★★THE MARINA
1327 Beach Drive, Victoria, 250-598-8555; www.marinarestaurant.com
International. Lunch, dinner, Sunday brunch. Reservations recommended. $16-35

★★OLD HOUSE RESTAURANT
1760 Riverside Lane, Courtenay, 250-338-5406; www.oldhouserestaurant.ca
International. Lunch, dinner. Reservations recommended. Outdoor seating. $16-35

★★★★RESTAURANT MATISSE
512 Yates St., Victoria, 250-480-0883; www.restaurantmatisse.com
Restaurant Matisse is a gem of a dining room that has become a destination for simple, traditional French fare among Victoria's dining elite. While French wines dominate the list, there is also a great selection of California bottles. French. Dinner. Closed Monday-Tuesday. Reservations recommended. $36-85

★★SPINNAKER'S BREW PUB
308 Catherine St., Victoria, 250-386-2739, 877-838-2739; www.spinnakers.com
International. Lunch, dinner. Reservations recommended. Outdoor seating. $16-35

★★★SOOKE HARBOR HOUSE
1528 Whiffen Spit Road, Sooke Harbor, 250-642-3421, 800-889-9688;
www.sookeharbourhouse.com
Considered one of the most unique restaurants in Canada, the bistro serves local organic seafood, meat and produce, with edible herbs and flowers from the garden.
International. Dinner. Closed Monday-Wednesday, December-February. Reservations recommended. Outdoor seating. $36-85

★WHITE HEATHER TEA ROOM
1885 Oak Bay Ave., Victoria, 250-595-8020; www.whiteheather-tearoom.com
Scottish. Closed Sunday-Monday. Reservations recommended. $15 and under

WHISTLER
See also Vancouver
The winning combination of Blackcomb and Whistler mountains makes this an internationally famous ski area—yet it's also packed full through the summer, as preppy golfers descend upon the village alongside mud-spattered, hardcore mountain bikers. Five lakes dot Whistler valley, offering ample opportunity to fish, swim, windsurf, canoe, kayak or sail. The alpine slopes for a time give way to extensive hiking and mountain biking trails, but even in summer there is skiing to be found—Whistler is where enthusiasts will find the only lift-serviced, summertime public glacier skiing in North America. Everything in Whistler is larger-than-life: the ideal getaway with opulent food and wine, an infectious party atmosphere and sumptuous accommodations, plus a staging ground for epics that is nothing short of extraordinary.

WHAT TO SEE
BLACKCOMB SKI AREA
4545 Blackcomb Way, Whistler, 604-687-1032, 866-218-9690;
www.whistlerblackcomb.com
This ski area features seven high-speed quad chairlifts, three triple chairlifts and seven surface lifts. There are more than 100 runs with the longest run at seven miles, with a vertical drop of 5,280 feet.

WHISTLER MUSEUM AND ARCHIVES
4333 Main St., Whistler, 604-932-2019; www.whistlermuseum.com
Discover the rich history of the thriving Whistler community through artifacts, photographs and stories from local community members.

SPECIAL EVENTS
CORNUCOPIA: WHISTLER'S CELEBRATION OF WINE AND FOOD
www.whistlercornucopia.com
Enjoy wine from more than 70 wineries from the province, neighboring U.S.

states and around the world. Food tastings, wine dinners and seminars will keep you busy.
November.

TELUS WORLD SKI & SNOWBOARD FESTIVAL
www.whistlerblackcomb.com/twssf/
This ten-day festival features outdoor concert series, action-sports photography and film events, demonstration days and festive parties.
Mid-April.

WHERE TO STAY
★★CRYSTAL LODGE
4154 Village Green, Whistler, 604-932-2221, 800-667-3363; www.crystal-lodge.com
159 rooms. Restaurant, bar. Business center. Fitness center. Pool. Pets accepted. $61-150

★★★THE FAIRMONT CHATEAU WHISTLER
4599 Chateau Blvd., Whistler, 604-938-8000, 866-540-4424; www.fairmont.com/whistler
The Fairmont Chateau Whistler is a skier's nirvana. During summer, its golf course and David Leadbetter Golf Academy lend the same status for golfers. The Vida Wellness Spa soothes the tired muscles of active visitors. Taste buds are tantalized at the resort's various restaurants.
550 rooms. Restaurant, bar. Business center. Fitness center. Pool. Spa. Pets accepted. Golf. Ski in/ski out. Tennis. $251-350

★★★★FOUR SEASONS RESORT WHISTLER
4591 Blackcomb Way, Whistler, 604-935-3400, 888-935-2460; www.fourseasons.com
This resort is nestled at the foot of the Blackcomb and Whistler mountains and offers a year-round getaway that features signature Four Seasons service and style. The resort is a five-minute walk to the ski lifts and a 10-minute stroll to the village center. The guest rooms are spacious, beautifully furnished and decorated. The dining room and lounge, Fifty Two 80 Bistro, delight with flavorful food and an extensive wine list and specialty cocktails. After a day of activity, retreat to the Spa, where body wraps, hydro-therapy, facials and massages will help you unwind.
273 rooms. Restaurant, bar. Business center. Fitness center. Pool. Spa. Pets accepted. $351 and up

★★★PAN PACIFIC WHISTLER MOUNTAINSIDE
4320 Sundial Crescent, Whistler, 604-905-2999, 888-905-9995; www.panpacific.com
Nestled at the foot of Whistler and Blackcomb mountains and facing Skier's Plaza, this all-suite boutique resort offers kitchens, fireplaces and balconies with beautiful views of the mountains of Whistler Village. After a day of skiing, retreat to the onsite spa for a hot stone massage, or swim in the heated outdoor pool.
121 rooms. Restaurant, bar. Business center. Fitness center. Pool. Spa. $251-350

★★SUMMIT LODGE & SPA

4359 Main St., Whistler, 604-932-2778, 888-913-8811; www.summitlodge.com
81 rooms. Restaurant, bar. Pool. Spa. Pets accepted. $251-350

★★★THE WESTIN RESORT AND SPA

4090 Whistler Way, Whistler, 604-905-5000, 888-634-5577; www.westinwhistler.com
Dramatic views are enjoyed from the privacy of airy suites, and guests retreat
to the comfort of the FireRock Lounge après-ski or the Aubergine Grille for
fresh cuisine. The Avello Spa & Health Club entices visitors with more than
75 treatments and the latest fitness equipment.
419 rooms. Restaurant, bar. Business center. Fitness center. Pool. Pets accepted. $251-350

WHERE TO EAT
★★★BEARFOOT BISTRO

4121 Village Green, Whistler, 604-932-3433; www.bearfootbistro.com
Only a hard day of skiing can justify this decadent feast for the senses. Each
of three or five courses is handcrafted from a huge range of rare, high-quality
ingredients including caribou and pheasant. Additionally, this is one of the
most beautiful locations in North America, making it a truly standout dining
experience.
International. Dinner. Reservations recommended. Bar. $86 and up

★★LA RUA

Le Chamois Hotel, 4557 Blackcomb Way, 604-932-5011; www.larua-restaurante.com
Seafood, steak. Dinner. Closed Tuesday and six weeks in October-November.
Reservations recommended. Outdoor seating. $36-85

★★RIMROCK CAFE

2117 Whistler Road, Whistler, 604-932-5565, 877-932-5589; www.rimrockwhistler.com
Seafood, steak. Dinner. Closed late October-mid-November. Reservations
recommended. Outdoor seating. $36-85

★★★ARAXI

4222 Village Square, Whistler, 604-932-4540; www.araxi.com
Tables encircle a giant stone urn, the centerpiece of this warm and friendly
dining room. A blend of French and Italian culinary styles and fine, regional
ingredients have gained this restaurant continent-wide recognition.
International. Dinner. Closed two weeks in early May, late October. Reservations recommended. Outdoor seating. $36-85

★★TRATTORIA DI UMBERTO

4417 Sundial Place, Whistler, 604-932-5858; www.umberto.com
Italian. Dinner. Reservations recommended. Outdoor seating. $36-85

★★★VAL D'ISERE

4314 Main St., Whistler, 604-932-4666; www.valdisere-restaurant.com
Impressive for both the food and the charming interior, this fine restaurant is
located in the north village plaza. The menu covers a wide range of culinary
influences and includes dishes such as venison flank steak with chanterelle

sauce and wild salmon baked in a potato crust.
French. Lunch (summer), dinner. Reservations recommended. Outdoor
seating. $36-85

★★★WILDFLOWER RESTAURANT
Fairmont Chateau Whistler, 4599 Chateau Blvd., Whistler, 604-938-8000, 866-540-4424;
www.fairmont.com/whistler
Tucked inside the Chateau Whistler, this restaurant features a local, organic-laden menu with weekly table d'hote signature dishes, an ever-popular coastal market buffet and a "Flavors of Asia" buffet on Friday and Saturday nights. International. Breakfast, dinner. Reservations recommended. Outdoor seating. $36-85

SPAS
★★★THE AVELLO SPA
Westin Resort & Spa, 4090 Whistler Way, Whistler, 604-935-3444;
www.whistlerspa.com
The Avello Spa takes a holistic approach in its well-being treatments. Massage accounts for most of the menu, with the signature massage treatments including the Avello hot rock massage, and Thai and Chinese therapies. Asian approaches to balance include Reiki, acupuncture, reflexology and shiatsu. A wide variety of hydrotherapy sessions are available, from herbal, milk, mustard, and mud to soaks using salts from the Dead Sea.

★★★★THE SPA AT FOUR SEASONS WHISTLER
Four Seasons Resort Whistler, 4591 Blackcomb Way, Whistler, 604-935-3400;
www.fourseasons.com/whistler/spa
This contemporary spa located inside the Four Seasons Resort Whistler offers a full menu of massages and body treatments designed to sooth and restore sore muscles after a day on the slopes. Chilly feet are wrapped in warm towels while muscles are warmed with hot stones during the après-ski massage. The men's fitness facial restores wind- and sun-burned skin while the British Columbia glacial clay wrap is a great way to warm up at the end of the day. Those who can't pry themselves from the comfort of their rooms can order up an in-room massage.

MANITOBA

MANITOBA IS LOCATED IN THE LONGITUDINAL CENTER OF THE COUNTRY, THOUGH IT IS CON-
SIDERED part of Western Canada and is the easternmost of Canada's three
prairie provinces. It is renowned for dramatic landscapes with golden fields,
granite ridges and sparkling lakes, a lively cultural heritage of fur trade-era
voyagers, accessible yet dramatic wildlife and warm, friendly people.

Sand dunes, ancient granite and amazing waterfalls are all crisscrossed
by extensive trail networks that attract hikers and bikers to broad valleys and
lush Canadian Shield forests. More than 10,000 trophy-sized fish are pulled
out of Manitoba's plentiful waters every year, with pristine fly-in as well
as road-accessible lodges peppering the north. Arctic grayling, brook trout,
lake trout, northern pike and walleye thrive here, and Winnipeg's Red River
offers some of the best giant channel cat fishing in the world. Recognized as
a birder's paradise, Manitoba attracts two-thirds of Canada's more than 500
species of birds. In spring, the birds fly north in amazing flocks in the hundreds of thousands over lakes, marshes and forests.

In contrast to Manitoba's off-the-beaten-track experiences, Winnipeg is
a multicultural city bursting with festivals, art, music and food. Restaurants serve everything from Ukrainian perogies to a fusion of regional and
western cuisine.

BRANDON

See also Winnipeg

Brandon, Manitoba's second-largest city, has a rich agricultural heritage and
reputation as a prosperous farming community, which it celebrates with the
province's largest agricultural fair.

WHAT TO SEE

COMMONWEALTH AIR TRAINING PLAN MUSEUM

Brandon Municipal Airport, Brandon, 204-727-2444; www.airmuseum.ca

This museum features a display of WWII aircrafts and vehicles; photos, uniforms, flags and other mementos of Air Force training conducted in Canada
from 1940 to 1945 under the British Commonwealth Air Training Plan.
Admission: adults $6, children $4. Hours vary by season. Tours by appointment.

SPECIAL EVENTS

MANITOBA LIVESTOCK EXPOSITION

Keystone Centre, 18th Street and Richmond Avenue, Brandon, 204-726-3590,

877-729-0001; www.brandonfairs.com

This is Manitoba's largest livestock show and sale and features a tractor pull
and rodeo.

November.

ROYAL MANITOBA WINTER FAIR
Keystone Centre, 18th Street and Richmond Avenue, Brandon, 204-726-3590,
877-729-0001; www.brandonfairs.com
Manitoba's largest winter fair features equestrian events, heavy horses and
entertainment.
Late March.

WHERE TO STAY
★★ROYAL OAK INN & SUITES
3130 Victoria Ave., Brandon, 204-728-5775, 800-852-2709; www.royaloakinn.com
96 rooms. Restaurant, bar. Fitness center. Pool. Pets accepted. $61-150

★★VICTORIA INN
3550 Victoria Ave., Brandon, 204-725-1532, 800-852-2710; www.vicinn.com
131 rooms. Restaurant, bar. Complimentary breakfast. Business center. Fitness center. Pool. Pets accepted. $61-150

CHURCHILL
Churchill is the only human settlement where visitors can come to see polar
bears in the wild. Fast and dangerous at more than 1,300 pounds and standing
up to 10 feet tall, the bears are a marvel to behold when they frequent the area
each fall. Wildlife admirers also come to this area of northern Manitoba to
see some of the 250 species of birds that pass through, and in the summer to
view beluga whales in the waters of the Churchill River.

WHAT TO SEE
ESKIMO MUSEUM
242 LaVerendrye Ave., Churchill, 204-675-2030; www.museumsmanitoba.com
This museum contains an impressive collection of Inuit carvings and artifacts, considered some of the oldest and finest in the world. Artifacts date
from 1700 B.C. to modern times.
Admission: by donation. June-mid-November; hours vary by season.

WAPUSK NATIONAL PARK OF CANADA
204-675-8863, 888-773-8888; www.pc.gc.ca
This park, southeast of Churchill, is home to one of the world's largest known
polar bear denning sites. Wapusk, the Cree word for white bear, is dedicated
to protecting the habitat for polar bears, as well as for the hundreds of thousands of birds that nest or migrate here each year. Unescorted visits to the
park are not recommended. For the most current list of tour operators, con-
tact the park office.

WINNIPEG
See also Brandon
Winnipeg, the provincial capital, is situated in the heart of the continent and
combines the sophistication and friendliness of east and west. Assiniboine,
Cree and Ojibwa tribes inhabited the formerly prairie-covered landscape
more than 6,000 years ago. These tribes met at the junction of the Assiniboine and Red rivers to trade. Today, Winnipeg, derived from the Cree word

for "muddy waters," is home to Canada's largest city-dwelling aboriginal community. A historic gathering place, it is still a destination that foreigners and Canadians alike visit to enjoy a wide range of attractions and cultural offerings. Among the city's popular sights and activities are relaxing cruises on the Assiniboine and Red rivers, Rainbow Stage Summer Theater in Kildonan Park, the Manitoba Theatre Centre, the Winnipeg Symphony, the Manitoba Opera and the renowned Royal Winnipeg Ballet. Sports fans will enjoy the Blue Bombers football team and the Manitoba Moose hockey team.

WHAT TO SEE
ASSINIBOINE FOREST NATURE PARK
2355 Corydon Ave., Winnipeg, 204-888-5466; www.winnipeg.ca
This park features colorful English and formal gardens, the Leo Mol Sculpture Garden, a conservatory with floral displays, a duck pond, playgrounds, a cricket and field hockey area, a miniature train, bike paths and a fitness trail featuring more than 39 species of mammals and more than 80 species of birds. The Assiniboine Park Zoo *(460 Assiniboine Park Drive, 204-986-2327; www.zoosociety.com)* has a collection of rare and endangered species, tropical mammals, birds and reptiles. the children's discovery area features a variety of young animals.
Park Admission: free. Zoo Admission: varies by season. Park: daily. Zoo: hours vary by season.

ASSINIBOINE PARK CONSERVATORY
Assiniboine Park, Winnipeg, 204-9864732; www.winnipeg.ca
The longest established conservatory in western Canada gives visitors a chance to view tropical trees and plants, exotic flowers and foliage not indigenous to the country.
Admission: free. Hours vary by season.

BIRDS HILL PROVINCIAL PARK
Highway 59, Winnipeg, 204-654-6730; www.gov.mb.ca
A 8,275-acre park situated on a glacial formation called an esker. The park has a large population of white-tailed deer and many orchid species. Interpretive, hiking, bridle and bicycle trails; in-line skating path; snowshoe, snowmobile and cross-country skiing trails.

DALNAVERT MUSEUM
61 Carlton St., Winnipeg, 204-943-2835; www.mhs.mb.ca
This is the restored Victorian residence of Sir Hugh John Macdonald, the premier of Manitoba in 1900, which depicts the lifestyle and furnishings of the period.
Admission: adults $5, seniors $4, children 5-17 $3. Wednesday-Friday 10 a.m.-5 p.m., Saturday 11 a.m.-6 p.m., Sunday noon-4 p.m.

FORKS
Downtown Winnipeg, 888-942-6302; www.theforks.com
Several key Winnipeg attractions are centered in the general location of what has been a gathering place for people for thousands of years. Come here to

shop, dine, explore museums and historic sites, or simply stroll along the beautiful Riverwalk.

THE FORKS MARKET

Downtown Winnipeg, 888-942-6302; www.theforks.com
Browse through more than 50 specialty shops for handicrafts, toys, gift items and more and dine on cuisine from around the world and local specialties.

THE FORKS NATIONAL HISTORIC SITE OF CANADA

401-25 Forks Market Road, Winnipeg, 204-983-6757; www.pc.gc.ca
Situated on 13.6 acres, the Forks National Historic site features a riverside promenade and walkways throughout. There are historical exhibits, a play-ground and special events. An adjacent area is open in winter for skating, and cross-country skiing.
Admission: adults $3.90, seniors $3.40, children 6-16 $1.90. Year-round.

FORT WHYTE CENTRE FOR FAMILY ADVENTURE AND RECREATION

1961 McCreary Road, Winnipeg, 204-989-8355; www.fortwhyte.org
Hike on self-guided trails through 400 acres of marshes, lakes and forests that are home to 27 species of birds and mammals. There is year-round fishing and canoe and boat rentals. Dine at Buffalo Stone café and shop for souvenirs at the Nature Shop. A 10,000-square-foot interpretive center showcases a variety of exhibits. Do not miss the Bison Prairie, with the largest urban-based herd of Plains bison in the country, or the Prairie Dog Exhibit. Admission: adults $6, seniors $5, students and children $4. Monday-Friday 9 a.m.-5 p.m., Saturday-Sunday 10 a.m.-5 p.m.

LEO MOL SCULPTURE GARDEN

Assiniboine Park, Winnipeg, 204-888-5466; www.partnersinthepark.org
Garden and gallery to view the bronze sculptures and other artwork by this acclaimed local artist. An onsite studio allows visitors to see how bronze sculptures are created.
May-early September, Tuesday-Sunday 10 a.m.-6 p.m.

THE MANITOBA CHILDREN'S MUSEUM

45 Forks Market Road, Winnipeg, 204-924-4000; www.childrensmuseum.com
Children can enjoy exploring and creating in seven galleries, each offering something unique for children to take part in. One such exhibit enables pre-schoolers to learn about the habitats of different animal species and another exhibit allows them to climb on a 17-foot oak tree. Travel into the past on a 1952 diesel locomotive and passenger coach, or into a fairytale wonderland. Admission: adults $6.75, seniors $6.25, children 2-17 $7. July-August, daily 9:30 a.m.-6 p.m.; September-June, Sunday-Thursday 9:30 a.m.-4:30 p.m., Friday-Saturday 9:30 a.m.-6 p.m.

MANITOBA MUSEUM OF MAN AND NATURE

190 Rupert Ave., Winnipeg, 204-956-2830; www.manitobamuseum.ca
Galleries here interpret Manitoba's human and natural history.

Admission: adults $8, seniors, students and children 3-17 $6.50, children 2 and under free. Labor Day-May, Tuesday-Friday 10 a.m.-4 p.m., Saturday-Sunday 11 a.m.-5 p.m.; mid-May-Labor Day, daily 10 a.m.-5 p.m.

MANITOBA OPERA ASSOCIATION

555 Main St., Winnipeg, 204-942-7479; www.manitobaopera.mb.ca
The strength of character of the Manitoba Opera comes from its ability to attract great international artists such as the Met's Leona Mitchell and La Scala's Eduard Tumagian, and to highlight local talent, such as Tracy Dahl and Phillip Ens. The Manitoba Opera Chorus is supported by Winnipeg Symphony Orchestra under the direction of internationally known conductors. Lavish sets and costumes bring the performances to life, while English subtitles, projected on an overhead screen, make foreign-language operas accessible and comprehensible to everyone.

PLANETARIUM

Manitoba Museum, 190 Rupert Ave., Winnipeg, 204-956-2830;
www.manitobamuseum.ca
Circular, multipurpose audiovisual theater. Wide variety of shows; subjects include cosmic catastrophes and the edge of the universe. Learn about science through hands-on exhibits.
Admission: adults $6.50, seniors, students and children $5. Hours vary by show.

ROSS HOUSE

Joe Zuken Heritage Park, 140 Meade St. N., Winnipeg, 204-943-3958; www.mhs.mb.ca
The oldest building in the original city of Winnipeg, the Ross house was the first post office in western Canada. Displays and period-furnished rooms depict daily life in the Red River Settlement.
Admission: free. June-August, Wednesday-Sunday 10 a.m.-5 p.m.

ROYAL CANADIAN MINT

520 Lagimodière Blvd., Winnipeg, 204-983-6429; www.mint.ca/royalcanadianmintpublic
One of the world's most modern mints, it has a striking glass tower and landscaped interior courtyard. Tour allows the viewing of the coining process and a coin museum.
Daily 9 p.m.-5 p.m. Closed Monday-Sunday early September-late May. Tours by appointment.

ROYAL WINNIPEG BALLET

Centennial Concert Hall, 555 Main St., Winnipeg, 204-956-0183, 800-667-4792;
www.rwb.org
This nationally acclaimed company performs throughout the year in Winnipeg and also presents Ballet in the Park during the summer.

ST. BONIFACE MUSEUM

494 Tache Ave., Winnipeg, 204-237-4500; www.virtualmuseum.ca
Located in the largest French-Canadian community west of Quebec, where Louis Riel, a founder of Manitoba, was born, this museum is housed in the

oldest structure in the city, dating to the days of the Red River Colony; it's the largest oak-log construction in North America.
Admission: adults $5, seniors, students and children 6-17 $3. Late March-late September, Monday-Friday 9 a.m.-5 p.m., Saturday-Sunday noon-4 p.m. Thursday until 8 p.m. late May-late September. Tours by appointment.

WINNIPEG ART GALLERY

300 Memorial Blvd., Winnipeg, 204-786-6641; www.wag.mb.ca
This is Canada's first civic gallery with eight galleries that present changing exhibitions of contemporary, historical and decorative art, plus the world's largest public collection of Inuit Art. Programming includes tours, lectures, films and concerts. There is also a restaurant here.
Admission: adults $8, seniors and students $6, children 6-12 $4. Tuesday-Sunday 11 a.m.-5 p.m., Thursday until 9 p.m.

SPECIAL EVENTS
FESTIVAL DU VOYAGEUR

Voyageur Park, Joseph and Messager streets, Winnipeg, 204-237-7692;
www.festivalvoyageur.mb.ca
In St. Boniface, Winnipeg's French Quarter, this winter festival celebrates the French-Canadian voyageur and the fur trade era.
Mid-February.

FOLKLORAMA

Winnipeg, 204-982-6210, 800-665-0234; www.folklorama.ca
Folklorama is a multicultural festival featuring more than 40 pavilions throughout the city. There is singing, dancing, food and cultural displays.
August.

RED RIVER EXHIBITION

3977 Portage Ave., Winnipeg, 204-888-6990; www.redriverex.com
This large event encompasses grandstand shows, band competitions, displays, agricultural exhibits, a parade, entertainment, a midway, petting zoo, shows and plenty of food.
June

WINNIPEG FOLK FESTIVAL

Birds Hill Provincial Park, 204-231-0096; www.winnipegfolkfestival.ca
More than 60 regional, national and international artists perform on nine stages. There is a children's village, a juried crafts exhibit and sale and an international food village.
Early July.

WINNIPEG FRINGE THEATRE FESTIVAL

Old Market Square, Winnipeg, 204-942-6537, 877-446-4500; www.winnipegfringe.com
More than 100 theater companies perform during North America's second-largest Fringe Festival.
July.

WHERE TO STAY
★★DELTA WINNIPEG
350 St. Mary Ave., Winnipeg, 204-942-0551, 888-311-4990; www.deltahotels.com
393 rooms. Restaurant, bar. Business center. Fitness center. Pool. Pets accepted. $151-250

★★★THE FAIRMONT WINNIPEG
2 Lombard Place, Winnipeg, 204-957-1350, 866-540-4466;
www.fairmont.com/winnipeg
The Fairmont Winnipeg's stylish interiors and central location have earned it a loyal following among leisure and business travelers. The city's large historic district, cultural attractions, restaurants, shops and businesses are all within walking distance from this hotel. The Velvet Glove restaurant is an ideal place for business meetings or private dinners with inspired Canadian cuisine and an exceptional wine list.
340 rooms. Restaurant, bar. Business center. Fitness center. Pool. Spa. Pets accepted. $151-250

★★HOLIDAY INN
2520 Portage Ave., Winnipeg, 204-885-4478, 877-863-4780; www.holidayinn.com
226 rooms. Restaurant, bar. Business center. Fitness center. Pool. $151-250

★★RADISSON HOTEL DOWNTOWN
288 Portage Ave., Winnipeg, 204-956-0410, 800-395-7046;
www.radisson.com/winnipegca
272 rooms. Restaurant, bar. Business center. Fitness center. Pool. Pets accepted. $61-150

WHERE TO EAT
★★AMICI
326 Broadway, Winnipeg, 204-943-4997; www.amiciwpg.com
Italian. Lunch, dinner. $36-85

★★ICHIBAN JAPANESE STEAKHOUSE AND SUSHI BAR
189 Carlton St., Winnipeg, 204-925-7400; www.ichiban.ca
Japanese. Dinner. $36-85

★★HY'S STEAK LOFT
1 Lombard Place, Winnipeg, 204-942-1000; www.hyssteakhouse.com
Steak. Lunch (Monday-Friday), dinner. $36-85

NEW BRUNSWICK

TRIUMPH OVER TRAGEDY PERSONIFIES THE GREAT ACADIAN ODYSSEY IN NEW BRUNSWICK—
and through the acadians' difficult historical journey, their "joie de vivre"
(joy of life) has sustained them and the spirit of this province for 250 years.
This indomitable spirit is celebrated in kitchen parties filled with fiddle
music, traditional cuisine, lively dance and storytelling. While not a purely
French population, New Brunswick's flavor is Gallic-inspired.

The largest of Canada's three Maritime provinces, New Brunswick is
bursting with the pride and color of the Acadian French (Cajuns' northern
cousins). Its rich historic past is reflected in major restorations such as the
Acadian Historical Village near Caraquet, Kings' Landing Historical Settlement near Fredericton and MacDonald Historic Farm near Miramichi. Despite the number of provinces with French-speaking locals, New Brunswick
is Canada's only official bilingual province, with about 33 percent of the
people speaking French.

There is much more to New Brunswick than history—including the Bay
of Fundy to the south (featuring some of the highest tides in the world and a
great variety of whales), the Reversing Falls in Saint John, Magnetic Hill in
Moncton, Hopewell Cape Rocks at Hopewell Cape and always the sea. The
four seasons of New Brunswick are some of the most vivid in the country.
Summers are breezy and hot, with record-breaking tides and the warmest salt
water north of Virginia, exposed ocean floors and vast expanses of sand dunes
ripe for picnics and exploring. Fall brings brilliant colors and the bounty of
the harvest amid some of the best whale-watching in the country. In winter,
enjoy endless frozen ponds and lakes, alpine and cross-country skiing, and the
world's longest network of groomed snowmobile trails. Spring visitors feast
on maple syrup and fiddleheads, and anglers are drawn to the world-famous
Atlantic salmon river, Miramichi, for the opening of the fishing season.

EDMUNDSTON

Known as the Gateway of the Maritimes, Edmundston is in northwest New
Brunswick, a few minutes from the province of Quebec, on the border of
Maine and at the doorstep of Atlantic Canada. Acadian culture predominates
in this cheerful and active town, with almost all of the population speaking
French and English.

WHAT TO SEE
ANTIQUE AUTOMOBILE MUSEUM
35 Principale St., Edmundston, 506-735-2637; www.tourismenouveau-brunswick.ca
This museum houses an extensive display of vintage vehicles and mechani-
cal marvels of the past 70 years.
Admission: adults $4, seniors and children 6-18 $3.25. Early June-mid-
September, daily 9 a.m.-8 p.m.

GRAND FALLS

25 Madawaska, Grand Falls, 506-475-7769, 877-475-7769; www.grandfalls.com

At 75 feet high, this is one of the largest cataracts east of Niagara. There is a fascinating gorge and scenic lookouts along the trail.
Mid-May-mid-October.

LES JARDINS DE LA REPUBLIQUE PROVINCIAL PARK

31 Principale St., Saint-Jacques, 506-735-2525; www.nbparks.ca

This park of 108 acres overlooks the Madawaska River. There is an amphitheater, which hosts music and film performances and a 20-acre botanical garden. There is a heated swimming pool, boat dock and launch; tennis, volleyball, softball, horseshoes, bicycle trails and a playground.
Mid-May-mid-September.

MONT FARLAGNE

360 Mont Farlagne Road, Edmundston, 506-739-7669, 888-837-7669; www.montfarlagne.com

Twenty-one trails open to downhill skiing and snowboarding, with five chair lifts, a snow park, restaurant and bar.
December-March.

NEW BRUNSWICK BOTANICAL GARDEN

15 Main St., Saint-Jacques, 506-737-4444; www.jardinbotaniquenb.com

Conceived and designed by a team from the prestigious Montreal Botanical Garden, this garden covers more than 17 acres. More than 30,000 annual flowers and 80,000 plants are on display.
Admission: adults $14, seniors and students $12, children 5-17 $7. May-September, hours vary by month.

ST. BASILE CHAPEL MUSEUM

Chapelle Street, Saint-Basile, 506-263-5971

This parish church is a replica of the first chapel built in 1786.
July-August, daily 11 a.m.-5 p.m.

SPECIAL EVENTS
INTERNATIONAL SNOWMOBILERS FESTIVAL

506-737-1866; www.isfim.net

This festival features snowmobile events on both sides of the international border in Madawaska, Maine and Edmundston. Highlights include a two-day Lucky Run, Fun Night and many more events for snowmobilers. Sledders from throughout the U.S. and Canada converge on the beautiful St. John Valley for three days of riding top-rated trails.
Early February.

JAZZ & BLUES FESTIVAL

Place de l'Hotel de Ville Park, Edmundston, 506-737-8188; www.jazzbluesedmundston.com

This is Edmundston's annual jazz festival which features a variety of different jazz and blues performances along with food and drink vendors.
Third weekend in June.

L'ACADIE DES TERRES ET FORÊTS EN FÊTE
Republic Provincial Park, Saint-Jacques, 506-739-0919;
www.acadiedesterresetforets.com
The performance celebrates 400 years of Acadian history through song, dance and theater. The representations are held on a natural site. Early July-mid-August.

LA FOIRE BRAYONNE
Place Brayonne, Edmundston, 506-739-6608; www.foirebrayonne.com
This French heritage festival features concerts, crafts, cultural activities and sporting events. Late July-early August.

FREDERICTON
See also Saint John
In the 1950s, the patron of this city, the late Lord Beaverbrook, raised Fredericton from a quiet provincial capital to a major cultural center. Born in Ontario, this British newspaper baron maintained a strong loyalty to New Brunswick, the province of his youth. Wander the elm tree-lined streets through the Green, a lovely park along the St. John River, and admire examples of Beaverbrook's generosity. Nestled along the tree-shaded Green sits Christ Church Cathedral, an 1853 example of decorated Gothic architecture. The art gallery that is Beaverbrook's namesake boasts a collection worthy of continent-wide pride.

WHAT TO SEE
BEAVERBROOK ART GALLERY
703 Queen St., Fredericton, 506-458-2028; www.beaverbrookartgallery.org
The collection here includes 18th- to 20th-century British paintings, 18th- and early 19th-century English porcelain, historical and contemporary Canadian and New Brunswick paintings; and a Hosmer-Pillow-Vaughan Collection of European fine and decorative arts from the 14th to 20th centuries. Admission: adults $8, seniors $6, students $3. Monday-Saturday 9 a.m.-5:30 p.m., Sunday noon-5:30 p.m., Thursday until 9 p.m. Closed Monday January-May.

HISTORIC GARRISON DISTRICT
Queen Street between Regent and York streets, Fredericton, 506-460-2129;
www.tourismfredericton.ca
In July and August, there are daily outdoor walking tours. Attractions include the New Brunswick School Days Museum, the York Sunbury Museum, the New Brunswick Sports Hall of Fame, and the Guard House and the Casemate Artisans Shops.

KINGS LANDING HISTORICAL SETTLEMENT
20 Kings Landing Road, Kings Landing, 506-363-4999; www.kingslanding.nb.ca
Settlement of 70 buildings, costumed staff of 100; recalls Loyalist lifestyle of a century ago. Carpenter's shop, general store, school, church, blacksmith shop, working sawmill and gristmill, inn; replica of a 19th-century wood

river craft. All restoration and work is done with tools of the period. Admission: adults $15.50, seniors $13.50, students $12.50, children 6-16 $10.50. Early June-mid-October, daily 10 a.m.-5 p.m.

MACTAQUAC PROVINCIAL PARK

1256 Route 105, Mactaquac, 506-363-4747; www.nbparks.ca
This park covers approximately 1,400 acres of farmland and forest overlooking the headpond of Mactaquac Dam. There is boating, swimming beaches, fishing, hiking, camping, golf, picnic areas, playgrounds, a restaurant and a store. Also in the vicinity are a historic village, a fish culture station and a generating plant.
Rates vary. Daily 8 a.m.-dusk.

ODELL PARK

397 Waggoners Lane, Fredericton, 506-458-8530; www.nbparks.ca
Odell Park is a unique example of the primeval forest of New Brunswick which is part of the original land grant. On its approximately 400 acres, there is a lodge, picnic area, play area, walking paths through woods, ski trail and an arboretum with 1.7-mile trail.
Daily dawn-10 p.m.

OFFICERS' SQUARE

397 Queen St., Fredericton, 506-460-2129; www.tourismfredericton.ca
This square features a park with Lord Beaverbrook statue. There are changing of the guard ceremonies (July-August); band concerts Tuesday and Thursday evenings (June-August) and theater in the park.

OLD OFFICERS' QUARTERS

397 Queen St., Fredericton; www.tourismfredericton.ca
These quarters features the typical architecture of Royal Engineers in the Colonial period which includes stone arches, iron handrails and a stone staircase. An older part near the river has thicker walls of solid masonry and hand-hewn timbers.

YORK-SUNBURY HISTORICAL SOCIETY MUSEUM

571 Queen St., Fredericton, 506-455-6041; www.yorksunburymuseum.com
Permanent and changing exhibits of military and domestic area history; seasonal exhibitions of history, and New Brunswick crafts and fine arts are featured at this museum.
Admission: adults $3, students $1. July-early September, Monday-Saturday 10 a.m.-5 p.m., Sunday noon-5 p.m.; April-June and early September-November, Tuesday-Saturday 1-4 p.m.; rest of year, by appointment.

SPECIAL EVENTS
HARVEST JAZZ AND BLUES FESTIVAL

Fredericton, 506-454-2583, 888-622-5837; www.harvestjazzandblues.com
This festival covers five days of performances from newer and more established local and international musicians at venues throughout Fredericton. Mid-September.

NEW BRUNSWICK HIGHLAND GAMES AND SCOTTISH FESTIVAL

Government House, 51 Woodstock Road, Fredericton, 506-452-9244, 888-368-4444;
www.highlandgames.ca

Immerse yourself in Scottish culture while listening to pipe bands, watching traditional dances, purchasing crafts and more.
Last weekend in July.

NEW BRUNSWICK SUMMER MUSIC FESTIVAL

Fredericton, 506-458-7836; www.cel.unb.ca/music

Classical musicians celebrate chamber music at these outdoor concerts held throughout the downtown.
Late August.

WHERE TO STAY

★★★DELTA FREDERICTON HOTEL

225 Woodstock Road, Fredericton, 506-457-7000, 888-462-8800;
www.deltahotels.com

This brownstone hotel sits directly in front of the St. John River. The guest rooms are spacious, and the décor reflects a combination of styles. Rooms offer views of the river or surrounding woods, and the onsite bar is a local favorite gathering spot.

222 rooms. Restaurant, bar. Business center. Fitness center. Pool. Spa. Pets accepted. $151-250

MONCTON

See also Fredericton

The Petitcodiac River and its branches twist and turn through this commercial and cultural center of the Atlantic provinces, becoming a mudflat clustered with sea gulls at the record-breaking low tides. Moncton is an excellent beginning for a tour to the northeast along the coast to beautiful Kouchibouguac National Park. Nearby, Shediac, "Lobster Capital of the World," boasts one of the finest beaches in Canada—Parlee Beach—with endless white sand dunes and the warmest ocean waters north of Virginia. Moncton, a bustling center with great shopping and plentiful amenities, hosts sailing regattas, hydroplane races, festivals, seafood and coastal relaxation.

WHAT TO SEE

FORT BEAUSEJOUR NATIONAL HISTORIC SITE

111 Fort Beauséjour Road, Aulac, 506-536-4399; www.pc.gc.ca

Built by the French between 1751 and 1755 during their long struggle with England for possession of Acadia. Attacked in 1755, the fort was captured by the British under Colonel Monckton who renamed it Fort Cumberland. Following its capture, the fort was strengthened and its defenses extended. During the American Revolution in 1776, it withstood an attack by revolutionaries. It was manned by a small garrison during the War of 1812. Three casements and a massive stone curtain wall have been restored. There are displays on history and the culture of Isthmus of Chignecto; and outdoor paintings showing the garrison as it existed in 18th century. There is a panoramic view of the site and surrounding salt marshes.

Admission: adults $3.90, seniors $3.40, children 6-16 $1.90. June-mid-October, daily 9 a.m.-5 p.m.

FUNDY NATIONAL PARK
Highway 114, Alma, 506-887-6000; www.pc.gc.ca/fundy
On the coast between Saint John and Moncton sits an extraordinary parcel of land—80 square miles of forested hills and valleys crisscrossed by miles of hiking trails. Cliffs front much of the rugged coastline, home of the highest tides in the world. To view this phenomenon, visit the beaches at Herring Cove, Point Wolfe and the picturesque town of Alma. Since the ocean water is cold enough for only the bravest of souls, swim in the heated saltwater pool or in one of the lakes. There is also golf, tennis, lawn bowling, picnicking, camping and cross-country skiing available. There are amphitheater programs and guided beach walks.
Admission: adults $7.80, seniors $6.80, children 6-16 $3.90.

HOPEWELL ROCKS PROVINCIAL PARK
Route 114 to Hopewell Cape, Albert County, 506-856-2940, 877-734-3429;
www.thehopewellrocks.ca
Unique cliffs, caves and flowerpot-shaped pillars of conglomerate rock are interspersed with shale and sandstone layers. The tourist information center has interpretive displays and tour guides are available. Visitors are advised to watch for caution signs, avoid loose cliff sections, stay off cliffs and return from the beach by the time posted at the stairs to avoid problems with rising tides. There are picnicking areas and a restaurant.
Admission: adults $8.50, seniors and students $7.25, children 5-18 $6.25.
Mid-May-mid-October, daily.

MAGNETIC HILL ZOO
125 Magic Mountain Road, Moncton, 506-877-7718; www.moncton.org/zoo
This 40-acre wild animal park and petting zoo represents many species, housing 400 animals including wildfowl, the great-horned owl, watusi, African lion, and many more.
Admission: varies by season. Mid-May-Labor Day, daily 9 a.m.-7 p.m.; Labor Day-October, daily 10 a.m.-6 p.m.; November-April, daily 10 a.m.-4 p.m.

PARLEE BEACH PROVINCIAL PARK
45 Parlee Beach Road, Pointe-du-Chêne, 506-533-3363; www.nbparks.ca
Parlee Beach boasts some of the warmest salt water north of Virginia, with vast sand dunes and clear swimming waters. Besides supervised swimming, enjoy volleyball, football and sand-sculpture competitions. The site includes restaurants, a canteen, an amphitheater, showers, washrooms, a playground, a picnic area and ample parking. Nearby you'll also find camping facilities, a marina, more restaurants, accommodations and cultural activities.
June-August, daily 8 a.m.-10 p.m.

TIDAL BORE

Tidal Bore Park, Moncton, New Brunswick, 506-853-3590; www.moncton.ca

A small tidal wave running upstream to usher in the Bay of Fundy tides on the normally placid Petitcodiac River. The water level rises more than 25 feet in an hour. The bore arrives twice daily.

SPECIAL EVENTS
ATLANTIC SEAFOOD FESTIVAL

506-855-8525; www.atlanticseafoodfestival.com

Enjoy all things seafood while listening to musicians from the Maritime provinces and observing the culinary skills of international celebrity chefs. Late August.

SHEDIAC LOBSTER FESTIVAL

Shediac, 506-532-1122; www.shediaclobsterfestival.ca

Since 1949, the Shediac Lobster Festival has drawn visitors from all over the world to feast on succulent lobster and soak up Acadian and maritime culture for five days in July. Ride the midway, watch the kids' parade and enjoy musical performances.
Early July.

WHERE TO STAY
★★★DELTA BEAUSEJOUR

750 Main St., Moncton, 506-854-4344, 800-268-1133; www.deltahotels.com

This stylish urban hotel is located in the heart of downtown Moncton, overlooking the Petitcodiac River. The spacious guest rooms feature contemporary décor. Guests can take advantage of bicycle rentals and walking maps available through the hotel.
310 rooms. Restaurant, bar. Fitness center. Pool. Pets accepted. $151-250

SAINT JOHN

See also Fredericton

The largest and oldest city in the province, this deep-sea port was founded by loyalists to the British crown after the American Revolution. Saint John is a vibrant arts and entertainment community with pristine parks, steep, history-lined streets, quality dining, shopping and festivals. The highest tides in the world rise here, where the powerful Saint John River changes its flow at the Reversing Falls—a natural wonder to watch, but even more so to ride in a specially designed jet boat. Day adventures from the city base include bird watching, whale watching, canoeing or kayaking the amazing Bay of Fundy ecosystem. Take a walking tour of the oldest incorporated city in Canada and shop at the historic Old City Market.

WHAT TO SEE
BARBOUR'S GENERAL STORE

King and Water streets, Saint John, 506-658-2855; www.tourismsaintjohn.com

This restored general store reflects the period between 1840 and 1940 and features 2,000 artifacts and a wide selection of old-fashioned grocery items, china, yard goods, farm implements and cooking tools. There is also a recre-

ated post office, a barbershop with a wicker barber's chair, a pharmacy with approximately 300 samples of cure-alls and a potbellied stove. Staff are outfitted in period costumes.
Admission: free. Mid-June-mid-September, daily 10 a.m.-6 p.m.

CARLETON MARTELLO TOWER NATIONAL HISTORIC PARK
454 Whipple St., Saint John, 506-636-4011, 888-773-8888; www.pc.gc.ca
These circular coastal forts were built for the War of 1812 and used in World War II as a fire command post for harbor defenses when a two-story superstructure was added. There is a restored 1840s powder magazine and a barrack room. Enjoy a panoramic view of the city, the harbor and the surrounding landscape. Guided tours of the tower are available.
Admission: adults $3.90, seniors $3.40, children 6-16 $1.90. June-early October, daily 10 a.m.-5:30 p.m.

FERRY SERVICE TO DIGBY, NOVA SCOTIA
877-762-7245; www.bayferries.com
This car and passenger ferry offers trips from Saint John, New Brunswick to Digby, Nova Scotia and allows you to feel the wind on your face and enjoy a trip on the water. Reservations required.

IRVING NATURE PARK
Sand Cove Road, Saint John, 506-653-7367; www.jdirving.com
This nature park features winding coastal road and hiking trails. Harbor seals, porpoises and many species of migrating birds can be viewed offshore. There are picnicking areas available to relax and enjoy the surrounding beauty.
Admission: free. May-early November, hours vary.

LOYALIST HOUSE
120 Union St., Saint John, 506-652-3590;
www.saintjohn.nbcc.nb.ca/host/loyalisthouse/
Built by David Daniel Merritt, a United Empire Loyalist from New York, this house has been the home to six generations. This gracious Georgian mansion remains much as it was when it was built in 1810-1817.
Admission: adults $3, children and students $1. Mid-May-June, Monday-Friday 10 a.m.-5 p.m.; July-mid-September, daily 10 a.m.-5 p.m.; rest of year, by appointment.

NEW BRUNSWICK MUSEUM
Market Square, Saint John, 506-643-2300, 888-268-9595; www.nbm-mnb.ca
Canada's oldest continuous museum contains everything from international fine art and decorative objects to exhibits detailing the human and natural history of New Brunswick. Exhibits include skeletons of a right whale, a mastodon and a geologic trail through time.
Admission: adults $6, seniors $4.75, children and students $3.25. Monday-Friday 9 a.m.-5 p.m., Thursday until 9 p.m., Saturday 10 a.m.-5 p.m., Sunday noon-5 p.m. Closed Monday November-mid-May.

REVERSING FALLS

Fallsview Park, Saint John, 506-658-2937; www.tourismsaintjohn.com

As the tides of the Bay of Fundy rise and fall, they cause the water of the St. John River to change the direction of its flow.

SAINT JOHN CITY MARKET

47 Charlotte St., Saint John, 506-658-2820; www.sjcitymarket.ca

This centralized market, dating to 1876, sells fresh meats and vegetables as well as indigenous baskets and handicrafts. Various vendors feature a breakfast on Saturday mornings with tasty treats such as waffles and pancakes. Monday-Friday 7:30 a.m.-6 p.m., Saturday 7:30 a.m.-5 p.m.

TRINITY ROYAL HERITAGE PRESERVATION AREA

115 Charlotte St., Saint John, 506-693-8558; www.trinityroyal.com

This 20-block heritage area, located in the city center, features 19th-century residential and commercial architecture, handicrafts and specialty goods as well as restaurants, galleries and more.

WHERE TO STAY

★★DELTA BRUNSWICK

39 King St., Saint John, 506-648-1981, 888-890-3222; www.deltahotels.com

254 rooms. Restaurant, bar. Fitness center. Pool. Pets accepted. $61-150

★★★HILTON SAINT JOHN

1 Market Square, Saint John, 506-693-8484, 800-561-8282; www.hilton.com

Connected by an above ground, sheltered pedway to the Saint John Trade and Convention Center, Market Square shopping mall, New Brunswick Museum, and Canada Games Aquatic Centre, this hotel overlooking the Saint John Harbor and waterfront is centrally located. Guest rooms feature white duvet-covered beds, large-view windows, large work desks and minibars.

197 rooms, Restaurant, bar. Business center. Fitness center. Pool. Pets accepted. $151-250

ST. ANDREWS

See also Saint John

Dramatic scenery frames this oceanside golf mecca, a playground of the rich and famous through the years and long recognized as one of North America's premier destinations for the game. Much unchanged over the past 100 years, St. Andrews is a town of character and charm, complemented by many historic sites including the Algonquin Hotel, a War of 1812 Blockhouse, the Charlotte County Courthouse and an impressive collection of period homes. The old downtown commercial core is a shopper's paradise, especially renowned for handicrafts and woolen products. The Public Wharf at the center of town acts as the gateway to the abundant recreational water activities of Passamaquoddy Bay. The Fundy Isles dot the bay, the most famous of which is Campobello. Here, Franklin Delano Roosevelt spent his summers from 1905 to 1921 when he was stricken with infantile paralysis. Tours of Roosevelt's cottage in the International Park are available. Nearby, a ferry leaves for Grand Manan Island, a popular vacation destination with picturesque lighthouses and tiny fishing villages nestled in the barren seaside cliffs.

WHAT TO SEE
ALGONQUIN GOLF COURSES
184 Adolphus St., St. Andrews, 506-529-8823; www.fairmontgolf.com/algonquin
Since 1894, this 18-hole championship course has offered wooded glades and beautiful shoreline views, as well as an executive nine-hole course. Late April-late October.

BLOCKHOUSE NATIONAL HISTORIC SITE
Harriet Street and Joe's Point Road, St. Andrews, 506-529-4270; www.pc.gc.ca
The sole survivor of coastal defenses built during the War of 1812, this historic site was restored in 1967.
Admission: adults and seniors $0.90, children 6-16 $0.40. June-August, daily 10 a.m.-6 p.m.

HUNTSMAN MARINE SCIENCE CENTER AQUARIUM & MUSEUM
1 Lower Campus, St. Andrews, 506-529-1202; www.huntsmanmarine.ca
This aquarium and museum features displays of coastal and marine environments with many fish and invertebrates found in waters of the Passamaquoddy Region. A "Touch Tank" allows visitors to handle marine life found on local rocky beaches. There are also displays of live animals including local amphibians, reptiles and a family of harbor seals. Explore exhibits on local geology and a seaweed collection.
Admission: adults $7.50, seniors $6.50, children 4-17 $5. Mid-May-August, daily 10 a.m.-5 p.m.; September, Thursday-Sunday 10 a.m.-5 p.m.

KINGSBRAE GARDEN
220 King St., St. Andrews, 506-529-3335, 866-566-8687; www.kingsbraegarden.com
This garden contains 27 acres of walking trails that pass more than 45,000 flowers, shrubs and other plants.
Admission: adults $9.75, seniors and students $8.25. Mid-May to early October, daily 9 a.m.-6 p.m.

ROSS MEMORIAL MUSEUM
188 Montague St., St. Andrews, 506-529-5124; www.townsearch.com/rossmuseum
This museum, housed in a circa-1824 redbrick Georgian mansion, houses the furniture and art collection of a prominent local family.
Admission: by donation. June-early October, Monday-Saturday 10 a.m.-4:30 p.m.; rest of year, by appointment.

WHERE TO STAY
★★★THE FAIRMONT ALGONQUIN
184 Adolphus St., St. Andrews, 506-529-8823, 866-540-4403;
www.fairmont.com/algonquin
This seaside resort overlooks Passamaquoddy Bay, with an area of tidal changes that varies 28 feet between the high and low tides. Guest rooms feature period décor in the main historic building and a more contemporary

style in the 1993 Prince of Wales wing. The fourth-floor rooms, originally the servants' quarters, offer the best views of the bay and surrounding country-side. Croquet, shuffleboard and bocce ball are among the activities offered. 234 rooms. Restaurant, bar. Fitness center. Pool. Spa. Pets accepted. Beach. Golf. Tennis. $151-250

★★★★KINGSBRAE ARMS

219 King St., St. Andrews, 506-529-1897; www.kingsbrae.com
Housed in a circa-1897 country house, this intimate inn overlooks the breath-taking Passamaquoddy Bay. Nearby are a renowned golf course, art galleries and the old town. Each suite has a gas fireplace, marble bathroom and a separate living room. The restaurant is popular with locals and visitors alike thanks to its focus on fresh, seasonal and local food, particularly seafood. Settle in for a pre-determined menu of several courses and enjoy a selection from the award-winning cellar.
9 rooms. Closed October-May. Restaurant. Pool. Pets accepted. $351 and up

WHERE TO EAT
★★THE LIBRARY LOUNGE & BISTRO

The Fairmont Algonquin, 184 Adolphus St., St. Andrews, 506-529-8823; www.fairmont.com/algonquin
American. Breakfast, lunch, dinner. Reservations recommended. Outdoor seating. $16-35

NEWFOUNDLAND AND LABRADOR

NEWFOUNDLAND AND LABRADOR OFFER SO MANY ICONIC SOUNDS AND SCENES, IT'S ALMOST impossible to pick a representative few: thousand-year-old icebergs, multicolored saltbox houses, fishing villages, fjords, lighthouses, whales, endless pubs and that Irish-origin lilt.

Wake up each day and walk outside, talk to the locals, tell them what mood you're in and see where it takes you. You might plan to tour the coastline by sea kayak one afternoon, but suddenly find yourself in a pub eating pan-fried cod. Or set out to tour a museum one morning and end up shopping along the oldest street in North America.

In Gros Morne National Park, exposed rock has been found that is 1.25 billion years old—as old as the planet itself. The mountains and fjords in this UNESCO World Heritage Site are 20 times older than the Rockies. Travel along some of the 10,500 miles of coastline to see 10,000-year-old icebergs drifting past or humpback whales in their annual migration to the north. See the Northern Lights from Labrador more than 240 nights a year, where endless wilderness shelters wildlife such as moose, black bears.

Thirty-five million seabirds gather in this province every year. Human visitors hike, bike, kayak, fish for Atlantic salmon and brook trout, dogsled, snowmobile, ski, golf on more than 20 courses, and visit archaeological and historic sites.

ST. JOHN'S

For more than 500 years, St. John's—the provincial capital and home of Canada's greatest number of per-capita pubs—has been visited by European explorers, adventurers, soldiers and pirates. First discovered in 1497 by John Cabot and later claimed as the first permanent settlement in North America for the British Empire by Sir Humphrey Gilbert, St. John's has a rich and colorful history. St. John's is cradled in a harbor carved from granite and surrounded by hills running down to the ocean. This city is bursting with old world charm, unique architecture, historic and natural attractions, and excellent facilities and services. And if that's not enough, a short drive brings visitors to spectacular coastlines, historic villages and a diverse selection of wildlife.

WHAT TO SEE
BOTANICAL GARDENS
Pippy Park, 306 Mount Scio Road, St. John's, 709-737-8590; www.mun.ca/botgarden
Memorial University's Botanical gardens cover 110 acres of land close to the heart of St. John's. It is unusual in its dual purposes of botanical garden and natural reserve. The gardens include a rock garden, peat and woodland beds, cottage garden, perennial garden, rhododendrons and a display of Newfoundland heritage plants. Five nature trails meander through a managed natural reserve.
Admission: varies by season. May-September, daily 10 a.m.-5 p.m.;
October-November, daily 10 a.m.-4 p.m.

CAPE SPEAR NATIONAL HISTORIC SITE

Route 11, Blackhead/Cape Spear, 709-772-5367; www.pc.gc.ca

Just six miles from St. John's, Cape Spear National Historic Site is situated at the most eastern point in North America. Here, overlooking the North Atlantic, stands the oldest surviving lighthouse (open mid-May-mid-October) in Newfoundland, a World War II coastal defense battery and the place where the light of dawn is first seen in North America.

Admission: adults $3.90, seniors $3.40, children $1.90. Daily.

THE FLUVARIUM

Pippy Park, Nagle's Place (North Bank of Long Pond), St. John's, 709-754-3474; www.fluvarium.ca

A unique facility on the shores of Long Pond in the heart of Pippy Park, this structure includes a series of nine panoramic viewing windows that give visitors a chance to see the secret underwater life of a river. This is the only year-round public fluvarium in North America. There are also exhibits that relate to freshwater ecology and guided tours are available year-round.

Admission: adults $5.50, seniors and students $4.50, children $3.50. Monday-Friday 9 a.m.-5 p.m., Saturday-Sunday noon-5 p.m.

GRAND CONCOURSE WALKWAYS

439 Allandale Road, St. John's, 709-737-1077; www.grandconcourse.ca

There are more than 74 miles of walkways connecting ponds, lakes and rivers in three municipalities making this one of the best walking networks in Canada.

INSTITUTE FOR OCEAN TECHNOLOGY

Prince Philip Drive, St. John's, 709-772-4939; www.iot-ito.nrc-cnrc.gc.ca

The Institute for Ocean Technology is an innovative research facility for ship technology and the oil and gas industries. Learn how scale-model ocean vessels are made and tested. See models of Hibernia and Terra Nova. View the ocean simulated indoors and the world's largest Ice Tank.

JOHNSON GEO CENTRE

175 Signal Hill Road, St. John's, 709-737-7880 , 866-868-7625; www.geocentre.ca

The Johnson Geo Centre tells the story of "Our Earth and Our People" through the remarkable geology of Newfoundland and Labrador. The large, glass-encased entry is the only part of the building above ground. Most of the 33,600 square feet of floor space is underground.

Admission: adults $11.50, seniors and students $9, children 5-17 $5.50. Monday-Saturday 9:30 a.m.-5 p.m., Sunday noon-5 p.m. Closed Monday mid-October-mid-May.

MILE ONE CENTRE & ST. JOHN'S FOG DEVILS

50 New Gower St., 709-758-1111; www.mileonecentre.com

Mile One Centre is a first-class multipurpose sports and entertainment facility located next to City Hall on New Gower Street in the heart of downtown St. John's. It is home to the Quebec Major Junior Hockey League, the St. John's Fog Devils and hosts numerous entertainment events, including concerts by top artists from around the world, ice shows, family shows, conventions and local hockey events.

OCEAN SCIENCE CENTRE OF MEMORIAL UNIVERSITY
Marine Drive (Route 30), Logy Bay, 709-737-3708; www.mun.ca/osc
The Ocean Sciences Centre is a cold ocean research facility operated in conjunction with Memorial University of Newfoundland. Located in Logy Bay, the Centre houses laboratories where research is conducted on the North Atlantic fishery, aquaculture, oceanography, ecology and physiology. Research is conducted on organisms ranging from bacteria to seals. In summer months, visitors experience an ocean life touch tank and Seal Facility.

THE ROOMS
9 Bonaventure Ave., St. John's, 709-757-8000; www.therooms.ca
Visit the new home housing the combined collections of the Provincial Archives of Newfoundland and Labrador, the Provincial Museum of Newfoundland and Labrador, and the Art Gallery of Newfoundland and Labrador. There are sixteen galleries and exhibit halls to explore as well as an 180-seat multimedia theater. There is also a restaurant and gift shop here.
Admission: adults $7.50, seniors and students $5, children 6-16 $4.
Monday-Saturday 10 a.m.-5 p.m., Wednesday until 9 p.m., Sunday noon-5 p.m. Closed Monday mid-October-May.

SIGNAL HILL NATIONAL HISTORIC SITE
Signal Hill Road, St. John's, 709-772-5367; www.pc.gc.ca
This site marks the spot where Marconi received the first transatlantic wireless signal in 1901. During the summer, watch cadets perform 19th-century British military drills.
Admission: adults $3.90, seniors $3.40, children 6-16 $1.90. Visitor center: Mid-May-mid-October, daily 10 a.m.-6 p.m.; mid-October-mid-May, Monday-Friday 8:30 a.m.-4:30 p.m.

ST. JOHN'S WATERFRONT
Harbor Drive, St. John's
To get a real sense of St. John's, a walk along the waterfront is a must. The harbor, located in the historic downtown, has provided shelter to explorers, merchants, soldiers, pirates and mariners of all kinds during the last 500 years. Historic buildings, coves, plaques and parks along the route help depict the history of St. John's.

NOVA SCOTIA

NOVA SCOTIA HAS BEEN DESCRIBED AS A "MUST-SEE" DESTINATION, AND CAPE BRETON has been lauded as the world's most scenic island. All this can be attributed to the surprising contradictions of this compact land: a slick and sophisticated urban scene populated with down-to-earth friendly folk; sumptuous accommodations with a rustic twist; and Zen-like Oceanside relaxation alongside the kind of raucous parties and festivals that are epic to the most seasoned of sailors.

In Nova Scotia, a rich and diverse past is not just showcased at museums and heritage sites. It still lives and breathes in communities throughout the province—with ancient forts, cannons, saltbox houses and fishing villages standing unchanged. Cape Breton Island, in particular, offers a chance to truly explore this province's vivid Celtic culture and history. Here is where they say "ciad mile failte," which means "a hundred thousand welcomes." Throughout each of Nova Scotia's scenic highways, a cosmopolitan experience—from art galleries, live theatre, shopping, spas and major sports events—is presented against a setting of colorful history and rich tradition.

Historic waterfronts are home to great restaurants, live music and popular festivals that use the harbor as a backdrop, including the International Buskers Festival, the Riverfront Music Jubilee and the Tall Ships Challenge. Spend the day shopping at a stylish boutique in Wolfville or Truro. Find the perfect souvenir to remember your trip with a stop at one of the many historic markets or quaint gift shops in the busy shopping districts in Yarmouth Sydney. Spring Garden Road in Halifax, one of the country's oldest retail thoroughfares, is where you'll find the season's must-haves.

Visit the rugged Atlantic Coast and the rich Annapolis Valley, which rolls down to the Bay of Fundy where the world's highest tides rise and fall. Follow the Northumberland Shore where you'll find the warmest waters north of Virginia and long stretches of beach. Witness the Highlands of Cape Breton rising above the sea. And follow the south shore from Halifax, a chain of seaside villages peppered with hidden coves, beaches, antique stores, crafts and bistros, and anchored by Lunenburg, home of the famed Bluenose schooner and UNESCO World Heritage Site. Two beautiful national parks (Kejimkujik National Park and Cape Breton Highlands National Park) and more than one hundred provincial parks add to the bounty.

ANTIGONISH

See also Baddeck

This harbor town, the commercial and cultural home base for northeast Nova Scotia, was settled by Highland Scottish immigrants and American Revolutionary War soldiers and their families. Antigonish is home to the oldest continuously run Highland Games in North America. Located just west of the Canso Causeway, the gateway to Cape Breton and its highlands, the town is surrounded by scenic rivers and hills.

WHAT TO SEE
SHERBROOKE VILLAGE
Sherbrooke, 902-522-2400, 888-743-7845; www.museum.gov.ns.ca/sv
This restored 1860s village reflects the area's former status as a prosperous river port. Historic buildings of that era are being restored and refurnished, including family homes, a general store, drugstore, courthouse, jail and post office. Watch demonstrations of blacksmith forging, water-powered sawmill operation or take horse-drawn wagon rides. Visitors can watch or try spinning, weaving and quilting. There is also a restaurant here.
Admission: adults $10, seniors $8, children $4.25. June-mid-October, daily 9:30 a.m.-5 p.m.

ST. NINIAN'S CATHEDRAL
Antigonish, 902-863-2338; www.antigonishdiocese.com
Built in 1867 in Roman Basilica style of blue limestone and sandstone from local quarries, the interior was decorated by Ozias LeDuc, the Paris-trained Quebec artist. Gaelic words, Tigh Dhe (House of God), appear inside and out, representing the large Scottish population in the diocese who are served by the cathedral.

SPECIAL EVENT
HIGHLAND GAMES
Columbus Field, 91 Main St., Antigonish; www.antigonishhighlandgames.com
This Scottish festival comprises the longest running Highland Games in North America. Events include pipe band concerts, Highland dancing, traditional athletic events and a massed pipe band tattoo.
Mid-July.

WHERE TO STAY
★★ CLAYMORE INN
137 Church St., Antigonish, 902-863-1050; www.claymoreinn.com
75 rooms. Restaurant, bar. Pool. $61-150

★★MARITIME INN
158 Main St., Antigonish, 902-863-4001, 888-662-7484; www.maritimeinns.com
32 rooms. Restaurant, bar. Pets accepted. $61-150

WHERE TO EAT
★★LOBSTER TREAT
241 Post Road, Antigonish, 902-863-5465
Seafood. Lunch, dinner. Closed January-April. $16-35

BADDECK
See also Antigonish
This tranquil, scenic village, situated midway between Canso Causeway and Sydney, is a good headquarters community for viewing the many sights on the Cabot Trail and around the Bras d'Or lakes. Fishing, hiking, swimming and picnicking are among favorite pastimes along the beautiful shoreline.

WHAT TO SEE
ALEXANDER GRAHAM BELL NATIONAL HISTORIC SITE OF CANADA

559 Chebucto St., Baddeck, 902-295-2069; www.pc.gc.ca

This site features three exhibition halls dealing with Bell's numerous fields of experimentation, including displays on his work with the hearing impaired, telephones, medicine, marine engineering and aerodynamics.

Admission: adults $7.80, seniors $6.55, children 6-16 $3.90. May-October, hours vary by month; rest of year, by appointment.

CELTIC MUSIC INTERPRETIVE CENTRE

5471 Route 19, Judique, 902-787-2708; www.celticmusicsite.com

Learn about the heritage and tradition of local music through photos, vintage recordings, interviews with musicians, live performances and exhibits. Admission: $12. Daily 9 a.m.-5 p.m.

CAPE BRETON HIGHLANDS NATIONAL PARK

16648 Cabot Trail, Cheticamp, 902-224-2306, 888-773-8888; www.pc.gc.ca

The famous Cabot Trail, a modern 184-mile paved highway loop beginning at Baddeck, is among the most scenic drives in North America. It runs through this national park, offering visitors spectacular vistas, beaches and trails. The hiking trail system is large and diverse, providing access to the area's remote interior as well as allowing you to explore its rugged coastline. Beaches and campgrounds are plentiful and golf is also popular, with the Highlands Links in Ingonish being one of the best 18-hole courses in Canada.

Admission: adults $7.80, seniors $6.80, children 6-16 $3.90. Daily; limited services mid-October-mid-May.

FORTRESS OF LOUISBOURG NATIONAL HISTORIC SITE

259 Park Service Road, Louisbourg, 902-733-2280; www.pc.gc.ca

This 11,860-acre park includes the massive Fortress erected by the French between 1719 and 1745 to defend their possessions in the new world. It is the largest reconstructed 18th-century French fortified town in North America. Explore the governor's apartment, soldiers' barracks, the chapel, the Dauphin Demi-Bastion, the King's storehouse, the engineer's house, several private dwellings and storehouses and the royal bakery. Sample 18th-century food amongst costumed guides who interpret the town as it was in 1744.

Admission: adults $17.60, seniors $14.95, children 6-16 $8.80. June-mid-October, hours vary; limited service late May and late October.

GAELIC COLLEGE

51779 Cabot Trail, St. Ann's, 902-295-3411; www.gaeliccollege.edu

This is the only institution of its kind in North America dedicated to preservation of Gaelic traditions. There are also special summer and winter programs.

GLENORA INN & DISTILLERY

Route 19, Glenville, 902-258-2662, 800-839-0491; www.glenoradistillery.com

This is the only distillery in North America to produce single malt whiskey. You can also explore a museum and grab a pint in the pub. There is also a

restaurant, inn and gift shop. Distillery tours are also offered.
Admission: adults $7. Early May-mid-October, daily 9 a.m.-5 p.m.

GREAT HALL OF THE CLANS
51779 Cabot Trail, St. Ann's, 902-295-3411; www.gaeliccollege.edu
The Great Hall of the Clans features a colorful historic display of Scot-origin clans, tartans and migrations. There is a genealogical area and audiovisual section where you can learn about the life and times of Highland pioneers and see relics of Cape Breton giant Angus MacAskill.
Admission: adults $7, students $5.50. June-September, hours vary.

WHERE TO STAY
★★★AUBERGE GISELE'S INN
387 Shore Road, Baddeck, 902-295-2849, 800-304-0466; www.giseles.com
Overlooking the Bras d'Or Lakes, the inn is close to the Bell Bay Golf Course, Highland Links and Uisge Ban Falls Park. The inn offers bike rentals as well as sailing tours of the lake. Enjoy international cuisine at the award-winning restaurant or a cocktail in the lounge.
75 rooms. Restaurant, bar. Closed mid-October-mid-May. $61-150

★★★KELTIC LODGE RESORT AND SPA
Middle Head Peninsula, Ingonish Beach, 902-285-2880, 800-565-0444;
www.signatureresorts.com
Perched high on a cliff overlooking the Atlantic Ocean, this resort provides a choice of rooms in the main lodge, inn or cottages. A top golf course sits next door, and guests can also enjoy kayaking, hiking, whale watching, beaches and complimentary bicycles. An Aveda spa offers massages and facials.
104 rooms. Restaurant, bar. Fitness center. Pool. Beach. Tennis. Closed mid-October-late May. $251-350

WHERE TO EAT
★★GRUBSTAKE
7499 Main St., Louisbourg, 902-733-2308; www.grubstake.ca
Steak, seafood. Lunch, dinner. Closed October-mid-June. $36-85

DIGBY
Best known for its delicious scallops and picturesque harbor, this summer resort has many historic landmarks that date back to its founding in 1783 by Sir Robert Digby and 1,500 Loyalists from New England and New York. This Annapolis Basin town is the ideal headquarters for adventures down the Digby Neck peninsula, whose Bay of Fundy shores measure the highest tides in the world. Off Digby Neck are Long Island and Brier Island, reachable by ferry—both are popular sites for rock collecting, whale watching and bird watching. Swim along sandy beaches and hike shoreline trails past lighthouses and wildflower-filled forests. A 35-mile drive to the northeast leads to Annapolis Royal and Port Royal, the first permanent European settlements in North America. Marking this is the restored fur-trading fort, the Habitation of Port Royal, built by Samuel de Champlain. With high, imposing cliffs, gently rolling farmland and quiet woodland settings, this seacoast drive creates a study in contrasts.

NOVA SCOTIA ★★★ ★★★ ★

WHAT TO SEE
POINT PRIM LIGHTHOUSE
Lighthouse and Bayview roads, Digby, 888-463-4429
Located on a rocky promontory, Point Prim has a view of the Bay of Fundy.
July-August.

TRINITY CHURCH
109 Queen St., Digby, 902-245-6744; www.unityserve.org/trinity
The only church in Canada built by shipwrights; the church cemetery is famous for inscriptions by pioneer settlers.
Monday-Friday; Sunday services.

SPECIAL EVENT
SCALLOP DAYS
Water Street, Digby, 902-245-4531; www.digbyscallopdays.com
This fest features scallop-shucking contests, a parade, a pet show, entertainment, sporting events , fishing, and water events.
Second week in August.

WHERE TO STAY
★★ADMIRAL DIGBY INN
441 Shore Road, Digby, 902-245-2531, 800-465-6262; www.digbyns.com
47 rooms. Restaurant, bar. Pool. Pets accepted. Closed mid-October-mid-May. $61-150

★★DIGBY PINES GOLF RESORT & SPA
103 Shore Road, Digby, 902-245-2511, 800-667-4637; www.signatureresorts.com
Built in 1929, this resort is located in a magnificent setting on a terraced hillside, overlooking the Annapolis Basin, just a mile from St. John's ferry terminal. Spacious public rooms feature many of the original furnishings. 147 rooms. Restaurant, bar. Fitness center. Pool. Spa. Golf. Tennis. Closed mid-October-mid-May. $151-250

WHERE TO EAT
★★FUNDY RESTAURANT
34 Water St., Digby, 902-245-4950, 866-445-4950; www.fundyrestaurant.com
Seafood. Breakfast, lunch, dinner. Outdoor seating. $16-35

GRAND PRÉ
See also Halifax
Grand-Pré is a heartland of Acadian culture in Canada—a rich tapestry of history in a pastoral setting of rolling hills, charming villages and vineyards. Founded by Acadian settlers who remained there until their expulsion began in 1755 (immortalized by Henry Wadsworth Longfellow with his epic poem, *Evangeline*), the village of Grand Pré has provided a home for immigrant farmers and artisans for more than 300 years. One of Nova Scotia's best-known wineries, Domaine de Grand Pré, is an evocative culinary destination. Grand-Pré is also Canada's first designated Historic Rural District.

WHAT TO SEE
ACADIAN MEMORIAL CHURCH
1 Annapolis Valley RR, Grand Pré, 902-490-5946; www.acadian-home.org
Featured here is a display commemorating the Acadian settlement and expulsion. There is an old Acadian Forge; a bust of Longfellow's Evangeline
statue; and a formal landscaped gardens with original French willows.

GRAND PRÉ NATIONAL HISTORIC SITE
Grand Pré, 902-542-3631; www.pc.gc.ca
Grand Pré commemorates the Acadian settlement from 1682 through 1755
and the Deportation of the Acadians, which began in 1755 and continued
until 1762. There are interpretive presentations and multimedia exhibits.
Grounds and gardens are open year-round.
Admission: adults $7.80, seniors $6.55, children 6-16 $3.90. Mid-May-
mid-October 9 a.m.-6 p.m.

WHERE TO STAY
★★★BLOMIDON INN
195 Main St., Wolfville, 902-542-2291, 800-565-2291; www.blomidon.ns.ca
Overlooking the Bay of Fundy, this inn was built as a sea captain's mansion
and has 4 acres of Victorian gardens and quaint rooms filled with antiques.
29 rooms. Restaurant. Complimentary breakfast. Tennis. $151-250

★★OLD ORCHARD INN
153 Greenwich Road South, Wolfville, 902-542-5751, 800-561-8090;
www.oldorchardinn.com
105 rooms. Restaurant, bar. Pool. Spa. Tennis. Pets accepted. $$151-250

★★★TATTINGSTONE INN
620 Main St., Wolfville, 902-542-7696, 800-565-7696; www.tattingstone.ns.ca
Victorian and Georgian period antiques fill the comfortable and inviting
rooms at this charming inn. Meals incorporate the locally grown produce.
10 rooms. Complimentary breakfast. Pool. Tennis. $61-150

HALIFAX AND DARTMOUTH
See also Grand Pré
The capital of Nova Scotia and the largest city in the Atlantic Provinces, of-
fers a delightful combination of old and new. Founded in 1749 as England's
stronghold in the North Atlantic, it is a bustling commercial, scientific and
educational center. Centrally situated in the province, Halifax is perfectly
suited as the starting point for the Evangeline and Glooscap Trails, the Light-
house Route and the Marine Drive with their scenic and historic sights. With
the world's second-largest natural harbor and an array of historical sites, fish-
ing villages, beaches and pubs within its municipal borders, this city prom-
ises some of the most diverse explorations of any urban center in Canada.

WHAT TO SEE
ART GALLERY OF NOVA SCOTIA
1723 Hollis St., Halifax, 902-424-7542; www.agns.gov.ns.ca
Located in the center of Halifax, this gallery features permanent collections and changing exhibits covering artists from Novia Scotia and elsewhere. They also offer programs and events throughout the year.
Admission: adults $10, seniors $8, students $5, children 6-17 $3, children 5 and under free. Daily 10 a.m.-5 p.m., Thursday until 9 p.m. Tours: Daily 2:30 p.m., Thursday 2:30 p.m. and 7 p.m.

BLACK CULTURAL CENTRE
1149 Main St., Dartmouth, 902-434-6223, 800-465-0767; www.bccns.com
History and culture of Africans in Nova Scotia, which was the destination for many on the Underground Railroad that led escaped slaves from American plantations. The area, not coincidentally, was also home to the first free black community in North America.
Admission: adults $6, seniors and students $4. September-May, Tuesday-Friday 9 a.m.-5 p.m., June-September, Tuesday-Friday 9 a.m.-5 p.m., Saturday 10 a.m.-3 p.m.

HALIFAX CITADEL NATIONAL HISTORIC PARK
Sackville and Brunswick streets, Halifax, 902-426-5080; www.pc.gc.ca
The most visited historic site in Canada, this historic park features a star-shaped hilltop fort built between 1828 and 1856. There are also restored signal masts, a library, barrack rooms, powder magazine, expense magazine, defense casement and garrison cell. Exhibits cover communications, the four Citadels and engineering and construction. There is also an Army Museum and orientation center. Visit the coffee bar, which serves typical 19th-century soldiers' food, take a guided tour and watch the changing of the guard.
Admission: adults $11.70, seniors $10.05, children 6-16 $5.80. Early May-October, hours vary; rest of year, grounds open without services.

HISTORIC PROPERTIES (PRIVATEERS WHARF)
Upper Water St., Halifax, 902-429-0530; www.historicproperties.ca
There are a variety of clothing, specialty shops, restaurants and pubs housed in several restored 18th-century buildings along the waterfront.

MARITIME MUSEUM OF THE ATLANTIC
1675 Lower Water St., Halifax, 902-424-7490; www.museum.gov.ns.ca/mma
The museum contains 1,675 exhibits displaying more than 24,000 artifacts from the nautical history of Nova Scotia, and an exhibit on the Titanic.
Admission: varies by season. November-April, Tuesday 9:30 a.m.-8 p.m, Wednesday-Saturday 9:30 a.m.-5 p.m., Sunday 1-5 p.m.; May-October, Monday 9:30 a.m.-5:30 p.m., Tuesday 9:30 a.m.-8 p.m., Wednesday-Saturday 9:30 a.m.-5:30 p.m., Sunday 9:30 a.m.-5:30 p.m.; Sunday June-September 9:30 a.m.-5:30 p.m.

NEPTUNE THEATRE

1593 Argyle St., Halifax, 902-429-7070, 800-565-7345; www.neptunetheatre.com

Home of an internationally recognized theater company, Neptune Theatre presents six main stage plays per season in Fountain Hall, which seats nearly 500. The Studio Theatre offers productions in a more intimate setting.
See Web site for ticket and schedule information.

NOVA SCOTIA MUSEUM OF NATURAL HISTORY

1747 Summer St., Halifax, 902-424-7353; www.museum.gov.ns.ca/mnh

This museum of natural history features permanent exhibits on man and his environment in Nova Scotia and offers changing exhibits.
Admission: adults $5.75, children 6-17 $3.75. Hours vary by season. Free Wednesday 5-8 p.m.

PIER 21

1055 Marginal Road, Halifax, 902-425-7770; www.pier21.ca

Pier 21 is Canada's Ellis Island. Between 1928 and 1971, more than one million immigrants and wartime evacuees took their first steps on Canadian soil here. Now a National Historic Site, the pier features traveling exhibits, live performances, the Wall of Ships, Immigrant Testimonial Stations and the Wall of Honor.
Admission: adults $8.50, seniors $7.50, students $6, children 6-16 $5.
Hours vary by season.

POINT PLEASANT PARK

5718 Point Pleasant Drive, Halifax, 902-421-6519; www.pointpleasantpark.ca

Visit ruins of several historic forts and monument in the heart of the city. There are also nature trails, a public beach and picnic areas to enjoy. Cross-country skiing is offered in the winter.
Daily 6 a.m.-midnight.

PRINCE OF WALES TOWER NATIONAL HISTORIC PARK

S. Tower Road, Point Pleasant Park, Halifax, 902-426-5080; www.pc.gc.ca

Known locally as Martello Tower, this fort was built in the late 1790s to protect British batteries and is said to be first tower of its type in North America. Exhibits portray the tower's history, architectural features and significance as a defensive structure.
Admission: free. July-early September, daily 10 a.m.-6 p.m.

PROVINCE HOUSE

1726 Hollis St., Halifax, 902-424-4661; www.gov.ns.ca/legislature

This is the oldest provincial parliament building in Canada. It houses the office of Premier and the legislative library. Guided tours are available.
July-August, Monday-Friday 9 a.m.-5 p.m., Saturday-Sunday 10 a.m.-4 p.m.; September-June, Monday-Friday 9 a.m.-4 p.m.

PUBLIC GARDENS

5711 Sackville St., Halifax, 902-421-6550; www.halifaxpublicgardens.ca

Created in 1836 by the Novia Scotia Horticultural Society, these formal Victorian gardens make up more than 16-acres with trees, flower beds, duck ponds and fountains. There is also a bandstand and concession area. The gardens were designated a National Historic Site in 1984. Before heading to the gardens, please note that pets are not allowed, and neither are bicycles. Jogging is also permitted.

Early May-mid-November, daily 8 a.m.-sunset.

SHEARWATER AVIATION MUSEUM

13 Bonaventure St., Shearwater, 902-720-1083; www.shearwateraviationmuseum.ns.ca
This museum features and extensive collection of aircraft and exhibits on the history of Canadian Maritime Military Aviation.

Admission: by donation. June-August, Monday-Friday 10 a.m.-5 p.m., Saturday-Sunday noon-4 p.m.; September-November and April-May, Tuesday-Friday 10 a.m.-5 p.m., Saturday noon-4 p.m.; rest of year, by appointment.

ST. GEORGE'S ROUND CHURCH

2222 Brunswick St., Halifax, 902-423-1059; www.roundchurch.ca
This Byzantine-style church was built in 1801 at the direction of Edward, Duke of Kent, father of Queen Victoria. Nearby is St. Patrick's Roman Catholic Church, a Victorian Gothic building. On Barrington Street is St. Paul's Church, the first church in Halifax and oldest Protestant church in Canada. Be sure to check out the "explosion window" on the Argyle Street side; during a 1917 explosion that destroyed a large portion of the city, the third window of the upper gallery shattered, leaving the silhouette of a human head.

SPECIAL EVENTS
ATLANTIC JAZZ FESTIVAL

Spring Garden Road at Queen Street, Halifax, 902-492-2225;
www.atlanticjazzfestival.ca
This nine day jazz festival features amateur musicians, established local artists as well as world-famous performers. There are more than 65,000 people who attend this festival for the many peformances and music workshops. July.

HALIFAX HIGHLAND GAMES & SCOTTISH FESTIVAL

Dartmouth Common, Dartmouth, 902-876-0189; www.halifaxhighlandgames.com
The games are the centerpiece at this five day celebration of Scottish culture, which includes competitions in piping, drumming, pipe bands and heavyweight events. There are theme concessions, food vendors and a beer tent with Celtic music onsite. July.

NOVA SCOTIA INTERNATIONAL AIR SHOW

902-465-2725; www.nsairshow.ca
This is one of the premier air spectaculars in North America. September.

NOVA SCOTIA INTERNATIONAL TATTOO

Halifax Metro Centre, 1800 Argyle St., Halifax, 902-451-1221; www.nstattoo.ca

The world's largest indoor variety show, with more than 2,000 Canadian and international performers, this 10-day event features military bands, pipes and drums, choirs, gymnasts, dancers and military displays and competitions. Late June-early July.

WHERE TO STAY

★★CAMBRIDGE SUITES HOTEL HALIFAX

1583 Brunswick St., Halifax, 902-420-0555, 800-565-1263; www.cambridgesuiteshotel.com

200 rooms. Restaurant, bar. Complimentary breakfast. Business center. Fitness center. $151-250

★★★CITADEL HALIFAX HOTEL

1960 Brunswick St., Halifax, 902-422-1391, 800-565-7162; www.citadelhalifax.com

This comfortable hotel offers a convenient location for both business and leisure travelers. It is adjacent to the Citadel Hill National Historic Site and the World Trade and Convention Centre.

267 rooms. Restaurant, bar. Business center. Fitness center. Pool. Pets accepted. $61-150

★★★DELTA BARRINGTON

1875 Barrington St., Halifax, 902-429-7410, 888-890-3222; www.deltahotels.com

Connected by the Downtown Link—an enclosed, above-ground pedestrian walkway—to two shopping centers, this downtown hotel is also a block from the waterfront. Comfortable guest rooms feature Nova Scotia country pine furniture and pillow-top mattresses. An enclosed central courtyard provides a view of greenery to inner rooms and corridors.

200 rooms. Restaurant, bar. Business center. Fitness center. Pool. Pets accepted. $151-250

★★★DELTA HALIFAX

1990 Barrington St., Halifax, 902-425-6700, 888-890-3222; www.deltahotels.com

Located in the heart of downtown, this hotel is adjacent to the Scotia Square Shopping Centre and connected to the pedway. Guest rooms are comfortable and include luxury bath amenities.

296 rooms. Restaurant, bar. Business center. Fitness center. Pool. Pets accepted. $151-250

★★★HALIFAX MARRIOTT HARBOURFRONT

1919 Upper Water St., Halifax, 902-421-1700, 800-943-6760; www.marriott.com

This hotel is the home of the only Halifax casino and is located in the heart of downtown. Rooms feature updated linens and pillowtop mattresses, plus large workspaces.

352 rooms. Restaurant, bar. Business center. Fitness center. Pool. Spa. Pets accepted. $151-250

★★★THE LORD NELSON HOTEL & SUITES

1515 S. Park St., Halifax, 902-423-6331, 800-565-2020; www.lordnelsonhotel.com
Conveniently located in downtown Halifax, the Lord Nelson is across the street from the Victorian-style Halifax Public Gardens, a block south of Citadel Hill and close to Dalhousie University.
260 rooms. Restaurant, bar. Business center. Fitness center. Pets accepted. $251-350

★★★OAK ISLAND RESORT AND SPA

36 Treasure Drive, Western Shore, 902-627-2600, 800-565-5075;
www.oakislandinn.com
This oceanfront resort approximately one hour's drive from Halifax overlooks Mahone Bay and its many islands, including the famous Oak Island, rumored to be the hiding place of Captain Kidd's buried treasure.
105 rooms. Restaurant, bar. Business center. Fitness center. Pool. Spa. Pets accepted. Tennis. $151-250

★★PRINCE GEORGE HOTEL

1725 Market St., Halifax, 902-425-1986, 800-565-1567; www.princegeorgehotel.com
This downtown hotel has classically decorated guest rooms with mahogany furnishings and comfortable beds. A covered walkway connects the hotel to the World Trade and Convention Centre, the Halifax Metro Centre, and the Halifax Casino.
203 rooms. Restaurant, bar. Business center. Fitness center. Pool. Pets accepted. $151-250

★★★THE WESTIN NOVA SCOTIAN

1181 Hollis St., Halifax, 902-421-1000, 888-679-3784; www.westin.ns.ca
This historic brick hotel, originally built as a Canadian National Railway hotel, is located just above the Halifax Harbor Waterfront. The hotel includes a lighted waterfront tennis court and conference and banquet facilities. The lobby is richly traditional in design and furnishings, and guest rooms are well stocked with amenities.
310 rooms. Restaurant, bar. Business center. Fitness center. Pool. Pets accepted. Tennis. $151-250

WHERE TO EAT
★★ROCCO'S

313 Prince Albert Road, Dartmouth, 902-461-0211; www.roccosrestaurant.ca
Italian. Breakfast (Monday-Friday), lunch (Monday-Friday), dinner, Sunday brunch. $16-35

★★★SALTY'S ON THE WATERFRONT

1869 Upper Water St., Halifax, 902-423-6818; www.saltys.ca
A blue-and-white-striped awning welcomes you to this casual seafood restaurant at the end of the Privateers, a 19th-century wharf, overlooking the Halifax Harbor in the Historic Properties area of downtown. Sample fresh lobsters or grilled swordfish sourced in local waters.
Seafood. Lunch (Monday-Friday), dinner. Outdoor seating. $36-85

ONTARIO

WHILE THE REST OF CANADA LOVES TO TEASE TORONTO FOR ITS BIG-CITY GRAVITY, THIS metropolitan hub and its surrounding province justify its ego. A colorful and endless mishmash of wilderness adventure, diverse cultures, urbane cosmopolitanism and rustic rural scenery, the province of Ontario has it all.

Ontario can be divided into north and south—the far northern wilderness dominated by lakes, forests and logging camps, while the southern is an agricultural, industrial and commercial hive inhabited by 90 percent of the population.

Toronto, the provincial capital, and Ottawa, the nation's capital, offer tourists a wide spectrum of vibrant and world-class theater, restaurants, galleries, museums and recreational facilities. The Stratford Festival in Stratford and the Shaw Festival in Niagara-on-the-Lake are not to be missed, and the same goes for the spectacular Niagara Falls. Ontario's many recreational areas, such as Algonquin and Quetico provincial parks and St. Lawrence Islands National Park, offer a bounty of camping, hiking and all varieties of outdoor adventure. To the north lie Sudbury and Sault Ste. Marie; to the northwest, Thunder Bay, Fort Frances and Kenora, which offer canoeing, fishing and hunting. Perhaps more appealing than any one attraction is the vast, unspoiled nature of the province itself. More than 400,000 lakes and magnificent forests form a huge vacationland just a few miles from the U.S. border stretching all the way to Hudson Bay.

BRANTFORD
See also Hamilton, Stratford
Brantford offers world-class gardens, museums and cultural attractions, scenic trails and paddling—all just an hour's drive from Toronto. Home to the Alexander Graham Bell Homestead National Historic Site, it was here that the great inventor conceived his idea for the telephone. Brantford is also the hometown of hockey legend Wayne Gretzky—and for the ultimate dose of Canada's national sport and spirit, view memorabilia from the career of The Great One alongside other local sports legends at the Gretzky Sports Hall of Recognition.

WHAT TO SEE
GLENHYRST ART GALLERY OF BRANT
20 Ava Road, Brantford, 519-756-5932; www.glenhyrst.ca
The gallery at this 16-acre estate contains changing exhibits of paintings, sculpture, photography and crafts from both local and international artists. Don't skip the beautiful grounds and nature trails surrounding the estate.
Tuesday-Friday 10 a.m.-5 p.m., Saturday-Sunday 1-5 p.m.

HER MAJESTY'S ROYAL CHAPEL OF THE MOHAWKS
301 Mohawk St., Brantford, 519-756-0240; www.mohawkchapel.ca
The first Protestant church in Ontario, the Mohawk Chapel is the only Royal Native Chapel in the world belonging to Six Nations people.
Daily 10 a.m.-5 p.m.

SANDERSON CENTRE FOR THE PERFORMING ARTS
88 Dalhousie St., Brantford, 519-758-8090, 800-265-0710;
www.sandersoncentre.on.ca
This 1919 vaudeville house has been restored and transformed to a theater featuring music, dance and dramatic performances.

WOODLAND CULTURAL CENTRE
184 Mohawk St., Brantford, 519-759-2650; www.woodland-centre.on.ca
Preserves and promotes the culture and heritage of the First Nations of the eastern woodland area. There are education, research and museum programs, art shows and annual festivals.

SPECIAL EVENTS
RIVERFEST
Lions Park Arena, 12 Edge St., Brantford, 519-751-9900
This three-day festival celebrates the Grand River with entertainment, fireworks and crafts.
Last weekend in May.

SIX NATIONS FALL FAIR & POWWOW
Ohsweken Fairgrounds, Fourth Line and Chiesswood, Brantford, 519-445-0783
Native dances, authentic craft and art exhibits are all part of this fall fair.
Weekend after Labor Day.

SIX NATIONS NATIVE PAGEANT
Seneca and Sour Springs roads, Brantford, 519-445-4528;
www.sixnationspageant.com
This pageant takes place at the Forest Theatre at Six Nations reserve, where Six Nations people reenact their history and culture.
First three weekends in August.

WHERE TO STAY
★★HOLIDAY INN BRANTFORD
664 Colborne St. E., Brantford, 519-758-9999, 800-465-4329
The rooms at this Holiday Inn are spacious. Guests also enjoy free hot breakfasts and Internet access.
98 rooms. Restaurant, bar. Pool. $61-150

WHERE TO EAT
★★★OLDE SCHOOL RESTAURANT
Paris Road West at 687 Powerline Road W., Brantford, 519-753-3131, 888-448-3131;
www.theoldeschoolrestaurant.ca
This steak and seafood restaurant, located in a relatively rural area, is housed in a 1850s schoolhouse with a bell tower and beautifully landscaped grounds. Before or after dinner, stop by the piano lounge.
Steak, seafood. Lunch. $251-350

GANANOQUE

See also Kingston

Nestled in the heart of the Thousand Islands, Gananoque is homebase for endless boating, sailing, canoeing, kayaking, jet skiing, scuba diving, water taxis and charters. St. Lawrence Islands National Park made up of nearly two-dozen beautiful islands, features nature trails, parks, beaches and island camping. Visitors can enjoy unique exhibits at the Historic Thousand Islands Village, a heritage center located on the waterfront. The Thousand Islands Playhouse is one of the region's most acclaimed professional theaters, featuring stage productions from May until October.

WHAT TO SEE
1000 ISLANDS CAMPING RESORT
1000 Islands Parkway, Gananoque, 613-659-3058; www.1000islandsinfo.com
This beautiful campground area with features a pool. Tent and trailer sites are available, as well as a playground, nature trails and miniature golf.

1000 ISLANDS SKYDECK
Hill Island, Lansdowne, 613-659-2335; www.1000islandsskydeck.com
The 400-foot tower offers views of the 1000 Islands and the St. Lawrence River. Visitors ride an elevator that takes 40 seconds to reach the first of three observation decks.
Mid-April-May, September-October, daily 9 a.m.-6 p.m.; June-August, daily 9 a.m.-8 p.m.

GANANOQUE BOAT LINE
6, Water St., Gananoque, 613-382-2144; www.ganboatline.com
Get out on the open water with a three-hour tour through the 1000 Islands with a stop at Boldt Castle. Mid-May-mid-October, schedule varies.

GANANOQUE HISTORICAL MUSEUM
10 King St. E., Gananoque, 613-382-4024
This former Victoria Hotel from 1863 allows you to explore how life was back then, with access to the parlor, dining room, bedroom, and kitchen all furnished in the Victorian style. Military and indigenous artifacts, china, glass, 19th- and 20th-century costumes are on display.
June-October, daily.

ST. LAWRENCE ISLANDS NATIONAL PARK
2 County Road 5, 14 miles east of Gananoque, Mallorytown, 613-923-5261,
800-839-8221; www.pc.gc.ca
Established in 1904, this park lies on a 50-mile stretch of the St. Lawrence River between Kingston and Brockville. It consists of 20 island areas and a mainland headquarters at Mallorytown Landing. The park offers boat launching facilities, beaches, natural and historic interpretive programs, island camping, picnicking, hiking and boating. A visitor reception center and the remains of an 1817 British gunboat are at Mallorytown Landing and open mid-May to mid-October. The islands can be accessed by water taxi or by rental boats at marinas along both the Canadian and American sides.
Monday-Friday 8 a.m.-4:30 p.m.

WHERE TO STAY
★★★GANANOQUE INN
550 Stone St. S., Gananoque, 613-382-2165, 800-465-3101; www.gananoqueinn.com
This historic inn is located on the banks of the St. Lawrence River in the heart of the Thousand Islands. Many of the rooms have fireplace and jacuzzis, and all are heavy on personalized charm and coziness.
57 rooms. Restaurant, bar. Spa. $61-150

★★★TRINITY HOUSE
90 Stone St. S., Gananoque, 613-382-8383, 800-265-4871; www.trinityinn.com
In the heart of the famous Thousand Islands, this fully restored 1859 home has antiques mixed together with modern amenities. Guests can wander through Victorian perennial gardens with herbs and flowers used by the chef in preparing the evening meals.
8 rooms. Complimentary breakfast. Restaurant, bar. Spa. $61-150

HAMILTON
See also Brantford, Toronto
Hamilton, linked to Toronto by the majestic Skyway Bridge, is a vibrant community with excellent dining, galleries and shopping. Emerging artists make their home downtown, a bustling engine of creative energy with a thriving gallery scene. Browse for antiques and collectibles, or wander through cobbled streets for a club scene that swings till the wee hours. The waterfront is a mecca for hikers, boarders and water sports enthusiasts, while buyers flock to the cornucopia of ethnic food stores and shops on Ottawa Street. Circling the cosmopolitan pleasures of the city is the splendor of the Royal Botanical Gardens, the famous Bruce Trail and an abundance of conservation areas, water parks and walking paths.

WHAT TO SEE
AFRICAN LION SAFARI

1386 Cooper Road, Flamborough, 519-623-2620, 800-461-9453; www.lionsafari.com
Drive-through this active wildlife park and spy exotic animals and bird shows, as well as training demonstrations.
Check Web site for details.

ART GALLERY OF HAMILTON
123 King St. W., Hamilton, 905-527-6610; www.artgalleryofhamilton.on.ca
This gallery boasts a collection of more than 8,000 sculptures and photographs covering several centuries by American, Canadian, British and European artists.
Tuesday-Wednesday noon-7 p.m., Thursday-Friday noon-9 p.m., Saturday-Sunday noon-5 p.m.

BATTLEFIELD HOUSE AND MONUMENT
77 King St., Stoney Creek, 905-662-8458; www.battlefieldhouse.ca
Devoted to the Battle of Stoney Creek, this 1795 settler's home and monument honors one of the most significant encounters of the War of 1812. Some rooms are furnished as a farm home of the 1830s and guides are dressed in

period costumes. June 15-Labor Day Tuesday-Sunday 11 a.m.-4 p.m.; Labor Day-June 14, Tuesday-Sunday 1-4 p.m.

CANADIAN FOOTBALL HALL OF FAME AND MUSEUM

58 Jackson St. W., Hamilton, 905-528-7566; www.cfhof.ca
Sports fans will rejoice once inside this national shrine to Canadian sports, tracing 120 years of football's history.

CHILDREN'S MUSEUM

1072 Main St. E., Hamilton, 905-546-4848; www.myhamilton.ca
The Children's Museum is a participatory learning center where children ages 2 to 13 can expand sensory awareness of the world. Hands-on exhibits will keep kids occupied for hours.
April-September, Tuesday-Saturday 9:30 a.m.-3:30 p.m.; October-March, Wednesday-Saturday 9:30 a.m.-3:30 p.m., Sunday 11 a.m.-4 p.m.

DUNDURN CASTLE

610 York Blvd., Hamilton, 905-546-2872; www.hamilton.ca
Home of Sir Allan Napier MacNab, Prime Minister of the United Provinces of Canada from 1854-1856, this 35-room mansion has been restored to its former splendor. Exhibits and programs run all year.
Canada Day-Labor Day, daily 10 a.m.-4 p.m.; Labor Day-Canada Day, Tuesday-Sunday noon-4 p.m.

FLAMBORO DOWNS

967 Highway 5 W., Flamborough, 905-627-3561; www.flamborodowns.com
Harness racing draws crowds here year-round with a grandstand that seats 3,000. The Confederation Cup race for the top three-year-old pacers in North America is held here every August.
Wednesday-Friday, Sunday-Monday 6 p.m.

HAMILTON'S FARMERS MARKET

55 York Blvd., Hamilton, 905-546-2096; www.hamilton.ca
Fresh produce, flowers, meat, poultry, fish, cheese and baked goods are brought from all over the Niagara garden belt.
Tuesday, Thursday 7 a.m.-6 p.m., Friday 8 a.m.-6 p.m., Saturday 6 a.m.-6 p.m.

ROYAL BOTANICAL GARDENS

680 Plains Road W., Hamilton, 905-527-1158; www.rbg.ca
Colorful gardens, natural areas and a wildlife sanctuary comprise Hamilton's many gardens, including a rock garden with seasonal displays, garden with herbaceous perennials, an arboretum containing world-famous lilacs in late May, a rose garden, a teaching garden, along with woodland, scented and medicinal gardens. At Cootes Paradise Sanctuary, trails wind around more than 1,200 acres of water, marsh and wooded ravines.

SPECIAL EVENTS
AROUND THE BAY ROAD RACE
The Around the Bay Road Race Inc., 1439 Upper Ottawa St., Hamilton, 905-624-0046; www.aroundthebayroadrace.com
Join in Canada's oldest footrace, dating back to 1894. Just dress accordingly—it's often chilly and wet.
Late March.

FESTIVAL OF FRIENDS
Main Street and Gage Avenue, Hamilton, 905-525-6644; www.creativearts.on.ca
A perfect outing for the kids, this festival is packed with musicians, artists, craftsmen, puppets, dancer, mimes and theater performances.
Second weekend in August.

WHERE TO STAY
★★★SHERATON HAMILTON HOTEL
116 King St. W., Hamilton, 905-529-5515, 888-627-8161; www.sheraton.com
Located in downtown Hamilton, this contemporary hotel has direct access to a shopping mall, the Convention Centre and Hamilton Place Concert Hall. Business travelers will appreciate the fitness center, business center and the wireless Internet access.
301 rooms. Restaurant, bar. Pets accepted. Pool. Business center. Fitness center. $151-250

WHERE TO EAT
★★★ANCASTER OLD MILL INN
548 Old Dundas Road, Ancaster, 905-648-1827; www.ancasteroldmill.com
Built in 1792, this building was originally a gristmill. Today it's a great spot to grab consistently good American fare with many organic options and farm fresh ingredients.
American. Outdoor seating. Lunch, Dinner, Sunday brunch. $36-85

KINGSTON
See also Gananoque
Nestled where the Rideau Canal and the St. Lawrence River meet Lake Ontario, Kingston is a freshwater sailor's dream, a city that exquisitely blends history and modern sophistication. Stroll through the bustling downtown and its boutiques and bistros, through its meandering waterfront with heritage-filled neighborhoods and breathtaking parklands.

WHAT TO SEE
AGNES ETHERINGTON ART CENTRE
University Avenue and Queen's Crescent, Kingston, 613-533-2190; www.aeac.ca
This family-friendly art center hosts ever-changing exhibitions of contemporary and historical art.
Tuesday-Friday 10 a.m.-4:30 p.m., Saturday-Sunday 1-5 p.m.

BELLEVUE HOUSE NATIONAL HISTORIC SITE

35 Centre St., Kingston, 613-545-8666; www.pc.gc.ca

This Italianate villa from 1840 was home of Sir John A. Macdonald, the first prime minister of Canada and is replete with restored and furnished period pieces, Multimedia displays and video presentation at the visitor center. April-May, daily 10 a.m.-5 p.m., June-Labor Day, daily 9 a.m.-6 p.m.; Labor Day-October, daily 10 a.m.-5 p.m.

FORT HENRY

1 Fort Henry Drive, Kingston, 613-542-7388, 800-437-2233; www.forthenry.com

One of Ontario's most spectacular historic sites, the present fortification was built in the 1830s and restored during the 1930s. During the guided tour, you'll see 19th-century British infantry and artillery drills; military pageantry; exhibits of military arms, uniforms, equipment and explore garrison life activities.

Mid-May-early October, daily 10 a.m.-5 p.m.

GRAND THEATRE

218 Princess St., Kingston, 613-530-2050; www.whatsonkingston.com/thegrand

This century-old, renovated theater hosts live theater, dance, symphonic and children's performances by professional companies and local groups. There is also a nice summer theater program.

Monday-Saturday 10:30 a.m.-5:30 p.m.

INTERNATIONAL ICE HOCKEY FEDERATION MUSEUM

277 York St., Kingston, 613-544-2355; www.ihhof.com

Hockey is a big deal in Canada, and this museum proves it with displays tracing the history of hockey from its beginning in Kingston in 1885 to the present.

Monday-Saturday 10 a.m.-4 p.m., Sunday noon-4 p.m.

MARINE MUSEUM OF THE GREAT LAKES AT KINGSTON

55 Ontario St., Kingston, 613-542-2261; www.marmuseum.ca

Ships have been built in Kingston since 1678. This museum explores the tales, adventures and enterprise of Inland Seas history. The museum features a ship building gallery, 1889 engine room, with dry dock engines and pumps; artifacts and changing exhibits. Library and archives. The Museum Ship Alexander Henry, a 3,000-ton icebreaker, is open for tours and bed and breakfast accommodations.

WHERE TO STAY

★★★ISAIAH TUBBS RESORT & CONFERENCE CENTRE

RR 1, West Lake Road, Picton, 613-393-2090; www.isaiahtubbs.com

This resort is located on the shores of West Lake and is open year-round. Adjacent to Sandbanks Provincial Park, it's ideal for families or business travelers seeking a little outdoor R&R.

70 rooms. Restaurant, bar. Pool. Tennis. $151-250

★★★MERRILL

343 Main St. E., Picton, 613-476-7451; www.merrillinn.com

This Victorian house was built in 1878 for Edwards Merrill, one of Canada's top barristers. Guest rooms are all decorated with period antiques, and the inn-keepers will make you feel like family.

13 rooms. Complimentary breakfast. Restaurant. $151-250

WHERE TO EAT
★★AUNT LUCY'S

1399 Princess St., Kingston, 613-542-2729; www.auntlucysdinnerhouse.com

Seafood, steak. Lunch, dinner, Sunday brunch. $16-35

KITCHENER-WATERLOO

See also Brantford, Hamilton, Stratford

The twin cities of Kitchener-Waterloo were settled in the early 1800s by Mennonites, Amish and Germans whose cultural heritage is still widely celebrated. A vigorous spirit of youth and industry pervades, and there's plenty of nightlife, restaurants, world-class cultural facilities, over 200 kilometers of community trails and lovely golf courses.

WHAT TO SEE
BINGEMAN PARK

425 Bingemans Centre Drive, Kitchener, 519-744-1555; www.bingemans.com

This recreation center on the banks of the Grand River includes a swimming pool, wave pool, water slides, bumper boats, a go-cart track, arcade, roller skating, miniature golf, golf driving range, batting cages, cross-country skiing, picnicking, restaurant, playground and camping facilities.

FARMERS MARKET

300 King St. E., Kitchener, 519-741-2287; www.kitchenermarket.ca

More than 100 vendors sell fresh produce, meat, cheese and handicrafts. Mennonite specialties are featured.

Saturday 7 a.m.-2 p.m.

GLOCKENSPIEL

King and Benton streets, Hamilton

Canada's first glockenspiel tells the fairy tale of Snow White. Twenty-three bells form the carillon. Performances last 15 minutes.

Four times daily.

JOSEPH SCHNEIDER HAUS

466 Queen St. S., Kitchener-Waterloo, 519-742-7752; www.region.waterloo.on.ca/jsh

The Joseph Schneider Haus Museum and Gallery is a community museum in downtown Kitchener that includes a Georgian-style frame farmhouse. Adjacent Heritage Galleries includes Germanic folk art and changing exhibits. Museum: July-September, Monday-Saturday 10 a.m.-5 p.m., Sunday 1-5 p.m.; September 2-December 24; also by appointment Wednesday-Saturday 10 a.m.-5 p.m., Sunday 1-5 p.m.

PIONEER MEMORIAL TOWER

Pioneer Tower Road and Lookout Lane, Kitchener-Waterloo, 519-571-5684;
www.kwtourism.ca

This tower stands as a tribute to industrious spirit of pioneers who first settled Waterloo County. Cemetery on grounds includes the graves of several original founders. It offers excellent view of Grand River.
May-October.

WATERLOO PARK

100 Westmount Road N., Waterloo, 519-725-0511; www.city.waterloo.on.ca

In this park, there is a log schoolhouse built in 1820, which is surrounded by a picnic area, lake and playground. There is also a small zoo and band concerts in the summer.

SPECIAL EVENTS
KITCHENER-WATERLOO MULTICULTURAL FESTIVAL

102 King St. W., Kitchener-Waterloo, 519-745-2531; www.kwmc.on.ca

Festival will celebrate the festival that Echo readers voted one of the best in the community.
Late June.

WATERLOO BUSKER CARNIVAL

100 Regina St. S., Kitchener-Waterloo, 519-747-8769; www.waterloo-buskers.com

Unique, long-standing and innovative, the Waterloo Busker Carnival is a volunteer driven International Street Performers Festival.
Late August.

WHERE TO STAY
★★★LANGDON HALL COUNTRY HOUSE HOTEL & SPA

1 Langdon Drive, Cambridge, 519-740-2100; www.langdonhall.ca

One would not guess that Langdon Hall Country House is a hotel as you approach the red brick mansion with graceful tall white columns that face a vast, manicured lawn. Country-style décor and antique charm awaits visitors, who will appreciate the variety of room styles, from the Stable Terrace to the Rose Suite. The house, formerly Eugene Langdon Wilks' vacation home more than 100 years ago, was designed in the classic American Federal Revival style, much of which is maintained today. The hotel is complete with wedding services, a spa and high-end restaurant, but the best feature is its 200-acre "backyard," home to the Cloister Garden, Maple Lane and the Woodland Walk.
52 rooms. Restaurant, bar. Fitness center. Business center. Spa. $251-350

★★★WATERLOO INN

475 King St. N., Waterloo, 519-884-0220, 800-361-4708;
www.waterlooinn.com

This hotel is close to the famous St. Jacob's Farmers Market, the Elora Gorge and the Stratford Festival. The rooms are charming and comfortable, with personal touches throughout.
155 rooms. Restaurant, bar. Pets accepted. Fitness center. Pool. $61-150

WHERE TO EAT
★★★CHARCOAL STEAK HOUSE
2980 King St. E., Kitchener, 519-893-6570; www.charcoalsteakhouse.ca
Consistently delicious steaks and a relaxing, serene atmosphere have made the Charcoal Steak House a Kitchener favorite for more than 50 years. The menu, which highlights Canadian steaks and fresh seafood, offers choices for all. A number of cocktails choices are offered in addition to an award-winning wine list.
Steak. Lunch, dinner, Sunday brunch. Reservations recommended. $36-85

★★★★THE DINING ROOM AT LANGDON HALL
Langdon Hall Coutry House Hotel & Spa, 1 Langdon Drive, Cambridge, 519-740-2100; www.langdonhall.ca
Executive chef Jonathan Gushue heads this lovely restaurant which features dishes made with fresh local ingredients. The Dining Room's true star is its dinner menu, but it is also open for breakfast, brunch and lunch. For dinner, try the robust herb-basted rainbow trout or the dry-aged Aberdine beef tenderloin. If you're really looking for an unforgettable dining experience, Gushue also prepares a $95 tasting menu with wine pairings, featuring poached Arctic char with local morels and a crispy St. Jacobs pig cheek, followed by delightful strawberry compote with lime sorbet.
American, French. Breakfast, lunch, dinner, Sunday brunch. Jacket required. Reservations recommended. $86 and up

SPA
★★★THE SPA AT LANGDON HALL
Langdon Hall Coutry House Hotel & Spa, 1 Langdon Drive, Cambridge, 519-624-3220; www.langdonhall.ca
Along with the traditional body and facial treatments, the Spa at Langdon Hall offers hydrotherapy sessions, which include de-stressing, detoxifying or a re-mineralizing bath. The private baths are powerful, with 100 jets that promise to relax the tightest knots. A detoxifying seaweed wrap will leave you feeling rejuvenated, and the Vichy Aroma Rain Body Therapy—a sea salt and jojoba body scrub under rainfall—is an invigorating treatment that results in super soft skin.

LONDON
See also Stratford
London is a busy, modern city with a charming small-town atmosphere. Located on the Thames River, its street names echo "the other" London, as does the contrast of Victorian architecture and contemporary skyscraperss. You'll find theaters, provincial parks and some of the best freshwater beaches in the world. Every summer evening, the lights dim and the curtain rises on stages throughout the area for the famous Stratford Festival, London's entertainment flagship.

WHAT TO SEE
DOUBLE-DECKER BUS TOURS
300 Dufferin Ave., London, 519-661-5000, 800-265-2602;www.doubledeckertours.com
Two-hour guided tour aboard authentic double-decker English bus with stops

at Storybook Gardens in Springbank Park and the Regional Art Museum. Tours depart from City Hall, Wellington Street and Dufferin Avenue. Reservations recommended.
July-Labor Day, daily.

FANSHAWE PIONEER VILLAGE
2609 Fanshawe Park Road E., London, 519-457-1296; www.fanshawepioneervillage.ca
This living history museum consists of 24 buildings and recreates the life of a typical 19th-century crossroads community in southwestern Ontario. There are log cabins, barns and a stable; blacksmith, weaver, harness, gun, woodworking and barber shops; general store, church, fire hall, school and sawmill and costumed interpreters.
Victoria Day Weekend-Thanksgiving, Tuesday-Sunday 10 a.m.-4:30 p.m.

GRAND THEATRE
471 Richmond St., London, 519-672-8800, 800-265-1593; www.grandtheatre.com
The contemporary façade houses a 1901 theater, built by Colonel Whitney of Detroit and Ambrose Small of Toronto. The interior has been restored to include proscenium arch, murals and cast plasterwork.
October-May.

GUY LOMBARDO MUSIC CENTRE AND MUSEUM
205 Wonderland Road S., London, 519-473-9003; www.guylombardomusic.com
The centre houses artifacts belonging to London-born musician, Guy Lombardo. Exhibits on other big-band era greats are featured as well.

MUSEUM OF ONTARIO ARCHAEOLOGY
1600 Attawandaron Road, London, 519-473-1360; www.uwo.ca/museum
This museum traces the prehistory of southwestern Ontario with more than 40,000 artifacts showing how indigenous people lived thousands of years before Columbus was born. There are archeological and ethnographic exhibits from southwestern Ontario, as well as a gallery, theater and native gift shop.
May-August, daily 10 a.m.-4:30 p.m.; September-December, daily 10 a.m.-4:30 p.m.; January-April, Saturday-Sunday 1-4 p.m.

STORYBOOK GARDENS
1958 Storybook Lane, Springbank Park, London, 519-661-5770; www.storybook.london.ca
Storybook Gardens is a family-oriented theme park featuring a children's playworld and zoo, within London's largest park of 281 acres.
Early May-mid-October, daily.

SPECIAL EVENTS
LONDON FRINGE THEATRE FESTIVAL
476 Richmond St., London, 519-433-3332; www.londonfringe.ca
This citywide festival features theater, spoken word, fims and visual art at various locations for ten days in June.
June.

WHERE TO STAY
★★★HILTON LONDON ONTARIO
300 King St., London, 519-439-1661; www.hiltonlondon.com
An attached heated walkway makes access to the convention center easy
from this hotel and the indoor pool provides a great break to the winter dol-
drums. The rooms are updated and spacious.
322 rooms. Restaurants, bar. Fitness center. Pool. Pet accepted. Business
center. $151-250

WHERE TO EAT
★★MICHAEL'S ON THE THAMES
1 York St., London, 519-672-0111; www.michaelsonthethames.com
French, Italian. Reservations recommended. $36-85

NIAGARA FALLS
See also Niagara-on-the-Lake, St. Catharines
More than 12 million people visit Niagara Falls each year, and not just to see
the the Falls. The area is also home to more than 70 award-winning wineries.
Visitors will also find dozens of excellent golf courses and over 200 kilome-
ters of spectacular cycling and hiking trails. You'll also get a better view of
Niagara Falls from this side of the border.

WHAT TO SEE
CANADA ONE FACTORY OUTLETS
7500 Lundy's Lane, Niagara Falls, 905-356-8989, 866-284-5781;
www.canadaoneoutlets.com
This outlet sells many nationally recognized brands of merchandise from
stores such as The Body Shop, Club Monaco, Guess and Tommy Hilfiger.

GUINNESS WORLD OF RECORDS MUSEUM
4943 Clifton Hill, Niagara Falls, 905-356-2299, 866-656-0310;
www.guinnessniagarafalls.com
Based on the popular book of records, hundreds of original exhibits, artifacts, and laser video galleries are on display, as well as recreations of many
of the world's greatest accomplishments.
Daily.

IMAX THEATRE NIAGARA FALLS
6170 Fallsview Blvd., Niagara Falls, 905-358-3611, 866-405-4629;
www.imaxniagara.com
This six-story-high movie screen shows Niagara: Miracles, Myths and Magic, a film highlighting the Falls. Daredevil Adventure has displays, exhibits
and some of the actual barrels used to traverse the Falls throughout history.

JOURNEY BEHIND THE FALLS
6650 Niagara Parkway, Queen Victoria Park, Niagara Falls, 905-354-1551;
www.niagaraparks.com
An elevator descends to a point about 25 feet above the river, with excellent
views of the Falls from below and behind; waterproof garments are supplied

for visitors.
Open year-round at 9 a.m.

LOUIS TUSSAUD'S WAXWORKS
4960 Clifton Hill, Niagara Falls, 905-356-2238; www.ripleysniagara.com
Louis Tussaud's Waxworks is a collection of instantly recognizable, true-to-life wax figures crafted by recognized wax artists from around the world. Life-size, historically costumed wax figures of the past and present are on display. If you're looking for a scare, head into the Chamber of Horrors.

MARINELAND
7657 Portage Road, Niagara Falls, 905-356-8250; www.marinelandcanada.com
See killer whales, dolphins and sea lions and then visit wildlife displays with deer, bears, buffalo and elk. There are also thrill rides, including one of the world's largest steel roller coasters as well as restaurants and picnic areas.

MINOLTA TOWER CENTRE
6732 Fallsview Blvd., Niagara Falls, 905-356-1501; www.niagaratower.com
This awesome 325-foot tower offers a magnificent 360-degree view of the Falls and surrounding areas. There are eight levels at top with specially designed glass for ideal photography; a Minolta exhibit floor; the Waltzing Waters water and light spectacle; gift shops; incline railway to the Falls and Top of the Rainbow dining rooms overlooking the Falls. Reservations are recommeded.

NIAGARA FALLS AVIARY
5651 River Road, Niagara Falls, 905-356-8888, 866-994-0090;
www.niagarafallsaviary.com
Wander through this 15,000-square-foot 1,394-square-meter conservatory amidst lush foliage. The environment simulates a tropical rainforest in which free-flying birds soar overhead. There are guided and self-guided tours and a restaurant.

NIAGARA FALLS MUSEUM
5651 River Road, Niagara Falls, 416-596-1396; www.niagaramuseum.com
One of North America's oldest museums, founded in 1827, it contains 26 galleries of rare, worldwide artifacts, including Niagara's Original Daredevil Hall of Fame, Egyptian mummy collection and dinosaur exhibit.

NIAGARA PARKS BOTANICAL GARDENS
2565 Niagara Parkway, Niagara Falls, 905-356-8554, 877-642-7275;
www.niagaraparks.com
The Botanical Gardens include nearly 100 acres of horticultural exhibits as well as a nature shop.

NIAGARA PARKS BUTTERFLY CONSERVATORY
2405 Niagara Parkway, Niagara Falls, 905-358-0025, 877-642-7275
Approximately 2,000 butterflies make their home in this 11,000-square-foot, climate-controlled conservatory filled with exotic greenery and flowing wa-

ter. Nearly 50 species of butterflies can be viewed from a 600-foot 180-meter network of walking paths. There is an outdoor butterfly garden and ift shop.

NIAGARA SPANISH AERO CAR
Niagara Falls, 905-354-5711; www.niagaraparks.com
The 1,800-foot cables support a car that crosses the whirlpool and rapids of the Niagara River. It's a five-minute trip each way.
Mid-April-mid-October, daily.

OLD FORT ERIE
350 Lake Shore Road, Fort Erie, 905-871-0540
Fort Erie is the site of some of the fiercest fighting of the War of 1812. It has been restored to the period and offers guided tours of the Glengarry Light Infantry by interpreters dressed in uniform.
May-November, daily 10 a.m.-6 p.m.

SKYLON TOWER
5200 Robinson St., Niagara Falls, 905-356-2651, 866-434-4202; www.skylon.com
Skylon Tower stands 775 feet above the base of the Falls. A three-level dome contains an indoor/outdoor observation deck and revolving and stationary dining rooms served by three external, glass-enclosed Yellow Bug elevators. There are also specialty shops at base of tower.

SPECIAL EVENT
WINTER FESTIVAL OF LIGHTS
Queen Victoria Park, Murray Street and River Road, Niagara Falls, 800-563-2557; www.wfol.com
Celebrate the start of the winter season with parades, fireworks, light displays and Disney shows.
Late November-late January.

WHERE TO STAY
★★★DOUBLETREE FALLSVIEW RESORT & SPA BY HILTON-NIAGARA FALLS
6039 Fallsview Blvd., Niagara Falls, 905-358-3817, 800-222-8733; www.niagarafallsdoubletree.com
Cathedral ceilings with wood beams, slate floors and freshly baked chocolate chip cookies welcome guests. The property is within walking distance to area attractions. The spacious guest rooms offer panoramic views of the upper Niagara River. Art lovers can check out the in-house gallery, Ochre Art Gallery. For pure relaxation, the Five Lakes AVEDA Day Spa is the place to go. Buchanans Chophouse is the perfect spot to unwind.
224 rooms. Restaurant, bar. Spa. Pool. Business center. Fitness center. $151-250

★★EMBASSY SUITES HOTEL NIAGARA FALLS/FALLSVIEW
6700 Fallsview Blvd., Niagara Falls, 905-356-3600, 800-420-6980; www.embassysuitesniagara.com
512 rooms. Complimentary breakfast. Restaurant, bar. Pool. $61-150

★★★HILTON NIAGARA FALLS
6361 Fallsview Blvd., Niagara Falls, 905-354-7887, 888-370-0325;
www.hiltonniagarafalls.com
Located in the heart of the bustling Niagara Falls tourist area, this hotel is near all the area attractions. The dramatic lobby features lots of pale ochre marble and blond wood and many of the guest rooms offer outstanding views.
516 rooms. Restaurant, bar. Pool. Business center. $151-250

★★★MARRIOTT NIAGARA FALLS FALLSVIEW
6740 Fallsview Blvd., Niagara Falls, 905-357-7300, 888-501-8916;
www.niagarafallsmarriott.com
Directly across from Horseshoe Falls, this is a prime Niagara Falls location. Area attractions, restaurants and shops are nearby. The interior of this elegant hotel has a light, sunny feel. The Falls can be viewed from many of the guest rooms as well as right in the lobby.
432 rooms. Restaurant, bar. Pool. Business center. $151-250

★★★RENAISSANCE FALLSVIEW HOTEL
6455 Fallsview Blvd., Niagara Falls, 905-357-5200, 888-238-9176;
www.renaissancefallsview.com
This hotel is very close to Niagara Falls and the Queen Victoria Park. The rooftop dining room provides views of the Falls.
262 rooms. Restaurant, bar. Pool. Business center. $151-250

★★★SHERATON FALLSVIEW HOTEL AND CONFERENCE CENTRE
6755 Fallsview Blvd., Niagara Falls, 905-374-1077, 800-618-9059; www.fallsview.com
Guests can walk to the falls and numerous area attractions, restaurants and shops. The large two-story lobby has a curved staircase with comfortable, casual seating. Guest rooms are attractive and feature deep blue bed coverings, luxurious linens and comfortable mattresses.
402 rooms. Restaurant, bar. Pets accepted. Pool. Business center. $151-250

WHERE TO EAT
★★BUCHANANS
6039 Fallsview Blvd., Niagara Falls, 905-353-4111; www.niagarafallsdoubletree.com
Steak. Breakfast, lunch, dinner. Reservations recommended. Outdoor seating. $16-35

★★MILLERY
5425 Robinson St., Niagara Falls, 905-357-1234, 800-263-6208;
www.oldstoneinn.on.ca
American. Lunch, dinner. Reservations recommended. $16-35

★★QUEENSTON HEIGHTS
14184 Niagara Parkway, Niagara Falls, 905-262-4274, 877-642-7275;
www.niagaraparks.com
American. Lunch, dinner. Reservations recommended. Outdoor seating. $16-35

★★VICTORIA PARK
6342 Niagara Parkway, Niagara Falls, 905-356-2217; www.niagaraparks.com
American. Closed mid-October-mid-May. Outdoor seating. $36-85

NIAGARA-ON-THE-LAKE
See also Niagara Falls, St. Catharines
Often called the loveliest in Ontario, this picturesque town has a long and distinguished history that parallels the growth of the province, which was once a busy shipping, shipbuilding and active commercial center. The beautiful old homes lining the tree-shaded streets testify to the area's prosperity, and the town's attractions include theater, historic sites, beautiful gardens and Queen Street's shops, hotels and restaurants. Delightful in any season, this is one of the best-preserved and prettiest remnants of the Georgian era.

WHAT TO SEE
BROCK'S MONUMENT
14184 Niagara River Parkway, Niagara, 905-468-4257
This monument emcompassess a massive, 185-foot memorial to Sir Isaac Brock, who was felled by a sharpshooter while leading his troops against American forces at the Battle of Queenston Heights in October 1812. A narrow, winding staircase leads to a tiny observation deck inside the monument. A walking tour of important points on the Queenston Heights Battlefield begins at Brock Monument; Brock and his aide-de-camp, Lieutenant-Colonel Macdonell, are buried here.
Mid-May-Labor Day, daily.

FORT GEORGE NATIONAL HISTORIC SITE
26 Queen St., Niagara-on-the-Lake, Niagara Parkway, 905-468-4257; www.pc.gc.ca
Once the principal British post on the frontier, this fort saw much action during the War of 1812. There are eleven restored, refurnished buildings and massive ramparts.
April-October, daily 10 a.m.-5 p.m.; rest of year, by appointment.

MCFARLAND HOUSE
15927 Niagara Parkway, Niagara-on-the-Lake, 905-356-2241
This Georgian brick home was used as a hospital in the War of 1812 and is furnished in the Loyalist tradition, 1835-1845.
July-Labor Day, daily; mid-May-June and Labor Day-September, Saturday-Sunday.

NIAGARA APOTHECARY
5 Queen St., Niagara-on-the-Lake, 905-468-3845; www.niagaraapothecary.ca
The apothecary is a restored pharmacy that operated on the premises from 1866-1964. It has a large golden mortar and pestle over the door, original walnut and butternut fixtures, apothecary glass and remedies of the past.
May-Labor Day, daily.

NIAGARA HISTORICAL SOCIETY MUSEUM

43 Castlereagh St., Niagara-on-the-Lake, 905-468-3912;
www.niagarahistorical.museum

Opened in 1907, this is the earliest museum building in Ontario. Items from the time of the United Empire Loyalists, War of 1812, early Upper Canada and the Victorian era are all on display.

May-October, daily 10 a.m.-5 p.m.; November-April, daily 1-5 p.m.; rest of year, Saturday-Sunday or by appointment.

ST. MARK'S ANGLICAN CHURCH

47 Byron St., Niagara-on-the-Lake, 905-468-3123; www.stmarks1792.com

The original church was damaged by fire after being used as a hospital and barracks during the War of 1812. Rebuilt in 1822 and enlarged in 1843, the church contains an unusual three-layer stained-glass window. The churchyard dates from earliest British settlement.

July-August, daily; rest of year, by appointment.

ST. VINCENT DE PAUL ROMAN CATHOLIC CHURCH

73 Picton St., Niagara-on-the-Lake, 905-468-1383

St. Vincent is the first Roman Catholic parish in Upper Canada and an excellent example of Gothic Revival architecture. It was enlarged in 1965 and an older part was largely preserved.

SPECIAL EVENT
SHAW FESTIVAL

Queen's Parade and Wellington Street, Niagara-on-the-Lake, 905-468-2153,
800-657-1106; www.shawfest.com

Shaw Festival Theatre, specializing in the works of George Bernard Shaw and his contemporaries, presents 10 plays each year in repertory. It is housed in three theaters, including the Court House Theatre, and staged by an internationally acclaimed ensemble company. A lunchtime theater featuring one-act plays by Shaw is also offered.

Mid-April-October.

WHERE TO STAY
★★★GATE HOUSE HOTEL

142 Queen St., Niagara-on-the-Lake, 905-468-3263; www.gatehouse-niagara.com

This property has a contemporary Italian design and is located within walking distance of shops, historic sites and the three theaters of the Shaw Festival. The rooms are small, but quaint and cozy.

10 rooms. Closed January-mid-March. Complimentary breakfast. Restaurant, bar. Pets accepted. $151-250

★★★OBAN INN

160 Front St., Niagara-on-the-Lake, 905-468-2165, 888-669-5566; www.obaninn.ca

Once the home of a Scottish ship captain, ithis is now a modern hotel set in a wonderfully quaint, historic property. The grounds, which overlook Lake Ontario, feature charming English-style gardens. Individually decorated guest rooms have four-poster beds and antique furnishings with nice touches

like turndown service. Take advantage of the complimentary in-town shuttle service when going sightseeing.
26 rooms. Complimentary breakfast. Restaurant, bar. Pets accepted. Spa. $151-250

★★★PILLAR AND POST

48 John St., Niagara-on-the-Lake, 905-468-2123, 888-669-5566; www.vintageinns.com
This unique inn is located in a restored turn-of-the-century fruit canning factory. The lobby is full of plants and antique furniture. Don't miss a visit to the 100 Fountain Spa.
122 rooms. Restaurant, bar. Spa. Pets accepted. Pool. Business center. $151-250

★★★PRINCE OF WALES

6 Picton St., Niagara-on-the-Lake, 905-468-3246, 888-669-5566; www.vintageinns.com
This historic treasure dates to 1864. Its unique character and formal charm make it one of Canada's most beloved hotels. A cozy day spa celebrates the English countryside in its treatment rooms and afternoon tea is a daily ritual. There is sophisticated dining at Escabeche restaurant, where a modern French menu tempts and delights.
112 rooms. Restaurant, bar. Spa. Fitness center. Pool. Business center. Pets accepted. $251-350

★★★QUEEN'S LANDING

155 Byron St., Niagara-on-the-Lake, 905-468-2195, 888-669-5566; www.vintageinns.com
Built with Victorian charm, this inn overlooks the Niagara River, opposite historic Fort Niagara. The Georgian-style theme carries from the lobby to the guest rooms with plush furnishings and wood detailing. The Tiara Restaurant offers peerless views of Niagara-on-the-Lake Harbour.
142 rooms. Restaurant, bar. Spa. Fitness center. Pool. $251-350

★★★WHITE OAKS CONFERENCE RESORT AND SPA

253 Taylor Road SS4, Niagara-on-the-Lake, 905-688-2550, 800-263-5766; www.whiteoaksresort.com
This large, modern resort has relaxation and comfort in mind. This is reflected in the guest room amenities such as Frette robes, nightly turndown service and pillow topped mattresses. The attitude is carried over to the full-service spa and LIV, the resort's concept restaurant.
220 rooms. Restaurant, bar. Spa. Pool. Golf. Tennis. Fitness center. Business center. $151-250

WHERE TO EAT
★★★CARRIAGES

48 John St., Niagara-on-the-Lake, 905-468-2123, 888-669-5566; www.vintageinns.com
This cozy, candlelit dining room of the Pillar and Post hotel features exposed beams and a working brick oven. The rack of Australian lamb is superb, as are many of the seafood options, including Marrakech salmon.
American. Breakfast, lunch, dinner, Sunday brunch.Outdoor seating. $36-85

★★★ESCABÉCHE

6 Picton St., Niagara-on-the-Lake, 905-468-3246, 888-669-5566; www.vintageinns.com
The formal dining room of the Prince of Wales hotel makes the Victorian experience truly memorable. Enjoy afternoon tea or a long, elaborate dinner. The wine list is equally impressive if you're in the mood to imbibe. International. Breakfast, lunch, dinner. Reservations recommended. $36-85

OTTAWA

See also Toronto
With its parks full of flowers, universities, museums and diplomatic embassies, Ottawa is one of Canada's most beautiful cities. Ottawa is also a city of waterways including the majestic Ottawa River, the fast-flowing Gatineau and the placid Rideau. But no waterway has defined Ottawa like the Rideau Canal, which is a playground for skaters in winter and for boaters in summer. The oldest continuously operated canal in North America, it celebrated its 175th anniversary in 2007. Filled with festivals, buskers, theater, music and dance, Ottawa also prides itself on a superb collection of museums—such as the Canadian Museum of Contemporary Photography, the Canadian Museum of Civilization, and the Bytown Museum, depicting Ottawa's rowdy, lumberjack past. The nation's capital showcases Canada's art, music, people and politics with grace and verve—in both English and French.

WHAT TO SEE

BEAVERTAILS

This popular Canadian pastry resembles the tail of a beaver and comes with a variety of sweet and salty toppings. The original kiosk, BeaverTails Pastry (69 George St., 613-241-1230; www.beavertailsottawa.com), that began serving this pastry is still operating in the ByWard Market district at the corner of George and William streets. The pastry is based on an ancient North American Voyageur recipe and is a descendant of the quick bread the Voyageurs baked (it's kind of like a flat doughnut).

BYTOWN MUSEUM

540 Wellington St., Ottawa, 613-234-4570; www.bytownmuseum.com
Located in the heart of downtown, the museum occupies Ottawa's oldest stone building and includes artifacts, documents and pictures relating to Colonel By, Bytown and the history and social life of the region. Tours by appointment only. April-May 16, Thursday-Monday 10 a.m.-2 p.m.; May 17-October 12, daily 10 a.m.-5 p.m.; October 13-November, Thursday-Monday 10 a.m.-2 p.m.; December-March, Monday-Friday by appointment only.

BYWARD MARKET

55 ByWard Market Square, Ottawa, 613-562-3325; www.byward-market.com
ByWard Market features a traditional farmer's market, located outside, that features food and produce vendors, arts and crafts vendors and more (they are here year-round but hours vary). The other part of the market, takes up four blocks with wide streets and is lined with boutiques, restaurants, salons, museums, bars, art galleries and outdoor cafés, including the famous BeaverTails Pastry kiosk.

Farmer's market: May-October, daily 7 a.m.-6 p.m.; ByWard Market: daily, hours vary.

CANADIAN MUSEUM OF NATURE

Metcalf and McLeod streets, Ottawa, 613-566-4700, 800-263-4433; www.nature.ca
Exhibits and displays focus on nature and the environment. Topics include dinosaurs, insects, gems and minerals, birds and mammals of Canada and the evolution of the planet.
Winter, Tuesday-Sunday 9 a.m.-5 p.m., Thursday until 8 p.m.; summer, daily 9 a.m.-6 p.m., Wednesday-Thursday until 8 p.m.

CANADIAN PARLIAMENT BUILDINGS

Wellington Street on Parliament Hill, Ottawa, 613-996-0896; www.parl.gc.ca
Neo-Gothic architecture dominates this part of the city. The House of Commons and Senate meet here; visitors may request free tickets to both chambers when Parliament is in session. A guided tour includes the House of Commons, Senate Chamber, and Parliamentary Library. The Centennial Flame, lit in 1967 as a symbol of Canada's 100th birthday is also here as is the Memorial Chapel, dedicated to Canadian servicemen who lost their lives in the Boer War, WWI, WWII and the Korean War. An observation deck is located atop the Peace Tower.

CENTRAL EXPERIMENTAL FARM

88 Prince of Wales Drive, Ottawa, 613-991-3044
This farm contains approximately 1,200 acres of field crops, ornamental gardens, an an arboretum. View a showcase of herds of beef and dairy cattle, sheep, swine, and horses. There is also a tropical greenhouse, the Canada Agricultural Museum *(www.agriculture.technomuses.ca)*, Clydesdale horse-drawn wagon and sleigh rides. Museum Admission: adults $6, seniors and students $5, children 3-14 $3, children under 3 free. March-October, daily 9 a.m.-5 p.m.; barn: daily 9 a.m.-5 p.m. Tropical Greenhouse: daily 9 a.m.-4 p.m. Gardens: daily.

MUSEUM OF CANADIAN SCOUTING

1345 Base Line Road, Ottawa, 613-224-5131; www.scouts.ca
Depicting the history of Canadian Scouting, this museum features exhibits on the life of Lord R.S.S. Baden-Powell, founder of the Boy Scouts. You'll find pertinent documents, photographs and artifacts.

NATIONAL ARTS CENTRE

53 Elgin St., Ottawa, 613-947-7000; www.NAC-CNA.ca
This center for performing arts houses a concert hall and two theaters for music, dance, variety and drama. It is the home of the National Arts Centre Orchestra, and features more than 800 performances each year. There is also a canal-side café and landscaped terraces with panoramic view of Ottawa.

NATIONAL AVIATION MUSEUM

11 Aviation Parkway, Rockcliffe Airport, Ottawa, 613-990-1985, 800-463-2038;
www.aviation.technomuses.ca

More than 100 historic aircraft, 49 of which are on display in the Walkway of Time, can be viewed here. Displays demonstrate the development of aircraft in peace and war, emphasizing Canadian aviation.

NATIONAL GALLERY OF CANADA

380 Sussex Drive, Ottawa, 613-990-1985, 800-319-2787; www.national.gallery.ca

Permanent exhibits include European paintings from the 14th century to the present; Canadian art from the 17th century to the present; contemporary and decorative arts, prints, drawings, photos and Inuit art. A reconstructed 19th-century Rideau convent chapel with Neo-Gothic fan-vaulted ceiling is the only known example of its kind in North America. There are also gallery talks, films, restaurants and a bookstore.

May-September, daily 10 a.m.-5 p.m., Thursday to 8 p.m.; October-April, Tuesday-Sunday 10 a.m.-5 p.m., Thursday to 8 p.m.

NATIONAL MUSEUM OF SCIENCE AND TECHNOLOGY

1867 St. Laurent Blvd., Ottawa, 613-991-3044; www.sciencetech.technomuses.ca

Explore more than 400 exhibits with many do-it-yourself experiments. Canada's role in science and technology are shown through displays on Canada in space, transportation, agriculture, computers, communications, physics and astronomy. Unusual open restoration bay allows viewing of various stages of artifact repair and refurbishment.

Labor Day-April, Tuesday-Sunday 9 a.m.-5 p.m.; May-Labor Day, Monday-Sunday 9 a.m.-5 p.m.

ONTARIO ★★★★

130

RIDEAU CANAL

34A Beckwith St. S., runs 125 miles between Kingston and Ottawa, Ottawa, 613-992-8142, 800-230-0016; www.pc.gc.ca

Constructed under the direction of Lieutenant-Colonel John By of the Royal Engineers between 1826 and 1832 as a safe supply route to Upper Canada. The purpose was to bypass the St. Lawrence River in case of an American attack. There are 24 lock stations where visitors can picnic, watch boats pass through the hand-operated locks and see wooden lock gates, cut stone walls and many historic structures. In summer, there are interpretive programs and exhibits at various locations. Areas of special interest include Kingston Mills Locks, Jones Falls Locks off Highway 15, Smith Falls Museum off Highway 15, Merrickville Locks on Highway 43 and Ottawa Locks. Boating is popular (mid-May-mid-October), and ice skating is possible mid-December-late February.

ROYAL CANADIAN MINT

320 Sussex Drive, Ottawa, 613-993-8990, 800-276-7714; www.rcmint.ca

See how Canadian coins are produced, as well as expansive collections of coins and medals. Guided tours and film; detailed process of minting coins and printing bank notes is shown.

VICTORIA MEMORIAL MUSEUM BUILDING

240 McLeod St., Ottawa, 613-566-4700; www.nature.ca

This castle-like structure houses a museum that interrelates man and his natural environment. It also houses the Canadian Museum of Nature. Natural history exhibits from dinosaurs to present day plants and animals can be viewed as well as an outstanding collection of minerals and gems.

SPECIAL EVENTS
CANADA DAY

90 Wellington St., Ottawa, 613-239-5000, 800-465-1867; www.canadascapital.gc.ca

The celebration of Canada's birthday includes events throughout the city, such as canoe and sailing regattas, concerts, dance performances, arts and craft demonstrations, children's entertainment and fireworks.
July 1.

CANADIAN TULIP FESTIVAL

Canadian Tulip Festival, 130 Albert St., Ottawa, 613-567-5757; www.tulipfestival.ca

This is part of a two-week celebration, culminated by the blooming of more than 3 million tulips presented to Ottawa by Queen Juliana of the Netherlands after she sought refuge here during WWII. Enjoy tours of flower beds, a craft market and demonstrations, kite flying, and a boat parade.
May.

OTTAWA INTERNATIONAL JAZZ FESTIVAL

61A Yorks St., Ottawa, 613-241-2633, 888-226-4495; www.ottawajazzfestival.com

Jazz artists from around the world perform at this week-long celebration.
Ten days in mid-July.

WINTERLUDE

90 Wellington St., Ottawa, 613-239-5000; www.canadascapital.gc.ca

This extravaganza is devoted to outdoor concerts, fireworks, skating contests, dances, music and ice sculptures.
Three weekends in February.

WHERE TO STAY
★★★THE FAIRMONT CHATEAU LAURIER

1 Rideau St., Ottawa, 613-241-1414, 800-441-1414; www.fairmont.com

This impressive castle enchants visitors with its setting overlooking Parliament Hill, the Rideau Canal and the Ottawa River. It is conveniently located in the city center. Enjoy elegant dining at Wilfrid's, while Zoe's Lounge is a more casual alternative. Guest services include a full-service fitness club with a stunning Art Deco pool.
429 rooms. Restaurant, bar. Spa. Pets accepted. Pool. Business center.
$151-250

★★★THE FAIRMONT LE CHATEAU MONTEBELLO

392 rue Notre Dame, Montebello, 819-423-6341, 800-441-1414;
www.fairmont.com

Stretched out along the banks of the Ottawa River, this log cabin-style lodge

★★★★★ ONTARIO

charms with spectacular scenery. From hiking, biking and boating, the recreational pursuits offered here are endless. Sybaritic-minded visitors enjoy the pampering treatments at the spa, while gastronomes savor the cuisine at the resort's dining rooms.

210 rooms. Restaurant, bar. Pets accepted. Pool. Golf. Tennis. Spa. Business center. $151-250

★★★GASTHAUS SWITZERLAND INN

89 Daly Ave., Ottawa, 613-237-0335; www.ottawainn.com

This charming inn is located in a restored 1872 house. Enjoy traditional Swiss hospitality during a visit to Canada's capital. Though some of the rooms are small, they all offer personalized touches and comfortable beds.

22 rooms. No hildren under 12. Complimentary breakfast. Restaurant. $61-150

★★★HILTON LAC-LEAMY

3 Blvd. Du Casino, Hull, 819-790-6444; www.hiltonlacleamy.com

It is located on the shore of Lake Leamy and Des Carrieres Lake, its connected to a casino, and it is close to Gatineau's shopping district and near an all-season walking/biking trail. This hotel has something for everyone: Various dining options abound with the French-style bistro, Le Cellier, or a fine dining experience at Le Baccara. The rooms are what you would expect from a Hilton: comfortable and well-appointed.

349 rooms. Restaurant, bar. Pool. Business center. $151-250

★★★MARRIOTT OTTAWA

100 Kent St., Ottawa, 613-238-1122, 800-853-8463; www.ottawamarriott.com

Located in the heart of downtown, the hotel is close to local attractions such as Canada's Parliament Buildings, the Rideau Canal, the Ottawa Congress Centre and the National Gallery of Canada. Enjoy a panoramic view of the city with your meal at the Merlot Rooftop Grill, a revolving restaurant

480 rooms. Restaurant, bar. Pets accepted. Pool. Business center. $

★★★MINTO PLACE SUITE HOTEL

185 Lyon St. N., Ottawa, 613-232-2200, 800-267-3377; www.mintosuitehotel.com

Minto Place Suite Hotel offers a convenient location, as just outside its doors you can explore Parliament Hill, the Casino Lac-Leamy and the Historic Byward Market. Guests can enjoy find dining at Prime 360, the hotel's steakhouse, unwind at the hotel's pool and whirlpool, and take advantage of the fitness center. Rooms are updated with modern amenities including Internet access, luxurious bedding and kitchenettes.

417 rooms. Pool. Fitness center. Restaurant, bar. $251-350

★★★THE WESTIN OTTAWA

11 Colonel By Drive, Ottawa, 613-560-7000, 800-937-8461; www.westin.com

Located only blocks from Parliament Hill and the historic Byward Market, this hotel is connected to the Rideau Center Shopping Complex and the Ottawa Congress Center. Guest rooms are decorated in neutral tones and many rooms have soaking tubs.

487 rooms. Restaurant, bar. Spa. Pets accepted. Pool. Business center. $151-250

WHERE TO EAT
★★★JOHN TAYLOR AT DOMUS CAFÉ
87 Murray St., Ottawa, 613-241-6007; www.domuscafe.ca

Under chef John Taylor, this café offers innovative dishes using local meats and produce. A member of the Slow Food movement, you'll find the freshest ingredients are used to prepare your meal. Enjoy dishes such as pan-roasted halibut with new red skin potatoes, warm wilted greens, zuccini and Swiss chard chutney; and grass-fed grilled Kerr farm flatiron steak with sweet corn polenta, wilted greens, mushrooms and tomato-apple chutney. They also offer an extensive award-winning wine list and a single malt scotch menu, including Canada's Glen Breton scotch.

French bistro. Lunch, dinner. Bar. Reservations recommended. $36-85

STRATFORD
See also Brantford, Kitchener-Waterloo

The names Stratford and Avon River can conjure up only one name—Shakespeare. And that is exactly what you will find in this lovely city. World-renowned, this festival of fine theater takes place here every year. For a relatively small town, Stratford offers up a wonderful variety of shows, concerts, plays, art galleries and spas—ideal for a weekend escape, and sealed with plentiful gardens and a Victorian city core.

WHAT TO SEE
CONFEDERATION PARK
52 Romeo St. N., Stratford, 519-273-3352; www.welcometostratford.com

This park features a rock hill, waterfall, fountain, Japanese garden and commemorative court.

GALLERY STRATFORD
54 Romeo St. N., Stratford, 519-271-5271; www.gallerystratford.on.ca

This public gallery is located within what was formerly the city's pump house. There are three galleries and one studio space along with a shop to pick up a souvenir. The galleries showcase both historical and contemporary works from Canadian artists as well as changing exhibits . Guided tours on request.

Admission: adults $5, students and seniors $4. Mid-April-mid-November, Tuesday-Sunday 10 a.m.-5 p.m.; Mid-November-mid-April, Tuesday-Sunday noon-4 p.m.

SHAKESPEAREAN GARDENS
Huron St., Stratford, 519-271-5140; www.welcometostratford.com

Fragrant herbs, shrubs and flowering plants common to William Shakespeare's time are featured in this garden.

★★★★★ ONTARIO

SPECIAL EVENT
STRATFORD SHAKESPEARE FESTIVAL
55 Queen St., Stratford, 519-273-1600, 800-567-1600; www.stratford-festival.on.ca
Contemporary, classical and Shakespearean dramas and modern musicals are performances at Festival, Avon, Studio and Tom Patterson theaters. April-November, matinees and evenings.

WHERE TO STAY
★★★QUEEN'S INN
161 Ontario St., Stratford, 519-271-1400; www.queensinnstratford.ca
This lovely Victorian inn is located on the main street of downtown, close to a variety of shops and restaurants. It features uniquely decorated rooms that feel like a home away from home.
32 rooms. Restaurant. Pets accepted. $61-150

★★★TOUCHSTONE MANOR
325 St. David St., Stratford, 519-273-5820; www.touchstone-manor.com
This 1938 inn is located in a quiet, residential neighborhood within walking distance of downtown and about a 1/2 hour walk to the Shakespeare Festival area. The rooms boast period antiques and personalized detailing.
4 rooms. Closed late December-late January. No children under 12. Complimentary breakfast. $251-350

WHERE TO EAT
★★★CHURCH RESTAURANT AND THE BELFRY
70 Brunswick St., Stratford, 519-273-3424; www.churchrestaurant.com
Housed in a 19th-century Gothic church, with wooden arches and stained-glass windows, this restaurant showcasese opulent French meals. This restaurant is the perfect backdrop for an elegant wedding or party.
French. Dinner. Reservations recommended. $251-350

★★★RUNDLES
9 Cobourg St., Stratford, 519-271-6442; www.rundlesrestaurant.com
Located on the river at ground zero for the Stratford Festival, this longtime favorite affords the most elegant dining in the area. Like the environment, the chef's food is simple and thoroughly enjoyable. Try the sautéed Quebec foie gras with quail satay, pickled mushrooms and ginger flavored sauce; and the pan-fried, organically farmed Irish salmon, braised with fennel and olive oil with vegetable-filled ravioli.
American. Lunch, dinner. Outdoor seating. $86 and up

TORONTO
See also Brampton, Hamilton
Toronto is one of Canada's leading industrial, commercial and cultural centers. Having earned its name from the native word for "meeting place," Toronto is an awesome cosmopolitan city—the United Nations recently deemed it the world's most ethnically diverse city. A performing arts powerhouse, the city presents everything from Broadway musicals to standup comedy and opera to dance. Good shopping can be found throughout the city, but Toron-

tonians are most proud of their Underground City, a series of subterranean malls linking more than 300 shops and restaurants in the downtown area. For professional sports fans, Toronto offers the Maple Leafs (hockey), Blue Jays (baseball), Raptors (basketball) and Argonauts (football). A visit to the harbor front, a boat tour to the islands, and an evening on the town should round out your stay.

WHAT TO SEE
ALLAN GARDENS
19 Horticultural Ave., Toronto, 416-392-7288; www.toronto.ca
Over 100 years old, these gardens cover more than 16,000 square feet of greenhouses. Therea re both indoor and outdoor botanical displays, a wading pool and picnicking areas.
Daily 10 a.m.-5 p.m.

BATA SHOE MUSEUM
327 Bloor St. W., Toronto, 416-979-7799; www.batashoemuseum.ca
When Mrs. Sonja Bata's passion for collecting historical shoes began to surpass her personal storage space, the Bata family established The Bata Shoe Museum Foundation. Architect Raymond Moriyama's award-winning five-story, 3,900-square-foot building now holds more than 10,000 shoes, artfully arranged in four galleries to celebrate the style and function of footwear throughout 4,500 years of history. One permanent exhibition, "All About Shoes," showcases a collection of 20th-century celebrity shoes; artifacts on exhibit range from ancient Egyptian sandals to Elton John's platforms.
Monday-Saturday 10 a.m.-5 p.m., Sunday noon-5 p.m.

BLOOR/YORKVILLE AREA
Bounded by Bloor Street West, Avenue Road, Davenport Road and Yonge Street,
Toronto, 416-928-3553; www.bloor-yorkville.com
The Bloor/Yorkville area is one of Toronto's most elegant shopping and dining sections, with nightclubs, music, designer couture boutiques and first-rate art galleries. The area itself is fun to walk around, with a cluster of courtyards and alleyways. There's also a contemporary park in the heart of the neighborhood with a huge piece of granite called The Rock. It was brought here from the Canadian Shield, a U-shaped region of ancient rock covering about half of Canada.
Monday-Friday 8:30 a.m.-5 p.m.

CANADA'S SPORTS HALL OF FAME
115 Princes' Blvd., Toronto, 416-260-6789; www.cshof.ca
Erected to honor the country's greatest athletes in all major sports, Canada's Sports Hall of Fame features exhibit galleries, a theater, library, archives and kiosks that show videos of Canada's greatest moments in sports. Don't miss the Heritage Gallery lower level, which contains artifacts showcasing the development of 125 years of sport. Also stop in at the 50-seat Red Foster Theatre, which projects films clips that highlight Canadian sports, such as *The Terry Fox Story.*

CASA LOMA

1 Austin Terrace, Toronto, 416-923-1171; www.casaloma.org

Grab an audio cassette and a floor plan and take a self-guided tour of this domestic castle, built in 1911 over three years at a cost of $3.5 million. As romantic as he was a shrewd businessman, Sir Henry Pellatt, who founded the Toronto Electric Light Company, had an architect create this medieval castle. Soaring battlements, secret passageways, flowerbeds warmed by steam pipes, secret doors, servants' rooms and an 800-foot tunnel are just some of the treats you'll discover.

Daily 9:30 a.m.-5 p.m.

COLBORNE LODGE

Colborne Lodge Drive and The Queensway, Toronto, 416-392-6916; www.city.toronto.on.ca

The successful 19th-century architect John Howard was just 34 when he completed this magnificent manor, named for the architect's first patron, Upper Canada Lieutenant Governor Sir John Colborne. It stands today as an excellent example of Regency-style architecture, with its stately verandas and lovely placement in a beautiful setting.

Check Web site for hours.

CN TOWER

301 Front St. W., Toronto, 416-868-6937; www.cntower.ca

Toronto's CN Tower is the tallest freestanding structure in the world. At 1,815 feet from the ground to the tip of its communications aerial, it towers over the rest of the city. Take the elevator to the top, where on a clear day it's said you can see the spray coming off Niagara Falls 62 miles away.

Daily 9 a.m-10 p.m., Friday-Saturday to 10:30 p.m.

DRAGON CITY SHOPPING MALL

280 Spadina Ave., Toronto, 416-596-8885

Located in the heart of Chinatown, the Dragon City Shopping Mall consists of more than 30 stores and services. Buy Chinese herbs, look at Asian jewelry, browse chic Chinese housewares and gifts, or admire Oriental arts and crafts. Afterwards treat yourself to a meal at Sky Dragon Cuisine in the Dragon City tower, an upscale Chinese restaurant with a beautiful view of the Toronto skyline.

EATON CENTRE

220 Yonge St., Toronto, 416-598-8560; www.torontoeatoncentre.com

This 3 million-square-foot building is a masterpiece of architecture and environment. Its glass roof rises 127 feet above the mall's lowest level. The large, open space contains glass-enclosed elevators, dozens of long, graceful escalators and porthole windows. There are more than 230 retailers here, including Abercrombie & Fitch, Banana Republic, The Gap, H&M, Pottery Barn and others. A flock of fiberglass Canadian geese floats through the air. Even if shopping isn't a favorite vacation activity, Eaton Centre is worth a trip.

ELGIN & WINTER GARDEN THEATRE CENTRE

189 Yonge St., Toronto, 416-872-5555; www.heritagefdn.on.ca

The 80-year history of the two theaters speaks more volumes than one of its excellent productions. Built in 1913, each theater was a masterpiece in its own right: The Elgin was ornate, with gold leaf, plaster cherubs and elegant opera boxes; the walls of the Winter Garden were hand-painted to resemble a garden and its ceiling was a mass of beech bows and twinkling lanterns. Through the years, the stages saw the likes of George Burns and Gracie Allen, Edger Bergen and Charlie McCarthy, Milton Berle and Sophie Tucker. The Ontario Heritage Foundation offers year-round guided tours on Thursdays at 5 p.m. and Saturdays at 11 a.m.

GEORGE R. GARDINER MUSEUM OF CERAMIC ART

111 Queen's Park, Toronto, 416-586-8080; www.gardinermuseum.on.ca

This museum contains one of the world's finest collections of Italian majolica, English Delftware and 18th-century continental porcelain.

HARBOURFRONT CENTRE

235 Queens Quay W., Toronto, 416-973-4600; www.harbourfront.on.ca

This 10-acre waterfront community is alive with theater, dance, films, art shows, music, crafts and children's programs. Most events are free. Daily.

HIGH PARK

1873 Bloor St. W. and Keele St., Toronto, 416-392-1111; www.highpark.org

High Park is an urban oasis with expansive fields for sports, picnicking and cycling; a large lake that freezes in the winter; a small zoo, swimming pool, tennis courts and bowling greens.

★★★★★ ONTARIO

HISTORIC FORT YORK

100 Garrison Road, Toronto, 416-392-6907; www.city.toronto.on.ca

It may not have seen a lot of action—just one battle during the War of 1812— but Fort York's place in Toronto's history is secure. It is the birthplace of modern Toronto, having played a major role in saving York (now Toronto) from being invaded by 1,700 American soldiers. Fort York contains Canada's largest collection of original War of 1812 buildings and is a designated National Historic Site.

ICE SKATING AT GRENADIER POND

1873 Bloor St., 416-392-6916; www.toronto.ca/parks

One of the most romantic ice-skating spots you'll find is Grenadier Pond in High Park, one of 25 parks offering free artificial rinks throughout the city. In addition to vendors selling roasted chestnuts, there's a bonfire to keep you toasty. Other free ice rinks include Nathan Phillips Square in front of City Hall and an area at Harbor front Centre. Equipment rentals are available on site.

KENSINGTON MARKET

College Street and Spadina Avenue, Toronto

This maze of narrow streets is lined with food shops, vintage clothing stores, restaurants and jewelry vendors. There are bargain hunters haggling, café owners enticing diners and little stores brimming with items from Asia, South America, the Middle East and Europe.

KORTRIGHT CENTRE FOR CONSERVATION

9550 Pine Valley Drive, Woodbridge, 905-832-2289; www.kortright.org

This environmental center has trails, a bee house, maple syrup shack, wildlife pond and plantings. Naturalist-guided hikes are available and there's cross-country skiing in winter. The site also includes a picnic area, cafe, and theater.

LITTLE ITALY

West of Bathurst Street between Euclid Avenue and Shaw Street, Toronto;
www.torontotourism.com

After the British, Italians make up the largest cultural group in Toronto. Though the Italian community moved north as it grew, the atmosphere of Little Italy remains. Restaurants and bars open onto the sidewalks.

MACKENZIE HOUSE

82 Bond St., Toronto, 416-392-6915; www.toronto.ca

The restored 19th-century home of William Lyon Mackenzie, first mayor of Toronto includes furnishings and artifacts of the 1850s and a print shop. January-April, Saturday-Sunday noon-5 p.m.; May-Labor Day, Tuesday-Sunday noon-5 p.m.; Labor Day-December, Tuesday-Friday noon-4 p.m., Saturday-Sunday noon-5 p.m.

MARTIN GOODMAN TRAIL

Toronto, 416-392-8186; www.city.toronto.on.ca/parks

Leave it to fitness-conscious Toronto not just to have a beautifully maintained waterfront, but to build a trail that takes you from one end to the other. The Martin Goodman Trail is a public jogging, biking, walking and in-line skating path that connects all the elements of the waterfront, traversing 13 miles. It also runs past several spots for bike and skate rentals.

MEDIEVAL TIMES

Exhibition Place, Dufferin Gate, Toronto, 416-260-1234; www.medievaltimes.com

This 11th-century castle was created to replicate an 11th-century experience, complete with knightly competitions and equestrian displays.

MOUNT PLEASANT CEMETERY

375 Mount Pleasant Road, Toronto, 416-485-9129;
www.mountpleasantgroupofcemeteries.ca

One of the oldest cemeteries in North America, the Mount Pleasant Cemetery is the final resting place of many well-known Canadians, including Sir Frederic Banting and Charles Best, the discoverers of insulin; renowned classical pianist Glenn Gould and Prime Minister William Lyon Mackenzie King, who led Canada through World War II. The grounds hold rare plants and shrubs as well as a Memorial Peony Garden.

ONTARIO PARLIAMENT BUILDINGS
Queen's Park, 111 Wellesley St. West, Toronto, 416-325-7500;
www.parliamenthill.gc.ca
Guided tours of the Legislature Building and walking tour of grounds are available. You can also see the gardens, art collections and historic displays.

ONTARIO PLACE
955 Lakeshore Blvd. W., Toronto, 416-314-9900; www.ontarioplace.com
This is a 96-acre cultural, recreational and entertainment complex on three artificial islands in Lake Ontario. It includes an outdoor amphitheater for concerts, two pavilions with multimedia presentations, Cinesphere theater with IMAX films year-round; three villages of snack bars, restaurants and pubs; miniature golf; lagoons, canals and two marinas; 370-foot water slide, showboat, pedal and bumper boats and rides.
Mid-May-early September.

ONTARIO SCIENCE CENTRE
770 Don Mills Road, Toronto, 416-696-1000; www.ontariosciencecentre.ca
Ten huge exhibition halls in three linked pavilions are filled with exhibits on space and technology. Stand at the edge of a black hole, watch bees making honey, test your reflexes, heart rate or grip strength, use pedal power to light lights or raise a balloon, hold hands with a robot, or land a spaceship on the moon. Throughout the museum there are slide shows and films that demonstrate various aspects of science and two Omnimax theaters show films.
Daily 10 a.m.-5 p.m.

PARAMOUNT CANADA'S WONDERLAND
9580 Jane St., Vaughan, 905-832-8131; www.canadaswonderland.com
This 300-acre theme park is situated 30 minutes outside Toronto and features more than 140 attractions including a 20-acre water park, live shows and more than 50 rides. The park is known for its roller coasters, from creaky old-fashioned wooden ones to The Fly, a roller coaster designed to make every seat feel as if it's the front car.

PIER: TORONTO'S WATERFRONT MUSEUM
245 Queen's Quay W., Toronto
Original 1930s pier building on Toronto's celebrated waterfront includes two floors of hands-on interactive displays, rare historical artifacts, re-creations of marine history stories, art gallery, boat-building center, narrated walking excursions, children's programs.
March-October, daily.

QUEEN STREET WEST
From University Avenue to Bathurst Street, Toronto
Come to Queen West for vintage clothing stores, trendy home furnishings, hip styles that used to be original grunge and street vendor bohemia, as well as the handiwork of many up-and-coming fashion designers. In between the boutiques are antique stores, used bookstores and terrific bistros and cafés.

RIVOLI

334 Queen St. West, Toronto, 416-596-1908; www.rivoli.ca

This offbeat, artsy performance club was opened in 1982 on the site of Toronto's 1920s Rivoli Vaudeville Theatre. The focus is on eclectic and cutting-edge music and performances and includes everything from grunge and rock to poetry readings and comedy. The Indigo Girls, Tory Amos and Michelle Shocked all made their Toronto debuts here. Don't forget to check out the 5,000-square-foot pool hall with 13 vintage tables, including a 1870s Brunswick Aviator and a 1960s futuristic AMF seen in the Elvis movie V*iva Las Vegas*.

ROYAL ONTARIO MUSEUM

100 Queen's Park, Toronto, 416-586-5549; www.rom.on.ca

When the Royal Ontario Museum opened its doors to the public in 1914, its mission was to inspire wonder and build understanding of human cultures and the natural world. And its collections in archaeology, geology, genealogy, paleontology and sociology have moved in that direction ever since. One of the most-visited galleries is the Nubia Gallery, built in 1998 after a ROM team discovered a new archaeological culture in the Upper Nubia region of Northern Sudan, unearthing the remains of a settlement dating to 1000-800 B.C. The discovery has been officially recognized by UNESCO as "Canada's contribution to the United Nations' Decade for Cultural Development."

SPADINA HISTORIC HOUSE AND GARDEN

285 Spadina Road., Toronto, 416-392-6910; www.toronto.ca/culture

Built for financier James Austin and his family, this 50-room house has been restored to its 1866 Victorian glory and is open to those who want to see how the upper crust spent quiet evenings at home. It's filled with the family's art, artifacts and furniture and until 1982 it was filled with the family itself; that's when the last generation of Austins left and the house was turned over to public ownership. Docents tend to the glorious gardens and orchard, which are open to the public in the summer.

ST. LAWRENCE MARKET

92 Front St. E., Toronto, 416-329-7120; www.stlawrencemarket.com

In 1803, Governor Peter Hunt designated an area of land to be market block. Today, the St. Lawrence Market provides a good snippet of the way Toronto used to be, with enough of the character of the original architecture to make you feel as though the old city were alive and well. The market itself, Toronto's largest indoor market, sells 14 different categories of foods, which include incredibly fresh seafood, poultry, meat, organic produce, baked goods, gourmet teas and coffees, plus fruits and flowers.

SAINTE-MARIE AMONG THE HURONS

East of Midland on Highway 12

Reconstruction of 17th-century Jesuit mission that was Ontario's first European community. Twenty-two furnished buildings include native dwellings, workshops, barn, church, cookhouse, hospital. Candlelight tours, canoe excursions. Café features period-inspired meals and snacks. Orientation center, interpretive museum. World-famous Martyrs' Shrine site of papal visit is located across the highway. Other area highlights include pioneer museum, replica indigenous village, Wye Marsh Wildlife Centre.

TASTE OF THE WORLD NEIGHBORHOOD BICYCLE TOURS AND WALKS

Station P Toronto, 416-923-6813; www.torontowalksbikes.com

Equal parts fact and food, the tour walks visitors through a forgotten hanging square, a hidden gallery and a lost pillory site. The eats include East Indian treats with new twists, decadent offerings with Belgian chocolate, sandwich samples at Carousel Bakery and a spread at St. Urbain Bagel. On Sunday, a different tour focuses on the contributions of 200 years of immigrant activity in the Kensington market, exploring Jewish and East Indian snacks, Lebanese treats and, of course, chocolate truffles. The tour company suggests a light breakfast with the St. Lawrence Tour and no breakfast with the Kensington tour.

Daily 9:30 a.m.-1 p.m.

TORONTO ISLAND PARK

9 Queens Quay, Toronto, South across Inner Harbor, 416-392-8186;
www.toronto.ca/parks/island

Just seven minutes by ferry from Toronto lie 14 beautiful islands ripe for exploration. Centre Island is the busiest, and home to Centreville, an old-fashioned amusement park with an authentic 1890s carousel, flume ride, turn-of-the-century village complete with a Main Street, tiny shops, firehouse and even a small, working farm. Alternately, all the islands are great for renting bikes and exploring the 612 acres of shaded paths.

★★★★★ ONTARIO

TORONTO MUSIC GARDEN

475 Queen's Quay W., Toronto, 416-973-3000; www.city.toronto.on.ca

In the mid-1990s, internationally renowned cellist Yo-Yo Ma worked with several other artists to produce a six-part film series inspired by the work of Johann Sebastian Bach's *Suites for Unaccompanied Cello*. The first film was entitled The Music Garden and used nature to interpret the music of Bach's first suite. Toronto was approached to create an actual garden based on The Music Garden and the result—Toronto Music Garden—now graces the waterfront, a symphony of swirls and curves and wandering trails. In the summertime, free concerts are given. Tours are offered, with a guide or self-guided with a hand-held audiotape.

141

TORONTO SYMPHONY ORCHESTRA

212 King Street W., Toronto, 416-598-3375; www.tso.ca

The Toronto Symphony features classical, pops and children's programs. There is wheelchair seating and audio enhancement for the hearing impaired.

TORONTO ZOO

361A Old Finch Ave., Scarborough, 416-392-5929; www.torontozoo.com

There are more than 5,000 animals representing over 450 species at the Toronto Zoo. Well-designed and laid out, four large tropical indoor pavilions and several smaller indoor viewing areas, plus numerous outdoor exhibits compose 710 acres of geographic regions, which can be explored on six miles of walking trails. When you're tired of walking, sit down for a refreshment or take a ride on a pony, camel or a safari simulator.

WOODBINE RACETRACK

555 Rexdale Blvd., Rexdale, 416-675-7223; www.woodbineentertainment.com

The only track in North America that can offer both standard-bred and thoroughbred racing on the same day, Woodbine is home to Canada's most important race course events. It hosts the $1 million Queens Plate, North America's oldest continuously run stakes race; the $1 million ATTO; the $1.5 million Canadian International; and the $1 million North America Cup for Standard-bred. It also has an outstanding grass course; it was here, in 1973, that Secretariat bid farewell to racing with his win of the grass championship. Woodbine has 1,700 slot machines and many different dining options.

SPECIAL EVENTS
BEACHES INTERNATIONAL JAZZ FESTIVAL

1798 Queen St. E., Toronto, 416-698-2152; www.beachesjazz.com

Since 1989, for four days, the Beaches community of Toronto has resonated with the sound of world-class jazz at the Beaches International Jazz Festival, a musical wonder that attracts nearly 1 million people to the water's edge. More than 40 bands play nightly, featuring over 700 musicians. The Festival also serves as a springboard for talented amateurs.
Mid-late July.

CANADIAN INTERNATIONAL

Woodbine Racetrack, 555 Rexdale Blvd., Rexdale, 416-675-7223, 888-675-7223; www.woodbineentertainment.com

World-class thoroughbreds compete in one of Canada's most important races.
Mid-late October.

CANADIAN NATIONAL EXHIBITION

Exhibition Place, Lake Shore Boulevard and Strachan Avenue, Toronto, 416-393-6300; www.theex.com

This gala celebration originated in 1879 as the Toronto Industrial Exhibition for the encouragement of agriculture, industry and the arts, though agricultural events dominated the show. Today sports, industry, labor and the arts are of equal importance to the exhibition. The "Ex," as it is locally known, is so inclusive of the nation's activities that it is a condensed Canada. A special 350-acre park has been built to accommodate the exhibition. Hundreds of events include animal shows, parades, exhibits, a midway and water and air shows. Virtually every kind of sporting event is represented, from frisbee-throwing to the National Horse Show.
Mid-August-Labor Day.

CELEBRATE TORONTO STREET FESTIVAL

Yonge Street, between Lawrence Avenue and Dundas Street, Toronto, 416-395-0490; www.city.toronto.on.ca

Each July, on the first weekend after Canada Day, Toronto's Yonge Street—

the longest street in the world—is transformed into more than 500,000 square feet (46,452 square meters) of free entertainment, with something for people of all ages and tastes. Each of five intersections along Yonge Street runs its own distinctive programming mix; one has nothing but family entertainment, another has world music, a third has classic rock and so forth. Jugglers, stilt-walkers and buskers enliven street corners.
Early July.

ROYAL AGRICULTURAL WINTER FAIR

Coliseum Building, Exhibition Place, Lake Shore Boulevard and Strachan Avenue, Toronto, 416-263-3400; www.royalfair.org
This is the world's largest indoor agricultural fair, which exhibits the finest livestock and features food shows. The Royal Horse Show features international competitions in several categories.
Early November.

SUNDAY SERENADES

5100 Yonge St., Toronto, 416-338-0338; www.city.toronto.on.ca
See if moonlight becomes you and play Fred and Ginger under the stars at Mel Lastman Square. Each Sunday evening in June and July you enjoy live big band and swing music. It's free, easy and lots of fun.
Mid-July–mid-August.

TORONTO INTERNATIONAL FILM FESTIVAL

Eaton Centre, 220 Yonge St., Toronto, 416-968-3456; www.tiffg.ca
This acclaimed film festival is a celebration of world cinema in downtown theaters and includes Canadian and foreign films, international moviemakers and stars.
Early September.

★★★★★ ONTARIO

TORONTO KIDS TUESDAY

100 Queen St. W., Toronto; www.city.toronto.on.ca
For four consecutive Tuesdays in July and August, Nathan Philips Square is turned into a kid's fantasyland. There's entertainment, face painting, coloring, chalk art, make-and-take crafts, make your own T-shirts, build-a-kite; activities depend on who is entertaining and what the theme of the day is. The Stylamanders bring zany choreography and championship yo-yo tricks, which was followed by a high-energy day of play, including interactive games with the Toronto Maple Leafs.
July–August.

TORONTO WINE AND CHEESE SHOW

6900 Airport Road, Mississauga, 800-265-3673; www.towineandcheese.com
A mainstay since 1983, the Toronto Wine and Cheese show brings a world of top-tier wines, beers, lagers, ales, single malt whiskies, cheeses and specialty food to town. Learn from famous chefs, sample an exquisite collection of cigars, find out how to buy the perfect bottle of wine and enjoy free seminars by well-known food and wine experts. Ages 19 and up only.
Mid-April.

WHERE TO STAY

★★★DELTA CHELSEA

33 Gerrard St. W., Toronto, 416-595-1975, 800-243-5732; www.deltachelsea.com
Located in the heart of downtown Toronto, guests are within minutes of the city's best theatre, shopping and attractions. After a long day, unwind in an elegant guest room with choice amenities and deep soaking tubs.
1,590 rooms. Restaurant, bar. Pets accepted. Pool. Business center. $251-350

★★★FAIRMONT ROYAL YORK

100 Front St. W., Toronto, 416-368-2511, 866-540-4489; www.fairmont.com
The Royal York became known as a city within a city, with its 1½ acres of public rooms including a 12,000-book library, a concert hall with a 50-ton pipe organ and 10 ornate passenger elevators. A $100 million project restored the guest rooms and public spaces to their original elegance and added a health club.
1,365 rooms. Restaurants, bar. Pets accepted. Pool. Business center. Fitness center. $251-350

★★★★FOUR SEASONS HOTEL TORONTO

21 Avenue Road, Toronto, 416-964-0411; www.fourseasons.com/toronto
The Four Seasons Hotel Toronto is in a prime location in the upscale neighborhood of Yorkville. Guest rooms feature elegant colonial décor, plush furnishings and charming views of Yorkville, or stunning views of the city's downtown. Not forgotten are business travelers who are pampered with the in-house business center and complimentary limousine service. Guests can relax by the heated indoor and outdoor pool, sauna, whirlpool and fitness center.
380 rooms. Restaurant, bar. Fitness center. Pool. Business center. Pets accepted. $351 and up

★★★★THE HAZELTON HOTEL

118 Yorkville Ave., Toronto, 416-963-6300, 866-473-6301; www.thehazeltonhotel.com
Sleek luxury with hints of old Hollywood glam permeates the rooms and suites of the Hazelton hotel. You can almost get lost in the spacious rooms, each with an average of 620 square feet with 9-foot-tall ceilings. The luxe experience extends beyond the rooms and into the Hazleton's signature restaurant, One, led by chef Mark McEwan. The hotel even has its very own built-in elegant mini-movie theater that seats 25 on plush, leather seats.
77 rooms. Restaurant, bar. Fitness center. Business center. $351 and up

★★★HILTON TORONTO

145 Richmond St. W., Toronto, 416-869-3456, 800-445-8667; www.toronto.hilton.com
Guests will enjoy the location of this hotel in Toronto's financial and entertainment districts. The guest rooms are draped in neutral tones and include work stations for busy business travelers.
600 rooms. Restaurant, bar. Pets accepted. Pool. Business center. Fitness center. $151-250

★★★HOTEL LE GERMAIN

30 Mercer St., Toronto, 416-345-9500, 866-345-9501; www.germaintoronto.com
Sleek lines, modern architecture and a two-level lobby define this new hotel.
Facilities such as a massage room, two rooftop terraces and a library with an
open-hearth fireplace enhance guests' stays. Four suites have fireplaces and
private terraces.
122 rooms. Complimentary breakfast. Restaurant, bar. Pets accepted. Fitness center. $151-250

★★★INTERCONTINENTAL HOTEL TORONTO CENTRE

225 Front St. W., Toronto, 416-597-1400, 800-422-7969; www.intercontinental.com
The downtown InterContinental caters to business travelers who need meeting space, business support and proximity to the adjacent Metro Toronto
Convention Centre. The hotel is great for leisure travelers too who want to
stay close to theater, dining and shopping venues. The rooms are sizeable and
pet-friendly, so Fido can come along.
586 rooms. Restaurant, bar. Pool. Business center. Pets accepted. Fitness
center. Spa. $351 and up

★★★INTERCONTINENTAL TORONTO

220 Bloor St. W., Toronto, 416-960-5200, 888-567-8725; www.intercontinental.com
Located in the exclusive Yorkville neighborhood, this modern hotel has guest
rooms designed to be both inviting and efficient. Thoughtful details are offered through out the hotel, such as an international newspaper service.
208 rooms. Restaurant, bar. Pets accepted. Fitness center. Pool. Business
center. $151-250

★★★LE ROYAL MERIDIEN KING EDWARD

37 King St. E., Toronto, 416-863-9700, 800-543-4300;
www.lemeridien-kingedward.com
Le Royal Meridien King Edward is the grande dame of Toronto. This historic
landmark opened in 1903 and has been hosting the world's elite ever since.
Sharing the hotel's affinity for England in its décor, the Cafe Victoria and
Consort Bar are essential elements of the superb King Edward experience.
298 rooms. Restaurant, bar. Pets accepted. Business center. Spa. Fitness
center. $251-350

★★★MARRIOTT BLOOR YORKVILLE

90 Bloor St. E., Toronto, 416-961-8000, 800-859-7180; www.marriott.com
Situated in the fashionable Yorkville neighborhood, this hotel's creative and
artistic décor makes it fit right in. Although it's located at perhaps the city's
busiest intersection, the hotel feels tucked away and serene. In-room amenities abound and are only enhanced by the attractions of the tourist-friendly
neighborhood.
258 rooms. Restaurant, bar. Business center. Fitness center. Pets accepted.
$251-350

★★★MARRIOTT TORONTO AIRPORT

901 Dixon Road, Toronto, 416-674-9400, 800-905-2811; www.marriott.com

Both business and leisure travelers will like this property's proximity to Pearson International Airport and many of the city's other top attractions. The property offers a variety of dining options. Mikada serves traditional Japanese dishes, while the Terrace's menu is Continental. Toucan's Lounge & Patio is a nice place to meet up with friends for a quick drink.
424 rooms. Restaurant, bar. Pets accepted. Pool. Business center. Fitness center. $151-250

★★★MARRIOTT TORONTO EATON CENTRE

525 Bay St., Toronto, 416-597-9200, 800-905-0667; www.marriotteatoncentre.com

In the financial district and near the theater district, this property attracts all types of visitors with its extensive offerings. There is a top-floor pool overlooking the city. Guest rooms are well lit and include custom duvets and a choice of pillows to fit your preference.
459 rooms. Restaurant, bar. Pool. Business center. Fitness center. $151-250

★★★METROPOLITAN HOTEL TORONTO

108 Chestnut St., Toronto, 416-977-5000, 800-668-6600; www.metropolitan.com

All of Toronto is within easy reach from the Metropolitan Hotel, close proximity to world-renowned shopping, art galleries and museums, the hotel has the services of a large property and the intimacy of a private residence. Fully-staffed fitness and business centers are also on hand to assist all guests. The Lai Wah Heen is a serene setting for its luscious Cantonese cuisine, which is considered an excellent example of authentic dim sum.
422 rooms. Pets accepted. Restaurant, bar. Fitness center. Pool. Business center. $351 and up

★★★THE MILLCROFT INN & SPA

55 John St., Alton, 519-941-8111, 800-383-3976; www.millcroft.com

This former knitting mill dating back to 1881 is situated on 100 acres on the Credit River and boasts some of the most impressive accommodations in the city. Rooms have personalized touches along with modern-day amenities such as flat-screen TVs and large Jacuzzi tubs. Be sure to visit the award-winning spa for a rejuvenating treatment or a relaxing herbal steam.
52 rooms. Complimentary breakfast. Restaurant, bar. Pool. Tennis. $151-250

★★NOVOTEL TORONTO CENTER

45 The Esplanade, Toronto, 416-367-8900; www.novotel.com

The Novotel Toronto Center in downtown Toronto is ideal for business or vacation travel. This three star hotel features an indoor pool, gym, restaurant, free WiFi and meeting facilities. Many attractions are nearby including the Air Canada Centre, Hockey Hall of Fame, Rogers Centre, Harbourfront Centre, Eaton Centre, St. Lawrence Market, Centre Island (ferry docks) and the financial district. Union Station and public transport nearby.
262 rooms. Bar. Pets accepted. $151-250

★★★PANTAGES SUITES HOTEL AND SPA

210 Victoria St., Toronto, 416-362-1777, 866-852-1777; www.pantageshotel.com
Unique amenities and services such as a complimentary meditation channel, yoga mats, 400 thread-count Egyptian cotton linens, 27-inch flat-screen TVs and in-room European kitchens. Guests are close to The Eaton Centre mall and other Toronto attractions and just two minutes from the subway and Toronto's underground walkway.
111 rooms. Complimentary breakfast. Fitness center. Pool. Business center. $251-350

★★★OLD MILL INN AND SPA

21 Old Mill Road, Toronto, 416-236-2641, 866-653-6455; www.oldmilltoronto.com
This Tudor-style inn and the adjacent meeting and conference facility exude old-world charm. In summer and winter, the setting is spectacular. The inn sits 15 minutes northwest of downtown Toronto in the Humber River Valley, which offers opportunities for hiking, biking and in-line skating.
57 rooms. Complimentary breakfast. Restaurant, bar. Fitness center. Business center. $251-350

★★★★PARK HYATT TORONTO

4 Avenue Road, Toronto, 416-925-1234, 800-977-4197; www.parktoronto.hyatt.com
The Park Hyatt Toronto calls the stylish Yorkville area home. Located at the intersection of Avenue Road and Bloor Street, this hotel has some of the world's leading stores just outside its doors. Public and private spaces have a rich feeling completed with handsome furnishings and a clean, modern look dominates the rooms and suites. The demands of the world dissipate at the Stillwater Spa. International dishes are the specialty at Annona, while the grilled steaks and seafood of Morton's of Chicago are always a treat.
346 rooms. Restaurant, bar. Business center. Fitness center. $251-350

★★RADISSON PLAZA HOTEL ADMIRAL

249 Queens Quay West, Toronto, 416-203-3333, 888-201-1718; www.radisson.com
157 rooms. Restaurant, bar. Pool. Business center. Fitness center. $151-250

★★★SHERATON CENTRE HOTEL

123 Queen St. W., Toronto, 416-361-1000, 800-325-3535; www.starwoodhotels.com
Though large in size, this hotel specializes in personalized service. Each guest room has been revamped with upgraded amenities and signature Sheraton Sweet Sleeper beds. The 2½-acre waterfall garden that runs through the new lobby emphasizes the urban oasis that is Toronto.
1,377 rooms. Restaurant, bar. Pets accepted. Pool. Fitness center. Business center. $151-250

★★★SHERATON GATEWAY HOTEL

Toronto International Airport, Terminal 3, Toronto, 905-672-7000, 800-325-3535;
www.sheraton.com
Pefect for a layover, the hotel is connected to Terminal 3 at Toronto International Airport. First-class soundproofing ensures a good night's sleep before an early flight. This glass-walled hotel is thoroughly modern, with every fa-

cility for the business traveler and comfort for the leisure traveler. 474 rooms. Restaurant, bar. Pets accepted. Pool. Business center. Complimentary breakfast. $151-250

★★★SOHO METROPOLITAN HOTEL
318 Wellington St. W., Toronto, 416-599-8800; www.metropolitan.com
This boutique hotel earns high marks for its urban chic interiors, stylish food, central location and smart technology. The accommodations appeal with clean, simple lines and light wood furnishings. The SoHo Metropolitan's Senses Bakery & Restaurant offers the contemporary gourmet experience with its artfully designed and creatively prepared cuisine.
366 rooms. Restaurant, bar. Pets accepted. Pool. Business center. $251-350

★★★THE SUTTON PLACE
955 Bay St., Toronto, 416-924-9221; www.suttonplace.com
You get an old Europe feel from the rich surroundings, including mahogany trim in the meeting rooms and crystal chandeliers. Original art and antiques grace the guest rooms and suites. Enjoy a drink in the elegant lobby bar.
294 rooms. Restaurant, bar. Spa. Pets accepted. Pool. Business center. Fitness center. $151-250

★★★ THE WESTIN BRISTOL PLACE TORONTO AIRPORT
950 Dixon Road, Toronto, 416-675-9444, 877-999-3223;
www.starwoodhotels.com/westin
Just five minutes from Pearson International Airport, this is a good choice for those on a short trip. The indoor pool and state-of-the-art workout facility will get you up and going in no time, and the proximity to downtown is convenient for those looking to experience the city's nightlife.
287 rooms. Restaurant. Pool. Business center. $151-250

★★★THE WESTIN HARBOUR CASTLE
1 Harbour Square, Toronto, 416-869-1600, 800-228-3000;
www.westin.com/harbourcastle
The striking towers of this hotel are among the most recognized landmarks in the city. The glass-walled foyer offers a wide, clear view of Lake Ontario. The hotel is close to a host of tourist attractions, including the Air Canada Centre, the CN Tower, the Eaton Centre and the theater district.
977 rooms. Restaurant, bar. Pets accepted. Pool. Tennis. Business center. Spa. $251-350

★★★THE WESTIN PRINCE TORONTO
900 York Mills Road, Toronto, 416-444-2511, 800-228-3000; www.westin.com
Located in the center of downtown Toronto, this hotel is just minutes from both the Ontario Science Centre and the Ford Centre for the Performing Arts. Activity is paramount here, as the hotel's 15 acres include tennis courts, an outdoor pool and walking trails. Guest rooms offer views of the Toronto skyline and the surrounding greenery.
381 rooms. Restaurant, bar. Fitness center. Pool. Tennis. Business center. $151-250

★★★WINDSOR ARMS HOTEL

18 St. Thomas St., Toronto, 416-971-9666, 877-999-2767; www.windsorarmshotel.com
The accommodations in this intimate and stylish hotel are sleek, modern and sublime. The Tea Room serves a traditional tea by day and at night is transformed into Toronto's only champagne and caviar bar. Club 22 entertains with piano entertainment and live bands and the Cigar Lounge offers decadent treats.
28 rooms. Complimentary breakfast. Restaurant, bar. Pets accepted. Pool. Spa. $$$

WHERE TO EAT

★★★360

301 Front St. W., Toronto, 416-362-5411; www.cntower.ca
As the name suggests, this restaurant completes a 360-degree rotation, offering a breathtaking view from the CN Tower. The scenery inside is attractive as well, with colorful décor and a fresh, seasonal menu.
International. Reservations recommended. $36-85

★★★AUBERGE DU POMMIER

4150 Yonge St., Toronto, 416-222-2220; www.aubergedupommier.com
Located north of the city, this restaurant in an industrial park manages to feel like it is actually in rural France. The attentive service and comfortable décor are pleasing. And the pommes frites are divine.
French, American. Reservations recommended. Lunch, dinner. $36-85

★★★BIAGIO

155 King St. E., Toronto, 416-366-4040; www.biagioristorante.com.
This modern Italian restaurant is situated in the historic St. Lawrence Hall near the theater district and serves specialties from the north. An ornate ceiling and a lovely patio with a fountain add to the ambience.
Italian. Outdoor seating. $36-85

★★★★CANOE

66 Wellington St. W., Toronto 416-364-0054; www.oliverbonacini.com
Canoe is a stunning venue in which to experience creative, satisfying regional Canadian cuisine. While dazzling ingredients tend to be sourced from wonderful local producers, many organic, the kitchen borrows flavors and techniques from the world at large, including Asia, France and the American South. The end product is inventive food and an equally original room. The five-course tasting menu is a rollercoaster of succulent flavors. The wine list is equally indulgent.
Canadian. Reservations recommended. Lunch, dinner. Bar. $36-85

★★★CENTRO GRILL & WINE BAR

2472 Yonge St., Toronto, 416-483-2211; www.centro.ca
A lot of tastes are rolled into one destination at this contemporary European restaurant with a downstairs sushi and oyster bar. A colorful, New Age-style dining room and a worldly menu means you'll never be bored with novelties like caribou chop with juniper berry oil, Alsatian spatzle and Arctic cloudberry sauce.
International. Reservations recommended. $36-85

★★★★CHIADO
864 College St., Toronto, 416-538-1910; www.chiadorestaurant.ca

Paying homage to the old seaside town but updating dishes for a more modern sensibility, Chiado features what might best be described as "nouvelle Portuguese cuisine." The food is first-rate and fabulous, featuring an ocean's worth of fresh fish simply prepared with olive oil and herbs, as well as innovative takes on pheasant, game and poultry. To add to the authenticity of the experience, Chiado has the largest collection of fine Portuguese wines in North America and a superb selection of vintage ports.

Spanish. Lunch, dinner. Reservations recommended. $36-85

★★★★THE FIFTH
225 Richmond St. W., Toronto, 416-979-3000; www.thefifthgrill.com

It takes work to make it to The Fifth. First, an alley entrance leads you to The Easy, an upscale nightclub and former speakeasy. Once inside The Easy, you are directed onto a Persian rug-lined vintage freight elevator. There, an attendant takes you to the fifth floor. Exit and you have finally arrived at The Fifth, a treasured contemporary French restaurant and supper club. The food is of the deliciously updated French variety, and the dishes are perfectly prepared, beautifully presented and easily devoured. Don't miss the sticky banana cake with rum butterscotch sauce for desert—it's heavenly.

French. Dinner. Closed Sunday-Wednesday. Bar. Reservations recommended. Outdoor seating. $86 and up

★★GRAZIE
2373 Yonge St., Toronto, 416-488-0822; www.grazie.ca

Italian. Lunch, dinner. $16-35

★★★HEMISPHERES
108 Chestnut St., Toronto, 416-599-8000; www.metropolitan.com/hemis

Hemispheres elevates hotel dining to a whole new level with its stylish interior and international fusion cuisine. The menu includes European and Continental classics, many with an Asian bent. Wine lovers will appreciate the well-rounded and extensive cellar.

International. Breakfast. Lunch, dinner. Reservations recommended. $16-35

★★★JOSO'S
202 Davenport Road, Toronto, 416-925-1903; www.josos.com

The walls are covered with the chef's racy art and celebrity pictures at this popular restaurant, which offers unique but excellent Mediterranean cuisine. Though it takes 20 minutes to prepare, the risotti is worth waiting for.

Meditteranean. Dinner. Outdoor seating. $36-85

★★★LA FENICE
319 King St. W., Toronto, 416-585-2377; www.lafenice.ca

The stark, modern dining room of this downtown restaurant recalls the chic design aesthetic of Milan. The pink and orange hues work to compliment the casual atmosphere and tasty Italian fare. The menu is large, so if you're undecided, just ask the helpful staff for house recommendations.

Italian. Reservations recommended. Lunch, dinner. $$36-85

★★★LAI WAH HEEN

108 Chestnut St., Toronto, 416-977-9899; www.laiwahheen.com

Lai Wah Heen, meaning "luxurious meeting place," is truly luxurious with its two-level dining room featuring black granite, 12-foot ceilings and solarium-style glass wall. Exotic herbs and spices, skillful use of tropical fruits and seafood dishes make for a Cantonese menu rich with Pacific Rim flair. Cantonese, Chinese. Reservations recommended. $16-35

★★★MISTURA

265 Davenport Road, Toronto, 416-515-0009; www.mistura.ca

Contemporary, seasonal Italian cuisine and a stylish, upscale environment are the hallmarks of this elegant Toronto restaurant. Past menu items like wild boar filled pasta with dried cherries have delighted guests along with fresh ingredients and artful presentation. Desserts are just as inventive. Italian. $16-35

★★★★NORTH 44 DEGREES

2537 Yonge St., Toronto, 416-487-4897; www.north44restaurant.com

Style, serenity and elegance infuse every aspect of North 44 Degrees. From the recently renovated loft-like dining room to the world-class New Continental cuisine, North 44 is a sublime and sexy dining experience. A sophisticated crowd fills the restaurant, named for the city's latitude, on most nights. Chef/owner Mark McEwan expertly blends the bright flavors of Asia with those of Italy, France and Canada. The service is smooth, refined and in perfect harmony with the cool space and stellar cuisine.
International. Reservations recommended. Dinner. Bar. $86 and up

★★★OLD MILL

21 Old Mill Road, Toronto, 416-236-2641, 866-653-6455; www.oldmilltoronto.com

The main dining room of the Old Mill Inn & Spa, a charming, English-style inn along the Humber River, features a warm and romantic atmosphere with beamed ceilings, a roaring fireplace, brick walls and soft lighting. Reinventing old classics like Beef Wellington Nouveau and Australian Lamb Souvlaki keeps diner guests guessing and the kitchen on their toes. There is a cover charge (Friday-Saturday from 8 p.m.)
International. Dinner. Jacket required (weekend dinner). Reservations recommended. Outdoor seating. $36-85

★★★★ONE RESTAURANT

The Hazelton Hotel, 116 Yorkville Ave., Toronto, 416-961-9600; www.onehazelton.com

One restaurant, housed in Toronto's grand Hazelton Hotel, means serious business. The main dining room caters to diners looking for quality food as well as sharp décor. Chocolate brown-leather booths line the walls of the main dining room, while the 16-seat Neil Young Room is reserved for those to discuss business, view presentations on the 52" plasma screen or just have an intimate meal with a small group. Red walls and mirrored doors make this room pop with sophistication. The menu is equally refined, thanks to chef Andrew Ellerby, whose roasted goose foie gras on warm toast will make you swoon, as will pastry chef Tony Accettola's apple charlotte with cinnamon ice cream.
American. Breakfast, lunch, dinner, Saturday-Sunday brunch. $86 and up

★★★OPUS RESTAURANT
37 Prince Arthur Ave., Toronto, 416-921-3105; www.opusrestaurant.com
This plush Yorkville restaurant is elegant, romantic and filled with the energy of Toronto's powerful and moneyed elite.
International. Dinner. Reservations recommended. Outdoor seating. $36-85

★★★ORO
45 Elm St., Toronto, 416-597-0155; www.ororestaurant.com
This restaurant has changed hands and names many times since it opened in 1922 and is famous for its patrons, who have included Ernest Hemingway and Prime Minister Jean Chrétien. The décor is contemporary and elegant, as is the food.
International. Lunch, dinner. Bar. $36-85

★★★PANGAEA
1221 Bay St., Toronto, 416-920-2323; www.pangaearestaurant.com
Vaulted ceilings and exotic floral arrangements set the stage for sophisticated continental cuisine using the wealth of each season's harvest. Tired Bloor Street shoppers will find this a great place to break for lunch or tea.
International. Lunch, dinner. Reservations recommended. Bar. $36-85

★★PIER 4 STOREHOUSE
245 Queen's Quay W., Toronto, 416-203-1440; www.pier4rest.com
Seafood. Reservations recommended. Outdoor seating. Lunch, dinner. $36-85

★★IL POSTO NUOVO
148 Yorkville Ave., Toronto, 416-968-0469; www.ilposto.ca
Italian. Reservations recommended. Outdoor seating. Lunch, dinner. $36-85

★★PROVENCE
12 Amelia St., Toronto, 416-924-9901; www.provencerestaurant.com
French. Outdoor seating. Lunch, dinner, Sunday Brunch. Reservations recommended. $36-85

★★RODNEY'S OYSTER HOUSE
469 King St. W., Toronto, 416-363-8105; www.rodneysoysterhouse.com
Seafood. Reservations recommended. Outdoor seating. $16-35

★★ROSEWATER SUPPER CLUB
19 Toronto St., Toronto, 416-214-5888; www.libertygroup.com
French. Reservations recommended. Outdoor seating. Lunch, dinner. $36-85

★★★★SCARAMOUCHE
1 Benvenuto Place, Toronto, 416-961-8011; www.scaramoucherestaurant.com
Up on a hillside overlooking the dazzling downtown lights, Scaramouche is the perfect hideaway for falling in love with food or your dining companion. This modern, bi-level space is known for its fantastic contemporary French fare and is often filled with dressed-up, savvy locals. The restaurant is di-

vided between a formal dining room upstairs and a modestly priced pasta bar downstairs.

French. Reservations recommended. $86 and up

★★★★SPLENDIDO

88 Harbord St., Toronto, 416-929-7788; www.splendido.ca

Splendido has hit its stride tobecome one of Toronto's best restaurants, with interpretations of international cuisines and a focus on clean, flavorful sauces and local Canadian ingredients. Several charming details like the Champagne cart and the selection of petit fours make this a fun and enjoyable dining experience. The extensive selection of cheeses also makes for a nice late afternoon snack.

International. Dinner. Closed Sunday-Monday, July-August. Reservations recommended. $36-85

★★★SUSUR

601 King St. W., Toronto, 416-603-2205; www.susur.com

This internationally acclaimed restaurant blends flavors of the East and West to create innovative, eclectic dishes. Tasting menus, available in five or seven courses, change on a daily basis to reflect the fresh ingredients available at local markets, so you'll be treated to a new dining experience with each visit.

International. Reservations recommended. $36-85

★★ZACHARY'S RESTAURANT

Westin Bristol Place Hotel, 50 Dixon Road, Etobicoke, 416-679-4394; www.zacharys.
sites.toronto.com

Continental. Dinner. Reservations recommended. $16-35

SPAS

★★★★THE SPA AT THE HAZELTON HOTEL

The Hazelton Hotel, 118 Yorkville Ave., Toronto, 416-963-6307;
www.thehazeltonhotel.com

Toronto's prized hotel keeps up the second-to-none hospitality at its spa and health club. Linda McDonald-Ferris leads this excellent spa, whose experience as a skincare specialist for the past 20 years shows in the quality treatments that the spa offers. For complete relaxation, start with the lemon sea salt body scrub, followed by a shiatsu massage and an exfoliating session known as the Body Glow. Waxing, manicure and pedicure are also available. After you're done pampering and primping, end your spa day with a dip in the gorgeous indoor lap pool, which is outfitted in imported mosaic tile.

★★★★STILLWATER SPA

Park Hyatt Toronto, 4 Avenue Road, Toronto, 416-925-1234;
www.parktoronto.hyatt.com

With its cool, crisp interiors—complete with a fireplace in the Tea Lounge and waterfalls and streams throughout the facility—and fabulous mind and body relaxation therapies, Park Hyatt Toronto's Stillwater Spa offers you an escape. The signature Stillwater massage customizes an aromatherapy blend to accompany a relaxing bodywork combination of Swedish massage, trigger-points pressure and stretching techniques.

WINDSOR

See also London

Windsor is located at the tip of a peninsula and is linked to Detroit by the Ambassador Bridge and the Detroit-Windsor Tunnel. Aside from its status as the Ambassador City, thanks to its proximity to the United States, Windsor is also known as the City of Roses for its many beautiful parks. The Sunken Gardens and Rose Gardens in Jackson Park boast more than 500 varieties of roses, while Coventry Garden and Peace Fountain has the only fountain floating in international waters. A cosmopolitan and determinedly bilingual city with many French influences, Windsor enjoys a symphony orchestra, theaters, a light opera company, art galleries, nightlife and all the amenities of a large city.

WHAT TO SEE
ART GALLERY OF WINDSOR
401 Riverside Drive W., Windsor, 519-977-0013; www.artgalleryofwindsor.com
Collections at this art gallery consist of Canadian art, including Inuit prints and carvings, with an emphasis on Canadian artists from the past and the present. There is also a children's gallery and gift shop.

COVENTRY GARDENS AND PEACE FOUNTAIN
Riverside Drive E. and Pillette Road, Windsor, 519-253-2300; www.citywindsor.ca
Coventry Gardens is a riverfront park and floral gardens with a 75-foot-high floating fountain. There is also a myriad 3D water displays with spectacular night illumination.
May-September, daily.

WILLISTEAD MANOR
1899 Niagara St., Windsor, 519-253-2365; www.willisteadmanor.com
This restored English Tudor mansion was built for Edward Chandler Walker, the son of famous distiller Hiram Walker, on 15 acres of wooded parkland. It has elegant interiors with hand-carved woodwork and furnished in turn-of-the-century style.
July-August, Sunday and Wednesday; September-June, first and third Sunday of each month.

SPECIAL EVENTS
FESTIVAL EPICURE: A CELEBRATION OF FOOD, WINE AND MUSIC
Riverside Festival Plaza, Windsor, 519-971-5005; www.festivalepicure.com
Sample food from local eateries and wine from regional wineries, Enjoy performances ranging from pop to bluegrass from local musicians.
Mid-July.

INTERNATIONAL FREEDOM FESTIVAL
Riverside Drive and Ouelette Avenue, Windsor, 519-252-7264
This two-week joint celebration by Detroit and Windsor includes many events, culminating in a fireworks display over the river.
Late June-early July.

WHERE TO STAY
★★★CAESARS WINDSOR HOTEL
377 Riverside Drive E., Windsor, 519-258-7878, 800-991-7777;
www.casinowindsor.com
An oasis from the frenetic casino activity, this hotel's guest rooms feature views of the Detroit skyline or the city of Windsor. A constant line-up of entertainers and a buzzing casino in the lobby will keep you busy.
758 rooms. Restaurant, bar. Casino. Pool. Fitness center. $251-350

★★★HILTON WINDSOR
277 Riverside Drive W., Windsor, 519-973-5555, 800-774-1500; www.hilton.com
The waterfront location is key for both business and leisure travelers. The hotel is also conveniently interconnected to the Cleary International Convention Centre and close to other local attractions. The casual Park Terrace Restaurant serves breakfast, lunch and dinner. The River Runner Bar is a great place to catch the game.
305 rooms. Restaurant, bar. Pool. Business center. Pets accepted. $151-250

★★RADISSON RIVERFRONT HOTEL WINDSOR
333 Riverside Drive W., Windsor, 519-977-9777, 888-201-1718; www.radisson.com
207 rooms. Restaurant, bar. Pets accepted. Pool. Fitness center. $151-250

WHERE TO EAT
★★COOK SHOP
683 Ouellette Ave., Windsor, 519-254-3377
Italian. Closed Monday; also two weeks in August. Reservations recommended. $16-35

★TUNNEL BAR-B-Q
58 Park St. E., Windsor, 519-258-3663, 877-285-3663; www.tunnelbarbq.com
American, steak. Breakfast, dinner. $16-35

PRINCE EDWARD ISLAND

CANADA'S SMALLEST PROVINCE RESTS IN THE GULF OF ST. LAWRENCE ON THE EAST COAST, between Nova Scotia and New Brunswick. The island is just 40 miles wide at its broadest point, narrowing to only four miles wide near Summerside and 140 miles long. Charlottetown and Summerside are the sole cities in the province. As charming as they are, it's no wonder this idyllic getaway, with its red soil, warm waters, fine white beaches and deep-cut coves, is more famed for its pastoral views and its promise of unspoiled, pristine relaxation.

Explore the Hillsborough River, one of the Canadian Heritage Rivers; scenic, red clay Heritage Roads; about 50 lighthouses; three scenic routes— Lady Slipper Drive, Blue Heron Drive and Kings Byway—that travel around the island's coastline; 30 nine-hole and 18-hole golf courses; and a wealth of shops selling everything from traditional crafts to handmade soaps and Mi'kmaq figurines. Deep-sea fish, dig for clams, watch for more than 330 species of birds and sea kayak the coastline. Or simply unwind on one of many beaches.

Prince Edward Island is divided into six day-tour regions. "North by Northwest" encompasses the area from North Cape to Cedar Dunes Provincial Park, an area of unspoiled beauty with secluded beaches, picturesque fishing and farming communities and quaint churches. "Ship to Shore" covers the southwest, which proudly stewards a prosperous shipbuilding heritage, fox farming and world-famous Malpeque oysters. Also here is the city of Summerside, located on the Bedeque Bay. "Anne's Land," the white-sand beaches and central north shore of the province, brings literary fans to the real-life paradise of the beloved Anne of Green Gables, heroine of books written by Lucy Maud Montgomery. "Charlotte's Shore" encompasses the south central region, highlighted by Charlottetown, the provincial capital, as well as scenic red cliffs and warm waters. "Bays and Dunes," in the northeast corner, offers the island's best coastline views, with miles of white-sand beaches and spectacular dunes bordering the scenic countryside. "Hills & Harbors," through the southeast, is home to some of the most pleasing vistas and peaceful fishing villages in the province.

The 80-minute ferry ride to and from the island is a relaxing, scenic journey that is popular with visitors and locals alike. Northumberland ferries *(877-635-7245; www.nfl-bay.com)* operate between Caribou, Nova Scotia and Wood Islands, Prince Edward Island about every 90 minutes from May to late December, weather permitting. A second ferry link, Corporation Transport Maritime Arien (www.ctma.ca), offers regular ferry service (about a five-hour trip) from Souris, Prince Edward Island to Cap-aux-Meules, Iles-de-la-Madeleine, Quebec except during February and March. For an equally interesting passage to Canada's beach-ridden gem, drive from New Brunswick to Prince Edward Island across the Confederation Bridge, the longest of its kind in the world.

CONFEDERATION BRIDGE

Not too long ago, the only way to get to Prince Edward Island was by air or water. That changed in 1997 when construction of the Confederation Bridge was completed. The bridge allows travel from New Brunswick to the town of

Borden-Carleton on Prince Edward Island. Built with more than 3.5 million tons of concrete and two million cubic yards of aggregate, the bridge has 44 main bridge spans, two traveling lanes and one emergency lane in either direction. There are 310 streetlights and 34 traffic lights (which remain green under normal conditions). The bridge is open only to motor vehicles; cyclists and pedestrians must use a shuttle to get across.

CONFEDERATION TRAIL

Those with enough pedal or foot power can travel the island from tip to tip on the Confederation Trail—a unique hiking, biking and snowmobile path that travels from Tignish on the west side of the island to Elmira on the east. The route totals more than 169 miles, with branch trails extending into Charlottetown, Souris, Georgetown and Montague. There is also a link to the Confederation Bridge in Borden-Carleton. The easily traveled stone dust surface took the place of the Prince Edward Island railway, which was abandoned in 1989. Travelers pass woods, rivers and pastoral scenes along the route, in between small island communities. There are many places to stop for refreshments and a well-earned break. Prince Edward Island is the first province in Canada to complete its section (the Confederate Trail) of the Trans Canada Trail.

CAVENDISH

See also Charlottetown

Located near the western end of Prince Edward Island National Park, Cavendish has more than 15 miles of world-famous beaches and is the heart and soul of Anne of Green Gables. Silky-white dunes, red sandstone cliffs and crystal blue water are all warmed by the Gulf Stream. Together with the allure of Canada's red-haired darling, Cavendish attracts thousands of visitors from around the world.

WHAT TO SEE

AVONLEA-VILLAGE OF ANNE OF GREEN GABLES

8779, Route 6, Cavendish, 902-963-3050; www.avonlea.ca

Families can spend a delightful day exploring Anne's world, meeting the novel's characters, visiting the barnyard, riding ponies and milking cows. There are three music shows a day, featuring musicians playing the spoons, fiddle and other fun instruments. There are events for visitors to take part in throughout the day, such as a barn dance, pig race, and other performances by the characters of Avonlea. Visit heritage buildings and Avonlea Gardens. Admission: adults $19.05, seniors $17.31, children $15.48. Mid-June-August, daily 10 a.m.-6 p.m. September, daily 10 a.m.-4 p.m. Reduced admission in September.

BIRTHPLACE OF LUCY MAUD MONTGOMERY

Routes 6 and 20, New London, 902-886-2099; www.gov.pe.ca

A replica of the "Blue Chest," the writer's personal scrapbooks containing copies of her many stories and poems, as well as her wedding dress and veil, are stored here.
May-November.

GREEN GABLES HERITAGE PLACE

Prince Edward Island National Park, Cavendish, 902-963-7874; www.pc.gc.ca
Famous as the setting for Lucy Maud Montgomery's *Anne of Green Gables*.
The surroundings portray the Victorian setting described in the novel. Tours
are available.
Admission: varies by season. Late March-early December, hours vary by
season. Rest of year, by appointment.

LUCY MAUD MONTGOMERY'S CAVENDISH NATIONAL HISTORIC SITE

Route 6, Cavendish, 902-963-7874; www.pc.gc.ca
The site where Montgomery, author of *Anne of Green Gables* and 22 other
novels, was raised by her grandparents from 1876 through 1911. The bookstore and museum houses the original desk, scales and crown stamp used in
the post office.
Admission: varies by season. Late March-early December, hours vary by
season. Rest of year, by appointment.

PRINCE EDWARD ISLAND NATIONAL PARK

Cavendish, 902-672-6350; www.pc.gc.ca
Prince Edward Island National Park is one of Eastern Canada's most popular
vacation destinations. Warm salt waters and sandy beaches abound. There are
several supervised beach areas for swimmers and miles of secluded shoreline
to explore. In addition to golf, tennis, bicycling and picnicking, the park
offers campfires, beach walks, an interpretation program highlighting the
natural and cultural features and stories of the area and more. Green Gables
and its association with Lucy Maud Montgomery's *Anne of Green Gables* is
a major attraction, with daily walks offered around the house and grounds.
Many private cabins, hotels and campgrounds border the park.
Daily. Visitor center: Mid-May-mid-June, daily 9 a.m.-6 p.m.; mid-June-
Labor Day, daily 8 a.m.-9 p.m.

WHERE TO STAY
★CAVENDISH CORNER

Routes 6 and 13, Cavendish, 902-367-3205, 877-963-2251;
www.resortatcavendishcorner.com
97 rooms. Restaurant. Fitness center. Pool. $61-150

★SILVERWOOD MOTEL

Green Gables Post Office, Cavendish Beach, 902-963-2439; www.silverwoodmotel.com
76 rooms. Restaurant. Pool. $61-150

WHERE TO EAT
★★NEW GLASGOW LOBSTER SUPPERS

Route 258, New Glasgow, 902-964-2870; www.peilobstersuppers.com
Seafood. Closed Mid-October-May. $16-35

PRINCE EDWARD ISLAND
★★★
★★★
★★★
★★

158

CHARLOTTETOWN

See also Cavendish

Having hosted the conference that led to the formation of Canada in 1864, Charlottetown today is a walkable, charm-filled heritage city with a scenic natural harbor, boating, yachting, swimming and plentiful seafood. Bistros, museums and artisan shopping, as well as a plethora of amenities, make this a traveler's headquarters.

WHAT TO SEE

BEACONSFIELD HISTORIC HOUSE

2 Kent St., Charlottetown, 902-368-6603; www.gov.pe.ca

This Mansard-style house, built in 1877 for a shipbuilder, is architecturally intact. It's the headquarters of the Prince Edward Island Museum and Heritage Foundation. They also host regular and annual events.

Admission: adults $4.25, students $3.25. Daily, hours vary by season.

CONFEDERATION CENTRE OF THE ARTS

145 Richmond St., Charlottetown, 902-628-1864, 800-565-0278;
www.confederationcentre.com

Canada's National Memorial to the Fathers of Confederation was opened by Queen Elizabeth II to honor the centennial of the 1864 Confederation Conference. It contains a provincial library, the Confederation Centre Museum and Art Gallery, theaters and the Robert Harris Collection of portraiture. There is also a courtyard restaurant and gift shop. This centre is also the home of the Charlottetown Festival, whish showcases musical theatre and comedy and runs from June to Setember.

FORT AMHERST/PORT-LA-JOYE NATIONAL HISTORIC PARK

Route 19, Charlottetown, 902-566-7626; www.pc.gc.ca

The only earthworks of the former French fort Port la Joye (built in 1720) are still visible at this site. Captured by the British in 1758, it was abandoned in 1768. There is a cafe, boutique and interpretive center here as well.

Admission: adults $3.90, seniors $3.40, children 6-16 $1.90. July-October.

FOUNDER'S HALL-CANADA'S BIRTHPLACE PAVILION

6 Prince St., Charlottetown, 902-368-1864; www.foundershall.ca

Learn about the nation's history beginning in 1864 in this 21,000-square-foot waterfront attraction, which features state-of-the-art displays and multimedia presentations.

Admission: adults $7, seniors and students $6, children $3.75. Hours vary by season.

GOVERNMENT HOUSE

Charlottetown, 902-368-5480; www.gov.pe.ca

Tour the lieutenant governor's official residence. The Victorian Fanningbank Historic House was built in 1832. Tours explain the history of the house and the room furnishings. Visitors are free to explore the lovely flower gardens around the property after the tour.

July-August, Monday-Friday 10 a.m.-4 p.m.

GREEN PARK SHIPBUILDING MUSEUM

Port Hill, 902-831-7947; www.gov.pe.ca/peimhf

Former estate of James Yeo, Jr., whose family members were leading ship-builders of the 19th century. The house has been restored to reflect life during the prosperous shipbuilding era. There are photos of famous ships and arti-facts in interpretive center as well as an audiovisual presentation in Museum Theater. There are also lecture series, concerts and annual events.

Admission: adults $5, students $3.50. June-early September.

ORWELL CORNER HISTORIC VILLAGE

Route 1, Charlottetown, 902-651-8515; www.orwellcorner.ca

This reconstructed rural crossroads community of late 19th century features a combined store, post office and farmhouse; a school, church, cemetery and barns. Watch farming activities as they were practiced 100 years ago. Ceilidhs (Scottish and Irish gatherings that feature dancing, story-telling and traditional live music) take place on Wednesday evenings as well as other events throughout the week.

Admission: adults $7.50, children 6-18 $3. Late May-mid-June, Monday-Friday 9 a.m.-5 p.m.; July-early-September, daily 9:30 a.m.-5:30 p.m.; early September-early October, Sunday-Thursday 9 a.m.-5 p.m.

PROVINCE HOUSE ★★★★★

165 Richmond St., Charlottetown, 902-566-7626; www.pc.gc.ca

This is the birthplace of the Canadian nation and a national historic site. Visit the confederation room where delegates met in 1864 to discuss the confed-eration. This National Historic Site still houses the Legislative Assembly for Prince Edward Island. Tours are available.

Admission: $3.40. Open year-round, hours vary by season.

ST. DUNSTAN'S BASILICA

45 Great George St., Charlottetown, 902-894-3486; www.stdunstans.pe.ca

Largest church on the island. Gothic cathedral with distinctive triple towers contains beautiful stained-glass windows and an impressive altar: It is 37 feet high, made of many types of marble and crowned with a beautiful rose window.

SPECIAL EVENTS
CHARLOTTETOWN FESTIVAL

Confederation Centre of the Arts, 145 Richmond St., Charlottetown, 902-566-1267;
www.confederationcentre.com

During this festival, you'll find original Canadian musicals, including Anne of Green Gables, as well as special gallery presentations and theater.
Late May-mid-October.

FESTIVAL OF LIGHTS
Charlottetown Waterfront, Charlottetown, 902-629-1864
This festival features buskers, children's concerts, and a children's midway. There is a fireworks display over Charlottetown Harbor on July 1 (Canada Day).
Late June-early July.

PRINCE EDWARD ISLAND STUDIO TOUR
94, Euston St., Prince Edward Island, 902-368-6300; www.peistudiotour.com
Shoppers delight at this annual event where they can purchase island-made crafts and giftware at more than 140 participating craft studios, galleries, shops and museums across the island, without paying the provincial sales tax. Pick up the official directory and a map at any Price Edward Island visitor information center.
Late September.

WHERE TO STAY
★★BEST WESTERN CHARLOTTETOWN
238 Grafton St., Charlottetown, 902-892-2461, 800-780-7234;
www.bestwesternatlantic.com
146 rooms. Restaurant, bar. Complimentary breakfast. Business center. Fitness center. Pool. Pets accepted. $61-150

★★THE CHARLOTTETOWN
75 Kent St., Charlottetown, 902-894-7371, 800-565-7633; www.rodd-hotels.ca
115 rooms. Restaurant, bar. Business center. Fitness center. Pool. Pets accepted. $251-350

★★★DELTA PRINCE EDWARD
18 Queen St., Charlottetown, 902-566-2222, 888-890-3222; www.deltahotels.com
Overlooking Charlottetown Harbor in an area of shops and restaurants, this large red-brick hotel is located at the foot of Queen Street at Peake's Wharf. Renovated guest rooms have a modern flair and are comfortable and well appointed. The hotel features its own marina, and guests can walk along the waterfront or take a harbor cruise from the hotel.
211 rooms. Restaurant, bar. Business center. Fitness center. Pool, Spa. Pets accepted. $251-350

★★RODD ROYALTY INN
Highways 1 and 2, Charlottetown, 902-894-8566, 800-565-7633; www.rodd-hotels.ca
121 rooms. Restaurant, bar. Pool. Pets accepted. $151-250

QUÉBEC

AN ENCLAVE OF EUROPE IN THE HEART OF NORTH AMERICA, QUÉBEC IS A DIVERSE AND colorful province that is fiercely proud of its French heritage. Delightfully blending Old and New World, and passionate politics with a unique joie de vivre, this nation within a nation hums with incredible cuisine and nightlife alongside glorious mountains, charming villages, First Nations culture and an untamed wilderness. French is the language used by the majority of Québecers, though English is spoken or understood almost everywhere in the province.

By reason of its history and culture, Québec has forged a unique personality. Québecers enjoy fine dining and entertainment as evidenced by the busy calendar of festivals and other events—but they also maintain a classic Canadian hardiness and sense of adventure. As a place where both European and North American cultural influences play out, Québec has always produced a fertile creative energy and cultural vitality. The result is a thriving literature, theatrical, art, sculpture and crafts scene.

Historic yet resolutely modern, vibrant and festive, the cities of Montréal, Québec and Gatineau embody urban Québec with their rich architectural heritage, dynamic cultural melting pot and splendid surroundings. The wider river region, centered around the historic St. Lawrence river (one of the largest in the world), is home to old coastal villages, islands, bird sanctuaries, marine mammals and lighthouses, all bound by rural and rugged coastline.

Further afield, Québecers have mastered the art of resort living and ecotourism. Québec's vast natural heritage comprises 27 national parks, numerous wildlife reserves and three biosphere reserves recognized by UNESCO. Eco-tourism and adventure tour guides can support your discovery of the most beautiful sites in Québec on foot, by canoe or by kayak. During the summer, enjoy golf, biking, tennis, hiking, swimming and water sports; and in winter, get outside to snowmobile, ski, skate and even dogsled. Whatever the day holds, fine cuisine will await you on the patio or by the hearth. For the more independent wanderer, Québec has pushed the boundaries of adventure since the days of the fur traders. In this vast territory, bears, deer and caribou are often the only inhabitants. Explore the province's length and breadth by canoe, snowmobile or seaplane, with nature as your travel companion.

MONT TREMBLANT
See also Montréal

In 1894, the provincial government of Québec established this 482-square-mile wilderness reserve as a park in order to protect its abundant wildlife, 300 lakes, three rivers, three major hydrographical basins, innumerable streams, waterfalls and mountains that reach as high as 3,120 feet. Today it is a center of fishing, hiking, canoeing, biking, swimming, sailing, snowmobiling, snowshoeing and cross-country and downhill skiing—and in the fall, people come here in droves for the foliage.

SPECIAL EVENTS
TREMBLANT INTERNATIONAL BLUES FESTIVAL
Mont Tremblant Provincial Park, 888-736-2526; www.tremblant.com
Ten days of the biggest blues festival in Canada features more than 400 artists in almost 200 performances on indoor and outdoor stages. Mid-July.

WHERE TO STAY
★★★FAIRMONT TREMBLANT
3045 Chemin de la Chapelle, Mont Tremblant, 819-681-7000; www.fairmont.com
The Fairmont's location at the base of the Laurentian Mountains makes it a skier's paradise, with ski in/ski out access to the slopes. Its plentiful menu of activities ensures that non-skiers are also cosseted. The guest rooms and suites offer a sophisticated twist on traditional ski lodge décor while incorporating creature comforts.
314 rooms. Restaurant, bar. Pool. Business center. $151-250

★★★LE WESTIN RESORT, TREMBLANT
100 Chemin Kandahar, Mont Tremblant, 819-681-8000, 888-736-2526;
www.westin.com
A resort for all seasons, this hotel has luxurious guest rooms, many with balconies and fireplaces, a separate entrance for skiers and an outdoor heated saltwater pool. Twenty outdoor tennis courts and two 18-hole golf courses challenge guests. After an activity-filled day, try Soto's Japanese cuisine or the American fare at Panache.
126 rooms. Complimentary breakfast. Restaurant, bar. Spa. Beach. Pool. Golf. Tennis. Business center. $151-250

WHERE TO EAT
★AUBERGE SAUVIGNON
2723 Chemin Principal, Mont Tremblant, 819-425-5466, 866-665-5466;
www.aubergesauvignon.com
French. Dinner. $36-85

★PIZZATERIA
118 Chemin Kandahar Village Center, Mont Tremblant, 819-681-4522;
www.pizzateria.com
Pizza. Lunch, dinner. $15 and under

MONTRÉAL
See also Mont Tremblant, Québec City
Blessed by its location on an island at the junction of the St. Lawrence and Ottawa rivers, Montréal has served for more than three centuries as a gigantic trading post. However, despite its status as a commercial, financial and industrial center, Montréal has an unconventional, eclectic heart. An internationally recognized patron of the fine arts, the city hosts several acclaimed festivals attended by the international elite, and its cosmopolitan flavor is enhanced by its two-thirds French-speaking population, as well as more than 80 ethnic communities that welcome visitors to colorful neighborhoods at-

tractions and markets.

Montréal is made up of two parts: the Old City, which is a maze of narrow streets, restored buildings and old houses that are best seen on foot; and the modern Montréal, with its many skyscrapers, museums, theaters, restaurants and nightlife. The boutiques and department stores of Sainte-Catherine Street are a shopper's paradise, while the café terraces of Crescent Street encourage peoplewatching. In the brisk winter, locals and visitors alike take refuge in Montréal's underground city, an impressive pedestrian network more than 19 miles long with hundreds of shops, restaurants, attractions and one of the most unique subway systems anywhere—in which each station has been decorated by a different architect for what's been called the largest underground art gallery in the world.

WHAT TO SEE
BIODOME DE MONTRÉAL
4777 Pierre-De Coubertin Ave., Montréal, 514-868-3000; www.biodome.qc.ca
The former Olympic Velodrome has been transformed into an environmental museum that combines elements of a botanical garden, aquarium, zoo and nature center. Four ecosystems—Laurentian Forest, Tropical Forest, Polar World and St. Laurent Marine—sustain thousands of plants and small animals. The Biodome also features a 1,640-foot nature path with text panels and maps.

CHÂTEAU RAMEZAY
280 rue Notre-Dame E., Montréal, 514-861-3708; www.chateauramezay.qc.ca
This historic building was constructed in the 18th century and was once the home of the governors of Montréal, the West Indies Company of France and the Governors General of British North America. It opened as a museum in 1895 and today is the oldest private museum in Québec. Collections include furniture, paintings, costumes, porcelain, manuscripts and art objects of the 17th through 19th centuries.

DORCHESTER SQUARE
1555 Peel St., Montréal
In the center of Montréal, this park is a popular meeting place. Also here is Mary Queen of the World Cathedral, a one third-scale replica of St. Peter's in Rome, as well as the information center of Montréal and Tourisme Québec.

FLORAL PARK
Le Notre-Dame, Montréal
This is the site of Les Floralies Internationales exhibition in 1980. Now permanent, it displays a collection of worldwide flowers and plants. There are walking trails, pedal boats, and canoeing; a picnic area and restaurant.
Third week in June-mid-September, daily.

FORT LENNOX NATIONAL HISTORIC SITE
Saint-Paul-de-l'ile-aux-Noix, 1 61st Ave., Montréal, 450-291-5700;
www.parcscanada.gc.ca
Located on le-aux-Noix, Fort Lennox was designed to protect against an

American invasion. Costumed guides provide visitors with insight into the history of these fortifications.

THE LAURENTIANS

www.laurentides.com

The Laurentian region, just 45 miles from Montréal, is a rich tourist destination. Surrounded by forests, lakes, rivers and the Laurentian Mountains, this area provides ample open-air activities year-round. Water sports abound in summer, including canoeing, kayaking, swimming, rafting, scuba diving and excellent fishing. Hunting, golfing, horseback riding and mountain climbing are also popular in warmer months, as is bicycling along the 125-mile P'tit train du Nord trail. Brilliant fall colors lead into a winter ideal for snow lovers. The Laurentian region boasts a huge number of downhill ski centers, 600 miles of cross-country trails and thousands of miles of snowmobiling trails. The territory of the Laurentian tourist zone is formed on the south by the Outaouais River, des Deux-Montagnes Lake and the Milles-iles River. On the east, its limits stretch from the limit of Terrebonne to Entrelacs. It is bounded on the north by Sainte-Anne-du-Lac and Baskatong Reservoir and on the west by the towns of Des Ruisseaux, Notre-Dame de Pontmain and Notre Dame du Laus.

LA FONTAINE PARK

Sherbrooke and Avenue du Parc Lafontaine, Montréal, 514-872-2644

Outdoor enthusiasts delight in this park for its many recreational opportunities. Along with paddle boating on two manmade lakes, visitors may enjoy footpaths and bicycle trails and, in winter, cross-country skiing, ice-skating and snowshoeing.

LA RONDE

Le Sainte-Helene, 22 Chemin Macdonald, Montréal, 514-397-2000; www.laronde.com

A 135-acre amusement park with 35 rides, including a 132-foot wooden roller coaster; arcades, entertainment on a floating stage; waterskiing; live cartoon characters, a children's village; a circus, boutiques and restaurants. Mid-May-late October.

MAISON ST. GABRIEL

Pointe-Saint-Charles, 2146 place de Dublin, Montréal, 514-935-8136;
www.maisonsaint-gabriel.qc.ca

Built in the late 17th century as a farm, this building also served as a school for Marguerite Bourgeoys, the founder of the Sisters of the Congregation de Notre-Dame, who looked after young French girls who were to marry the early colonists. The site includes vegetable, herb and flower gardens. The house itself has period furnishings and tools and items of French-Canadian heritage, including woodcuts from ancient churches and chapels. Mid-April-late June, September-mid-December, Tuesday-Sunday 1-5 p.m.; late June-early September, Tuesday-Sunday 11 a.m.-6 p.m.

MCCORD MUSEUM OF CANADIAN HISTORY

690 rue Sherbrooke Ouest, Montréal, 514-398-7100; www.mccord-museum.qc.ca
This museum features extensive and diverse collections, including the most important First Nations collection in Québec, Canadian costumes and textiles and the Notman photographic archives.

MONTRÉAL BOTANICAL GARDEN

4101 rue Sherbrooke East, Montréal, 514-872-1400; www.ville.montreal.qc.ca/jardin
Within 180 acres of this botanical garden, there are more than 26,000 species and varieties of plants, with 30 specialized sections include roses, perennial plants, heath gardens, flowery brooks, bonsai, carnivorous plants and an arboretum. They have one of the world's largest orchid collections and seasonal flower shows. The bonsai and penjing collections are two of the most diversified in North America. There are also Chinese and Japanese gardens, a restaurant and a tearoom.
Admission: varies; see Web site for information. Daily 9 a.m.-6 p.m.

MONTRÉAL MUSEUM OF FINE ARTS

1379-80 rue Sherbrooke Ouest, Montréal, 514-285-2000, 800-899-6873;
www.mmfa.qc.ca
Canada's oldest art museum, founded in 1860, has a wide variety of displays ranging from Egyptian statues to 20th-century abstracts. A Canadian section features old Québec furniture, silver and paintings.
Admission: adults $15, seniors $10, students $7.50, children 12 and under free. Tuesday 11 a.m.-5 p.m., Wednesday-Friday 11 a.m.-9 p.m., Saturday-Sunday 10 a.m.-5 p.m.

MONTRÉAL PLANETARIUM

1000 rue Saint-Jacques Ouest, Montréal, 514-872-4530;
www.planetarium.montreal.qc.ca
See the stars at the Montréal Planetarium, where a 385-seat theater holds multimedia astronomy shows with projectors creating features of the night sky. Just outside the theater are temporary and permanent exhibits on the solar system, meteorites, fossils and other astronomy-related topics.
Hours and prices vary; see Web site for information.

THE MONTRÉAL SCIENCE CENTRE

King-Edward Pier, 333 rue de la Commune Ouest, Montréal, 514-496-4724,
877-496-4724; www.centredessciencesdemontreal.com/en
Uncover the mysteries of science and technology through multimedia and hands-on exhibits, an IMAX theater and more.
Hours and prices vary; see Web site for information.

MUSEÉ D'ART CONTEMPORAIN DE MONTRÉAL

185 rue Sainte-Catherine Ouest, Montréal, 514-847-6226; www.macm.org
This is Canada's only museum devoted exclusively to modern art.
Admission: adults $8, seniors $6, students $4, children 12 and under free.
Tuesday-Sunday 11 a.m.-6 p.m., Wednesday until 9 p.m.

NOTRE-DAME BASILICA
110 rue Notre-Dame Ouest, Montréal, 514-842-2925, 866-842-2925;
www.basiliquenddm.org

Completed in 1829, this church features Le Gros Bourdon, a bell cast in 1847 and weighing 24,780 pounds. Built of Montréal limestone, the basilica is neo-Gothic in design with a beautiful main altar, pulpit and numerous statues, paintings and stained-glass windows.

Admission: adults $5, children 7-17 $4, children 6 and under free. Monday-Friday 8 a.m.-4:30 p.m., Saturday 8 a.m.-4 p.m., Sunday 12:30 p.m.-4 p.m.

NOTRE-DAME-DE-BON-SECOURS CHURCH
400 rue St. Paul E., Montréal, 514-282-8670

Founded in 1657 by teacher Marguerite Bourgeoys and rebuilt 115 years later, this is one of the oldest churches still standing in the city. With its location near the Port of Montréal, parishioners often prayed here for the safety of the community's sailors. In recognition of this, many fishermen and other mariners presented the church with miniature wooden ships, which hang from the vaulted ceiling today. The tower offers views of the river and city. Housed here is the Marguerite Bourgeois museum, which features objects pertaining to early settlers.

THE OLD FORT
This is the oldest remaining fortification of Montréal, built between 1820 and 1824 and only the arsenal, powder magazine and barracks building still stand. Two military companies dating to the 18th century, La Compagnie Franche de la Marine and the 78th Fraser Highlanders, perform colorful military drills and parades.

Late June-August, Wednesday-Sunday.

OLD (VIEUX) MONTRÉAL
Bounded by McGill, Berri, Notre-Dame streets and the St. Lawrence River

The city of Montréal evolved from the small settlement of Ville-Marie founded by de Maisonneuve in 1642. The largest concentration of 19th-century buildings in North America is found here; several original dwellings remain while many other locations are marked by bronze plaques. The expansion of this settlement led to what is now known as Old Montréal. The area roughly forms a 100-acre quadrangle, which corresponds approximately to the area enclosed within the original fortifications.

OLD PORT OF MONTRÉAL
333 Rue de la Commune St., Montréal, 514-496-7678, 800-971-7678;
www.oldportofmontreal.com

This Old Port is a departure point for boat cruises, and a recreation and tourist park hosting exhibitions, special events and entertainment.

OLYMPIC PARK
4141 Pierre de Coubertin Ave., Montréal, 514-252-4141, 877-997-0919;
www.rio.gouv.qc.ca

The stadium was the site of the 1976 Summer Olympic Games and is now home to les Alouettes de Montréal football team. The world's tallest inclined tower (626 feet, leaning at a 45-degree angle) is here. Tours of the stadium are given daily.

PARC DU MONT-ROYAL

Cote des Neiges and Remembrance roads, Montréal, 514-843-8240; www.lemontroyal.qc.ca
Designed by Frederick Law Olmsted, the creator of Central Park in New York City, Parc du Mont-Royal is also a park located in the heart of a city. Popular with visitors to Montréal, it offers something for everyone: cycling, hiking, picnicking, paddle boating, cross-country skiing and snowshoeing. Bikes, paddleboats, skis and snowshoes may be rented at the park.
Daily 6 a.m.-midnight.

PARC JEAN-DRAPEAU

1 Circuit Gilles-Villeneuve, Montréal, 514-872-6120; www.parcjeandrapeau.com
This park consists of two islands in the middle of the St. Lawrence River. In order to access the park, visitors take the Jacques-Cartier Bridge or Metro subway. St. Helen's Island was the main anchor site for the Expo '67. It is now a 342-acre multipurpose park with three swimming pools, picnicking areas, cross-country skiing, and snowshoeing. Notre Dame Island, to the south, was partly built up from the riverbed and was an important activity site for Expo '67. The Gilles-Villeneuve Formula 1 racetrack is located here as well as a beach. You can rent paddleboats and go windsurfing and sailing as well.

PLACE D'ARMES

Rue St. Jacques, Montréal
A square of great historical importance and the center of Old Montréal, the founders of Ville-Marie encountered the Iroquois here in 1644 and rebuffed them. In the square's center is a statue of de Maisonneuve, the first governor of Montréal. At one end is the St. Sulpice seminary of 1685, with an old wooden clock. At 119 St. Jacques Street is the Bank of Montréal. This magnificent building contains a museum (open Monday-Friday) with a collection of currency, mechanical savings banks, photographs and a reproduction of an old-fashioned teller's cage. Some of the most important financial houses of the city are grouped around the square.

PLACE DES ARTS

260 Boulevard de Maisonneuve Oeste, 514-842-2112; www.pdarts.com
This four-theater complex is the heart of Montréal's artistic life. L'Opera de Montréal, the Montréal Symphony Orchestra, les Grands Ballets Canadiens and La Compagnie Jean-Duceppe theatrical troupe have their permanent homes here. Other entertainment includes chamber music, recitals, jazz, folk singers, variety shows, music hall, theater, musicals and modern and classical dance.

PLACE JACQUES-CARTIER

Between rue Notre-Dame and rue de la Commune, Montréal
Named for the discoverer of Canada, this was once a busy marketplace. Today, restaurants, cafés, bars, cyclists, in-line skaters and street performers are

found around the plaza, which is closed to traffic. The oldest monument in the city, the Nelson Column, is in the square's upper section.

POINTE-À-CALLIÈRE, THE MONTRÉAL MUSEUM OF ARCHAEOLOGY AND HISTORY

350 Place Royale, Montréal, 514-872-9150; www.pacmuseum.qc.ca

Built in 1992 over the site of the founding of Montréal, the main museum building, the Eperon, actually rests on pillars built around ruins dating from the town's first cemetery and its earliest fortifications, which are now in its basement. Two balconies overlook this archaeological site and a 16-minute multimedia show is presented using the actual remnants as a backdrop. From here, visitors continue underground, amid still more remnants, to the Archaeological Crypt, a structure that allows access to many more artifacts and remains; architectural models beneath a transparent floor illustrate five different periods in the history of Place Royale. The Old Customs House Ancienne-Douane houses thematic exhibits on Montréal in the 19th and 20th centuries. There are permanent and changing exhibits.

RUE SAINT-PAUL

This is the oldest street in Montréal. The mansions of Ville-Marie once stood here, but they have been replaced by commercial houses and office buildings.

ST. JOSEPH'S ORATORY OF MONT ROYAL

3800 Chemin Queen Mary, Montréal, 514-733-8211; www.saint-joseph.org

The chapel was built as a tribute to St. Joseph in 1904. A larger crypt church was completed in 1917. Today, the main church is a famous shrine attracting more than two million people who make pilgrimages here yearly. A basilica with a seating capacity of 2,200 was founded in 1924. There is a dome that towers over the city and a 56-bell carillon, which made in France—both are outstanding. The Oratory's museum features 200 nativity scenes from 100 different countries.

SPECIAL EVENTS
CANADIAN GRAND PRIX

Parc Jean-Drapeau, Montréal, 514-350-0000

Held annually since 1967, this Formula 1 race took place on the Mont-Tremblant Circuit until 1977. At that time, the track was considered too dangerous and the then-named le-Notre-Dame Track was built. The first race at the new track was held in 1978 and was won by Gilles Villeneuve, Canada's first F1 driver. In 1982, when Villeneuve was killed during practice laps at the Belgian Grand Prix, the track was renamed in his honor. If you wish to attend this event, make sure to purchase tickets well in advance; they can be extremely hard to come by.
Mid-June.

FETE NATIONALE

82 rue Sherbrooke Ouest, Montréal, 514-849-2560; www.fetenationale.qc.ca

St. Jean-Baptiste, patron saint of the French Canadians, is honored with three days of festivities surrounding the provincial holiday. The celebration includes street festivals, a bonfire, fireworks, musical events and parades. Mid-June.

MONTRÉAL BIKE FEST
1251 rue Rachel E., Montréal, 514-521-8356, 800-567-8356; www.velo.qc.ca
An entire week of events celebrating the bicycle, ending when 40,000 cyclists ride through the streets of Montréal.
Late May-early June.

MONTRÉAL INTERNATIONAL JAZZ FESTIVAL
822 rue Sherbrooke E., Montréal, 514-871-1881, 888-515-0515;
www.montrealjazzfest.com
More than 1,200 musicians and 1 million music lovers from around the world gather to celebrate jazz and other types of music. The 10-day fest includes more than 350 indoor and outdoor concerts.
Late June-early July.

WORLD FILM FESTIVAL
1432 de Bleury St., Montréal, 514-848-3883; www.ffm-montreal.org
Montréal's World Film Festival was organized to celebrate all types of cinema, from documentaries and drama to comedy and science fiction. Amateur and well-known filmmakers alike participate in the event, which screens films from nearly 70 countries.
Late August-early September.

WHERE TO STAY
★★★AUBERGE DU VIEUX-PORT
97 rue de la Commune E., Montréal, 514-876-0081, 888-660-7678;
www.aubergeduvieuxport.com

This historic landmark building served several functions before becoming a full-service inn. Rooms have contemporary furnishing and loft-like exposed beams and brick walls. Les Ramparts restaurant serves up fine, French cuisine and a rooftop terrace offers a panoramic view of the St. Lawrence River. Guests are pampered with a full breakfas and afternoon wine and cheese.
27 rooms. Complimentary breakfast. Restaurant, bar. $151-250

★★★AUBERGE HANDFIELD
555 Blvd. Richelieu, St. Marc-Sur-Richelieu, 450-584-2226;
www.aubergehandfield.com
This country inn, located 45 minutes from central Montréal, offers comfortable rooms with views of the garden or nearby river. The onsite restaurant serves full, traditional dinners drawing on local ingredients as well as an extensive Sunday brunch.
56 rooms. Restaurant, bar. Fitness center. Pool. Spa. $61-150

★★★CHATEAU VERSAILLES HOTEL
1659 rue Sherbrooke Ouest, Montréal, 888-933-8111, 514-933-8111;
www.versailleshotels.com
Located at the start of Montréal's famous Miracle Mile shopping district and

the foot of Mont Royal, this 1800s hotel features unique rooms in four reno-vated Victorian townhouses. The property is also just minutes by metro to the Molson Centre and the Place des Arts.

65 rooms. Complimentary breakfast. Restaurant, bar. Pets accepted. Fitness center. Business center. $151-250

★★COURTYARD MONTRÉAL DOWNTOWN

410 rue Sherbrooke Ouest, Montréal, 514-844-8855, 800-449-6654; www.marriott.com

157 rooms. Complimentary breakfast. Restaurant, bar. Pool. $61-150

★★★DELTA MONTRÉAL

475 President Kennedy Ave., Montréal, 514-286-1986, 877-286-1986;
www.deltamontreal.com

This modern, inviting hotel is located in the heart of downtown, near the Convention Centre and the Place des Arts. Have a game on the squash courts at Delta's elaborate spa and sports center, then enjoy French cuisine at Le Bouquet or relax at Le Cordial, the hotel's full-service bar.

456 rooms. Restaurant, bar. Pets accepted. Fitness center. Pool. Business center. $61-150

★★★FAIRMONT THE QUEEN ELIZABETH

900 Blvd. Rene Levesque Ouest, Montréal, 514-861-3511, 800-441-1414;
www.fairmont.com

This contemporary hotel is located in the city center, above the train station and linked to the underground system of shops and restaurants. The hotel's Beaver Club is a favorite for its gourmet meals and the convivial, Mediter-ranean-inspired Le Montréalais Bistrot-Bar-Restaurant is a more casual spot for dinner or drinks.

1,039 rooms. Restaurant, bar. Pets accepted. Fitness center. Pool. Business center. $151-250

★★★HILTON MONTRÉAL, BONAVENTURE

900 de la Gauchetiere Ouest, Montréal, 514-878-2332, 800-267-2575;
www.hiltonmontreal.com

This hotel is perched on top of the Place Bonaventure Exhibition Hall. There are rooftop gardens to explore and a year-round outdoor pool. The central city location is perfect for sightseeing in Old Montréal, gambling at the ca-sino or shopping the underground boutiques.

395 rooms. Restaurant, bar. Pets accepted. Fitness center. Pool. Business center. $151-250

★★★HILTON MONTRÉAL DORVAL AIRPORT

12505 Cote de Liesse, Dorval, 514-631-2411; www.dorval.hilton.com

Perfect for business or leisure travelers, this hotel has a location that is only a two-minute drive to the airport. Guests can relax in either the pool or Jacuzzi and then retreat to their renovated, contemporary rooms. Dine at Au Coin du Feu and enjoy the seafood and steak menu, then have a cocktail at Eclipse.

486 rooms. Restaurant, bar. Pets accepted. Fitness center. Pool. Business center. $61-150

★★★HOSTELLERIE LES TROIS TILLEULS

290 rue Richelieu, St. Marc-Sur-Richelieu, 514-856-7787; www.lestroistilleuls.com
This 1880s farmhouse is located 30 minutes south of Montréal on the
Richelieu River. The inn has comfortable rooms with down duvet-topped
beds. The onsite Spa Givency offers a full menu of treatments including hot
stone massages, facials and body wraps.
41 rooms. Restaurant, bar. Pool. Tennis. Business center. $61-150

★★★HOTEL DU FORT

1390 rue du Fort, Montréal, 514-938-8333, 800-565-6333; www.hoteldufort.com
Located steps from rue Sainte Catherine, this property is close to the city's
top attractions, shops and restaurants. Understated guest rooms offer city
views and traditional furnishings in neutral tones. Room service options include menus from area restaurants.
124 rooms. Complimentary breakfast. Restaurant, bar. Business center.
$61-150

★★★HOTEL GAULT

449 rue Ste. Héléne, Montréal, 514-904-1616, 866-904-1616; www.hotelgault.com
You might not expect to find an ultramodern hotel in a historic neighborhood,
but Hotel Gault is exactly that. Inside, you'll find interiors of glass, concrete
and steel, balanced with warm woods. Sound proofed guest rooms feature
flat-screen TVs, CD and DVD players and comfortable workstations, and
some have private terraces. A variety of living spaces are available.
30 rooms. Restaurant, bar. Fitness room. Business center. $151-250

★★★HOTEL INTERCONTINENTAL MONTRÉAL

360 rue Ste Antoine Ouest, Montréal, 514-987-9900;
www.montreal.intercontinental.com
This sophisticated, elegant hotel is located across from the Convention Center
in downtown Montréal. It's a short walk from the popular Old Town. Rooms
are comfortable and traditional with plush bedding and ample workspaces. The
hotel's building houses shops and businesses, with the guest rooms starting on
the 10th floor.
357 rooms. Pets accepted. Restaurant, bar. Fitness room. Pool. Business
center. $61-150

★★HOTEL LE CANTLIE SUITES

1110 rue Sherbrooke Ouest, Montréal, 514-842-2000, 800-567-1110;
www.hotelcantlie.com
251 rooms. Restaurant, bar. Pool. Business center. $151-250

★★★HOTEL LE GERMAIN

2050 rue Mansfield, Montréal, 514-849-2050, 877-333-2050; www.hotelgermain.com
This distinctive boutique hotel offers hospitality, comfort and relaxation in
an elegant setting. The convenient downtown location makes it close to shopping, museums, concert halls and movie theaters. Guest rooms feature original photos by Louis Ducharm and elegant, comfortable décor.
101 rooms. Complimentary breakfast. Restaurant, bar. Pets accepted. Fitness
center. $151-250

★★★★HOTEL LE ST. JAMES

355 Saint Jacques St., Montréal, 514-841-3111, 866-841-3111;
www.hotellestjames.com

At the majestic Hotel Le St. James, each room and suite is individually decorated with antiques and art. Housed in a former bank, the building's imposing façade features ornate moldings and details fully restored to their 1870s grandeur. The convention center, downtown business area, Old Port area and the St. Lawrence River are a short stroll away from the hotel. The hotel's restaurant features regional, market-driven fare for lunch, dinner and afternoon tea.

61 rooms. Restaurant, bar. Spa. Pets accepted. Fitness center. Business center. $351 and up

★★★HOTEL L'EAU À LA BOUCHE

3003 Blvd. Sainte-Adele, Sainte-Adèle, 450-229-2991; www.leaualabouche.com

Located just 45 minutes from Montréal, Hotel L'Eau à la Bouche is amid the greenery of the Laurentian Mountains. Rooms offer mountain views. The property includes a heated outdoor pool and a full-service spa. Having a meal at the hotel's restaurant, where the award-winning cuisine of chef Anne Desjardins is served, is a must.

25 rooms. Restaurant, bar. Spa. Fitness center. $151-250

★★★HOTEL NELLIGAN

106 rue St. Paul Ouest, Montréal, 514-788-2040, 877-788-2040;
www.hotelnelligan.com

This boutique hotel features exposed-brick and stone walls which hint at its lengthy history, but the hotel provides all the modern touches expected at an urban hotel. A wine and cheese reception is offered daily and Verses, the hotel's restaurant, serves French fare in a hip and trendy setting.

105 rooms. Complimentary breakfast. Restaurant, bar. Fitness center. Business center. $151-250

★★★HOTEL OMNI MONT-ROYAL

1050 rue Sherbrooke Ouest, Montréal, 514-284-1110, 800-843-6664;
www.omnihotels.com

This elegant property is centrally located in the historic Golden Square Mile in the heart of downtown and at the foot of Mont Royal. Shops, museums, nightlife and fine dining are within walking distance. Pets are not only welcome at the hotel, they receive specially designed treats.

299 rooms. Restaurant, bar. Spa. Pets accepted. Fitness center. Pool. Business center. $151-250

★★★HOTEL PLACE D'ARMES

55 Saint-Jacques Ouest, Montréal, 514-842-1887, 888-450-1887;
www.hotelplacedarmes.com

Steps from Old Montréal's centuries-old charm into new millennium mod at Le Place d'Armes Hotel and Suites. The boutique hotel's ultramodern décor makes for a refreshing departure of the more traditional hotels in the area. Service is polished and professional. The onsite restaurant serves a full breakfast daily so you can start your day right.

135 rooms. Complimentary breakfast. Restaurant, bar. Spa. $251-350

★★★HOTEL ST. PAUL

355 rue McGill, Montréal, 493-062-9011, 866-380-2202; www.hotelstpaul.com

Set in a restored Beaux Arts building, the Hotel St. Paul is all about contemporary cool. Lighting above guest room doors revolve around two themes: earth (lit in red) and sky (lit in blue). The spare accommodations feature large windows, modern furnishings and animal-print accents. The onsite restaurant, Cube, serves fresh seasonal cuisine.

120 rooms. Complimentary breakfast. Restaurant, bar. Pets accepted. Fitness center. Business center. $151-250

★★★HYATT REGENCY MONTRÉAL

1255 Jeanne-Mance, Montréal, 514-982-1234, 866-816-3871; www.montreal.hyatt.com

This lively urban retreat, located in the Cultural District, is part of the elaborate shopping, dining and entertainment center Complexe des Jardins and is located adjacent to Place des Arts. It offers underground access to the Montréal Convention Center.

605 rooms. Restaurant, bar. Fitness center. Pool. Business center. $151-250

★★★LE SAINT SULPICE HOTEL MONTRÉAL

414 rue Saint Sulpice, Montréal, 514-288-1000, 877-785-7423; www.lesaintsulpice.com

Step back in time at this luxury hotel, located in the historic section of Montréal, just steps from the Notre-Dame Basilica and the Old Port. Sample steaks and seafood as well as regional specialties in S Le Restaurant. The Essence Health Center features beautifying treatments in addition to modern exercise equipment.

108 rooms. Complimentary breakfast. Restaurant, bar. Spa. Fitness center. $251-350

★★★LOEWS HOTEL VOGUE

1425 rue de la Montagne, Montréal, 514-285-5555, 800-465-6654;
www.loewshotels.com

The fresh spirit and chic modernity of the Loews Hotel Vogue breathes new life into old-world Montréal. The accommodations provide sleek shelter with silk upholstered furnishings while creature comforts like oversized bathrooms appeal to every guest. Stop in at L'Opéra Bar, a lively after-dark gathering spot.

142 rooms. Restaurant, bar. Pets accepted. Business center. $151-250

★★★MARRIOTT MONTRÉAL CHATEAU CHAMPLAIN

1050 de la Gauchetiere Ouest, Montréal, 514-878-9000, 800-200-5909;
www.marriott.com

Charming Art Nouveau décor adorns the guest rooms which ahve views of the Cathedral, Parc Mont Royal and Old Montréal. Hospitality rules at the Mediterranean-flavored Le Samuel de Champlain restaurant, while Le Senateur Bar satisfies discriminating tastes.

611 rooms. Restaurant, bar. Fitness center. Pool. $151-250

★★NOVOTEL

1180 rue de la Montagne, Montréal, 514-861-6000, 800-668-6835;
www.novotelmontreal.com

228 rooms. Restaurant, bar. Pets accepted. Fitness center. Business center.
$61-150

★★★PETITE AUBERGE LES BONS MATINS

1401 Argyle Ave., Montréal, 514-931-9167, 800-588-5280; www.bonsmatins.com

Guests stay in rooms in adjoining restored century-old townhomes in the
heart of Montréal. This inn is located close to main thoroughfares Sainte-
Catherine Street and Crescent Street and just steps away from the Lucien
L'Allier metro stop. Antiques and paintings by a family artist decorate rooms,
each of which have private baths with bathrobes and natural bath products. A
full gourmet breakfast is served daily in the dining room.
21 rooms. Pets accepted. Complimentary breakfast. $151-250

★★★SOFITEL MONTRÉAL

1155 Rue Sherbrooke Ouest, Montréal, 514-285-9000; www.sofitel.com

Modern and elegant, this hotel is set at the foot of Parc Mont Royal on Sherbrooke Street and close to galleries, boutiques and the historic center of the
city. Enjoy morning croissants and evening cocktails in Le Bar or dine on
Provençal-inspired cuisine in Renoir.
258 rooms. Restaurant, bar. Pets accepted. Business center. Fitness center.
$251-350

WHERE TO EAT

★★★AU PIED DE COCHON

536 Ave. Duluth E., Montréal, 514-281-1114; www.restaurantaupieddecochon.ca

The "Pig's Foot" serves hearty regional cuisine with an emphasis on beef,
lamb, venison, duck and yes, pork. There are several varieties of foie gras
and fish, along with local favorite sides like poutine (fries doused in gravy).
The cozy atmosphere and historic Montréal location make for an authentic
dining experience.
French. Dinner. Closed Monday. Reservations recommended. $36-85

★AU TOURNANT DE LA RIVIERE

5070 Salaberry, Carignan, 450-658-7372; www.restaurantautournantdelariviere.com
French. Dinner, Sunday Brunch. $36-85

★★AUBERGE HANDFIELD

555 Blvd. Richelieu, St. Marc-Sur-Richelieu, 450-584-2226, 800-361-6162;
www.aubergehandfield.com

French. Dinner. Closed Monday; also mid-January-early May. Reservations
recommended. Outdoor seating. $36-85

★★★BISTRO À CHAMPLAIN

75 Chemin Masson, Ste. Marguerite, 450-228-4988; www.bistroachamplain.com

Located on the edge of Lake Masson in the Laurentian Mountains, this elegant, rustic restaurant serves a varied menu with everything from braised
caribou to grilled steak making an appearance on the menu. A lengthy wine

list and views of a nearby lake add to the ambience.
French. Dinner. Closed Monday-Tuesday. Reservations recommended. $36-85

★★★CAFE FERREIRA
1446 rue Peel, Montréal, 514-848-0988; www.ferreiracafe.com
This restaurant is one of the most stylish dining rooms in Montréal. The friendly staff serve up wonderful Portuguese cuisine, with an emphasis on fresh fish and a comprehensive selection of Portuguese wines and ports. Portuguese. Dinner. Closed Sunday. Bar. Reservations recommended. Outdoor seating. $$$

★★★CHEZ L'EPICIER
311 rue Saint-Paul East, Montréal, 514-878-2232; www.chezlepicier.com
This cozy and informal French restaurant is located in a building in Old Montréal that dates to the late 1800s. The restaurant uses fresh, local produce for its daily-changing menu, and its food products are available for sale in a neighborhood market setting.
French. Lunch, dinner. Closed two weeks in January. Reservations recommended. $$$

★★★CHEZ LA MERE MICHEL
1209 rue Guy, Montréal, 514-934-0473; www.chezlameremichel.com
In a city with volumes of competition, this fine French restaurant has succeeded in its downtown historic-home location since 1965. The classic and well prepared menu includes a fantastic strawberry Napoleon for dessert.
French. Dinner. Closed Sunday. $36-85

★★GLOBE
3455 St. Laurent, Montréal, 514-284-3823; www.restaurantglobe.com
French. Reservations recommended. $$$

★★JARDIN NELSON
407 Place Jacques-Cartier, Montréal, 514-861-5731; www.jardinnelson.com
Italian. Lunch, Saturday-Sunday brunch. Closed November-mid-April. Reservations recommended. Outdoor seating. $16-35

★★THE KEG STEAKHOUSE & BAR
25 rue St. Paul East, Montréal, 514-871-9093; www.kegsteakhouse.com
Steak. Dinner. Bar. Reservation recommended. $36-85

★★★★L'EAU A LA BOUCHE
3003 Blvd. Sainte-Adèle, Sainte-Adele, 450- 229-2991; www.leaualabouche.com
Tucked into forests surrounding the Laurentian Mountains, near the village of Sainte-Adèle, you will find L'eau a la Bouche, a charming little restaurant located on the property of the Hotel L'eau a la Bouche. The gourmet menu is built around local produce, fish, meat and homegrown herbs and vegetables, woven together and dressed up with a perfect dose of French technique and modern flair. Attentive, thoughtful service and a vast wine list make this luxurious dining experience unforgettable.
French. Breakfast, dinner. Bar. $36-85

★★LA GAUDRIOLE
825 rue Laurier E., Montréal, 514-276-1580; www.lagaudriole.com
French. Closed first week in January, mid-July-early August. Reservations recommended. $36-85

★LA LOUISIANE
5850 Sherbrooke St. W., Montréal, 514-369-3073; www.lalouisiane.ca
Cajun. Dinner. Closed Monday. $16-35

★★★LA MAREE
404 Place Jacques Cartier, Montréal, 514-861-9794; www.restaurant.ca
Situated in Old Montréal, this romantic dining room offers classic French cuisine in an ornate, Louis XIII atmosphere. The historic 1808 building is just the place to enjoy old-fashioned, formal service and a great bottle of wine from the cellar.
French. Reservations recommended. Outdoor seating. $36-85

★★★LA RAPIERE
1155 rue Metcalfe, Montréal, 514-871-8920
Southwestern French cooking with a personal touch is the draw at this sophisticated restaurant in downtown Montréal. Cassoulet, foie gras and other specialties are served in a typical country-French setting.
French. Dinner. Jacket required. Closed Sunday; also mid-July-mid-August, 15 days in December. Reservations recommended. $36-85

★★★LALOUX
250 Pine Ave. E., Montréal, 514-287-9127; www.laloux.com
One of Montréal's most appealing Parisian-style bistros, this cozy spot delivers traditional bistro fare in a crisp, white-tableclothed environment. In addition to an excellent steak frites, you can sample hearty dishes like mushroom and herb casserole or seafood risotto with leeks and spinach. Polish it all off with a classic French dessert such as chocolate pot de crème.
French. Reservations recommended. Outdoor seating. $36-85

★★LE CAFE FLEURI
Hyatt Regency Montréal, 1255 rue Jeanne Mance, Montréal, 514-841-2010; www.montreal.hyatt.com
French. Breakfast, lunch. Outdoor seating. $16-35

★★★LE LUTETIA
1430 rue de la Montagne, Montréal, 514-288-5656; 800-361-6262; www.hoteldelamontagne.com
Located in the popular l'Hotel de la Montagne, this restaurant serves breakfast only in a formal rococo setting. The service is gracious and accommodating, and the creative dishes make a special occasion out of the simplest meal of the day.
French. Breakfast. Reservations recommended. $36-85

★★★LE MAS DES OLIVIERS

1216 rue Bishop, Montréal, 514-861-6733; www.lemasdesoliviers.ca

This small, traditional French restaurant has been offering rich cuisine in a provençal setting for more than 30 years. Settle in to the rustic room, with its white tablecloth-topped tables and exposed brick walls, and dig into classic dishes such as frog's legs with garlic or rack of lamb with herbs de Provence and mustard sauce.

French. Dinner. Reservations recommended. $36-85

★★LE PARCHEMIN

1333, rue University, Montréal, 514-844-1619; www.leparchemin.com

French. Lunch, dinner. Closed Sunday. Reservations recommended. $36-85

★★★LE PIÉMONTAIS

1145 Ave. de Bullion, Montréal, 514-861-8122; www.lepiemontais.com

Experience authentic, Italian cuisine at this comfortable, elegant restaurant. Fresh pastas appear on the menu nightly, from linguine to gnocchi. The wine list features bottle from the Piedmont region of Italy and service is prompt and professional.

Italian. Lunch, dinner. Closed Sunday; mid-July-mid-August. Reservations recommended. $36-85

★★★LE PIMENT ROUGE

1170 Peel St., Montréal, 514-866-7816; www.lepimentrouge.com

The spicy cuisine of China's Szechwan province is served in an airy, contemporary restaurant located in the former Windsor Hotel. Signature dishes include spicy peanut butter dumplings, a recipe the restaurant is credited with inventing in Montréal. Le Piment Rouge also stocks more than 3,000 wines.

Chinese. Dinner. $16-35

★★★LES CAPRICES DE NICOLAS

2072 rue Drummond, Montréal, 514-282-9790; www.lescaprices.com

The intimate candlelight and a romantic indoor/outdoor garden combine to make this restaurant a special occasion destination. Given the classic, formal service, it is a pleasant surprise to find the French dishes on the menu refreshingly updated with light, vibrant flavors and seasonal market produce. A wine list of 500 labels adds to the excitement.

French. Dinner. Jacket required. Reservations recommended. $36-85

★★★LES CONTINENTS

InterContinental Montréal, 360, rue St. Antoine Ouest, Montréal, 514-847-8729, 800-361-3600; www.intercontinental.com

Located on the second floor of the Hotel InterContinental Montréal, Les Continents has beautiful views of Jean-Paul Riopelle Park and the colorful Convention Centre. The menu features contemporary French cuisine with Canadian influences.

French, Canadian. Breakfast, lunch, dinner. $36-85

★★★LES REMPARTS

93, rue de la Commune East, Montréal, 514-392-1649; www.restaurantlesremparts.com

Located in the basement of the Auberge du Vieux-Port, on the site of Mon-

tréal's original fortress, this French restaurant offers a comfortable, cozy atmosphere with professional, attentive service. The restaurant is decorated with candles on each table, stone floors and exposed brick walls with parts of the old fort's stonework on display.
French. Reservations recommended. Outdoor seating. $36-85

★★★MED BAR AND GRILL

3500 Blvd. St. Laurent, Montréal, 514-844-0027; www.medgrill.com
If you're seeking a spot to see-and-be-seen, or a chic place to linger over cocktails while perched amidst Montréal's most stylish set, Med Bar and Grill is an excellent option. The food is upscale but remains fun and inviting. Classic dishes of the Mediterranean are given a modern spin here, reflecting the seasons and incorporating the regions bountiful produce.
Mediterranean. Dinner. Closed Sunday-Monday. Reservations recommended. $36-85

★★MIKADO

399 Laurier West, Montréal, 514-279-4809; www.mikadomontreal.com
Japanese. Lunch, dinner. Bar. Reservations recommended. $16-35

★★MOISHE'S

3961 Blvd. St. Laurent, Montréal, 514-845-3509; www.moishes.ca
Steak. Dinner. Reservations recommended. $36-85

★★★NUANCES

1 Ave. de Casino, Montréal, 514-392-2708, 800-665-2274; www.casinosduquebec.com
This stylish, modern bistro, located within the Montréal Casino, is swathed in soothing earth tones and decorated with original works that were custom-designed for the space by local artists. The upscale menu stars exquisitely updated French cuisine with a cast of nature's best seasonal products.
French. Lunch, dinner. Jacket required. Reservations recommended. $36-85

★★★QUEUE DE CHEVAL

1221 Blvd. Rene-Levesque Ouest, Montréal, 514-390-0090; www.queuedecheval.com
Prime, dry-aged meats are the showstoppers at Queue de Cheval, a rustic, chateau-styled steakhouse accented with rich maple wood and tall, vaulted ceilings in the heart of Montréal. The menu also has a generous raw bar, a terrific selection of salads and vegetarian appetizers and a fresh fish market.
Steak. Lunch, dinner. Reservations recommended. Outdoor seating. $36-85

★★RESTAURANT CHEZ LÉVÈQUE

1030, rue Laurier Ouest, Montréal, 514-279-7355; www.chezleveque.ca
French. Reservations recommended. $16-35

★★RESTAURANT SHO-DAN

2020, rue Metcalfe, Montréal, 514-987-9987; www.sho-dan.com
Japanese. Lunch (weekdays only), dinner. $16-35

★★★RISTORANTE DA VINCI
1180, rue Bishop, Montréal, 514-874-2001; www.davinci.ca
This charming restaurant offers an authentic atmosphere, warm, attentive service and well-prepared traditional dishes made with fresh ingredients. The menu includes everything from freshly prepared pasta to grilled steaks. Italian. Dinner. Closed Sunday. Reservations recommended. Outdoor seating. $36-85

★★ROSALIE RESTAURANT
1232, rue de la Montagne, Montréal, 514-392-1970; www.rosalierestaurant.com
French bistro. Lunch (Monday-Friday) dinner. Reservations recommended. Outdoor seating. $16-35

★★★★TOQUE!
900 place Jean-Paul Riopelle, Montréal, 514-499-2084; www.restaurant-toque.com
Toque! is a graceful, luxurious, contemporary French restaurant located across from the Convention Centre and Jean-Paul Riopelle Park. Plates are garnished with such impeccable attention to detail that you may spend several minutes debating whether or not to ruin the presentation. The talented and hospitable chef, Norman Laprise, wields magic with a whisk and uses locally farmed ingredients to create a miraculous menu of sophisticated, avant-garde French fare.
French. Closed Sunday-Monday; also two weeks in late December-early January. Reservations recommended. $36-85

QUÉBEC CITY
See also Montréal
Nestled on a historic rampart, Québec, the provincial capital, is historic, medieval and lofty, a place of mellowed stone buildings and weathered cannons, horse-drawn calches, ancient trees and narrow, steeply angled streets. Once the "Gibraltar of the North," Québec's Upper Town is built high on a cliff and surrounded by fortress-like walls. One of the split-level city's best-known landmarks, Le Chateau Frontenac, is a hotel towering so high that it's visible 10 miles away. The Lower Town surrounds Cape Diamond and spreads up the valley of the St. Charles River, a tributary of the St. Lawrence. The two sections are divided by a funicular, which affords magnificent views of the harbor, river and hills beyond. The most ardently French of all Canadian cities, Québec City is a place where it's not uncommon to encounter folks who don't (or won't) speak English, and who proudly stick to their Gallic Traditions. The historic streets of Québec City provide an easy clue as to what this city looked like in Colonial days, and the cafés and shops tucked within them deliver hours of distractions.

WHAT TO SEE
ARTILLERY PARK NATIONAL HISTORIC SITE
2 d'Auteuil St., Québec City, 418-648-4205; www.pc.qc.ca
A 4-acre site built by the French to defend the opening of the St. Charles River. By the end of the 17th century, it was known as a strategic site and military engineers began to build fortifications here. Until 1871, the park housed French and British soldiers, eventually becoming a large industrial complex.

BASILICA OF STE. ANNE-DE-BEAUPRE

10018 Royale Ave., Québec City, 418-827-3781; www.ssadb.qc.ca

This basilica is noted as the oldest pilgrimage in North America. The first chapel was built on this site in 1658. The present basilica, built in 1923, is made of white Canadian granite and is regarded as a Romanesque masterpiece, with capitals that tell the story of Jesus' life in 88 scenes and vaults, which are decorated with mosaics. Unusual techniques were used for the 240 stained-glass windows that are outlined in concrete.

GASPÉ PENINSULA

357, route de la Mer Sainte-Flavie, Québec City, 418-775-2223, 800-463-0323;
www.tourisme-gaspesie.com

Jutting out into the Gulf of St. Laurent, the Gaspé Peninsula is a region of varying landforms including mountains, plateaus, beaches and cliffs. It is blessed with abundant and rare wildlife and some unique flora, including 12-foot-tall, centuries-old fir trees. The rivers, teeming with trout, flow to meet the salmon coming from the sea. Called "Gespeg" meaning "land's end" by the aborigines, the area was settled primarily by Basque, Breton and Norman fishermen, whose charming villages may be seen clinging to the shore beneath the gigantic cliffs. The French influence is strong, although English is spoken in a few villages.

GRAND THEATRE

269 Blvd. Rene-Levesque, Québec, 418-643-8131; www.grandtheatre.qc.ca

This ultramodern theater has giant mural by sculptor Jordi Bonet in the lobby. It is the home of the Québec Symphony Orchestra and Opera and features theatrical performances and concerts.

ILE D'ORLÉANS

490, côte du Pont, Saint-Pierre-de-l'Île-d'Orléans, Québec City, 418-828-9411;
www.iledorleans.com

This 23-mile-long island was visited by Champlain in 1608 and colonized in 1648. Old stone farmhouses and churches of the 18th century remain. Farms grow an abundance of fruits and vegetables, especially strawberries, for which the island is famous.

JEANNE D'ARC GARDEN

835 Wilfrid Laurier, Québec City, 418-649-6159

This floral jewel was created in 1938 by landscape architect Louis Perron. It combines the French Classical style with British-style flower beds and features more than 150 species of annuals, bulbs and perennials.

LA CITADELLE

Côte de la Citadelle, Québec City, 418-694-2815; www.lacitadelle.qc.ca

Forming the eastern flank of the fortifications of Québec, construction on La Citadelle began in 1820 and continued until 1850. Vestiges of the French regime, such as the Cap Diamant Redoubt and a powder magazine can still be seen. There are panoramic views to check out and 50-minute guided tours are available. Be sure to catch the changing of the guard (late June-Labor Day, daily 10 a.m.), which is always interesting. Beating the Retreat, a recreation of a 16th-century ceremony takes place late July through August on Friday and Saturday evenings.

Admission: adults $10, seniors and students $9, children 7-17 $5.50, children 7 and under free. April-October, hours vary.

LAURENTIDES WILDLIFE RESERVE

Québec City, 418-686-1717; www.sepaq.com

A variety of animals including moose, wolves, bears and numerous birds can be found here. Nature fans will find many recreational opportunities such as canoeing, fishing, hunting and camping, as well as boat, ski and snowshoe rental. There are also 140 cabins and 134 campsites located here.

Late May-Labor Day, mid-December-mid-April.

MONT-SAINTE-ANNE PARK

2000 Blvd. Beau-Pré, Beaupré, 418-827-4561; www.mont-sainte-anne.com

Take a trip on a gondola that travels to a summit of the mountain at 2,625 feet, affording a beautiful view of St. Lawrence River. Enjoy skiing and cross-country skiing here in winter. In spring and summer, there are two 18-hole golf courses, bicycle trails and campsites. The migration of 250,000 snow geese occurs in spring and fall at nearby wildlife reserve Cap Tourmente. Daily.

MUSÉE DE LA CIVILISATION

85, rue Dalhousie, Québec, 418-643-2158; www.mcq.org

At the entrance is La Debacle, a massive sculpture representing ice breaking up in spring. Separate exhibition halls present four permanent and several changing exhibitions dealing with the history of Québec and the French Canadian culture, as well as cultures of other civilizations from around the world.

MUSÉE NATIONAL DES BEAUX-ARTS DU QUÉBEC

Parc des Champs-de-Bataille, Québec city, 418-643-2150; www.mnba.qc.ca

This museum features collections of ancient, modern and contemporary Québec paintings, sculpture, photography, drawings and decorative arts.

Admission: adults $15, seniors $12, students $7, children 12-17 $4, children 12 and under free. June-Labor Day, daily 9 a.m.-6 p.m., Wednesday until 9 p.m.; Labor Day-May, Tuesday-Sunday 9 a.m.-5 p.m., Wednesday until 9 p.m.

MUSEUM OF THE ROYAL 22E REGIMENT

La Citadelle, Côte de la Citadelle, Québec City, 418-694-2815; www.lacitadelle.qc.ca

While at La Citadelle, be sure to check out this portion which is also onsite but can be toured with a guide. Located in a powder magazine from 1750, flanked on both sides by massive buttresses, this museum contains replicas of old uniforms of French regiments, war trophies, 17th-20th-century weapons and a diorama of historic battles under the French. You can also visit old military prison here, which contains insignias and a rifle and bayonet collections. Only the last cell was left intact.

Admission: adults $10, seniors and students $9, children 7-17 $5.50, children 7 and under free. April-October, daily. Changing of the guard: mid-June-Labor Day, daily 10 a.m.

NATIONAL ASSEMBLY OF QUÉBEC

Grande-Allee and Honore-Mercier Avenue, Québec City, 418-643-7239;
www.assnat.qc.ca

Take a 30-minute guided tour of Québec's Parliament Building, constructed between 1877 and 1886. Guides provide an inside look into the proceedings of the Québec National Assembly, while explaining the building's architectural features.

NATIONAL BATTLEFIELDS PARK

835 Wilfrid Laurier, Québec City, 418-648-4071

Two hundred fifty acres along edge of bluff overlooking St. Lawrence River from Citadel to Gilmour Hill. Also called the Plains of Abraham, the park was site of 1759 battle between the armies of Wolfe and Montcalm and the 1760 battle of Sainte Foy between the armies of Murray and Levis. The visitor center presents history of the Plains of Abraham from the New France period to the present. In the park are two Martello towers, part of the fortifications, a sunken garden, many statues and the Jeanne d'Arc Garden.

NOTRE-DAME DE QUÉBEC BASILICA-CATHEDRAL

20 De Buade St., Québec City, 418-694-0665; www.patrimoine-religieux.com

View the richly decorated Cathedral, over 350 years old and the crypt, where most of the governors and bishops of Québec are buried.
Guided tours: Early May-early November, daily.

PLACE-ROYALE

27 Notre Dame St., Québec City, 418-646-9072; www.mcq.org

This site encompasses the earliest vestiges of French civilization in North America. Once a marketplace and the city's social center, it has been restored to its historic appearance. Today, visitors come to enjoy the many restaurants and retail stores, as well as theater performances that take place during summer.

QUÉBEC AQUARIUM

1675 Ave. des Hotels, Sainte-Foy, 418-659-5264; www.sepaq.com/paq/en

Overlooking the St. Lawrence River, this aquarium features an extensive collection of tropical, fresh and saltwater fish, marine mammals and reptiles. Admission: adults $15.50, seniors $14.50, children 6-17 $8.25, children 3-5 $5.50, children 2 and under free. June-Labor Day, daily 10 a.m.-5 p.m.; Labor Day-May, daily 10 a.m.-4 p.m.

QUÉBEC CITY WALLS AND GATES

Encompassing Old Québec, these eighteenth-century walls and gates encircle the only fortified city in North America. It includes the Governor's Promenade and provides a scenic view of The Citadel, St. Lawrence River and Levis.

ST. ANDREW'S PRESBYTERIAN CHURCH

5 Cook St., Québec City, 418-694-1347; www.standrewsquebec.ca

Serving the oldest English-speaking congregation of Scottish origin in Canada, which traces back to 1759, this church was built in 1810. Its interior is distinguished by a long front wall with a high center pulpit, as well as stained-glass windows and historic plaques. The original petition to King George III asking for a "small plot of waste ground" on which to build a Scotch church is on display in the Church Vestry. A spiral stairway leads to the century-old organ.

July-August.

SPECIAL EVENTS
CARNAVAL DE QUÉBEC

290, rue Joly, Québec City, 418-626-3716; www.carnaval.qc.ca

This internationally acclaimed French Canadian festival, billed as the world's biggest winter carnival, is celebrated throughout Old Town. Activities include parades, a canoe race on the St. Lawrence River, a dogsled race, a snow and ice sculpture show, a soapbox derby and the "snow bath," where participants brave the snow in their bathing suits.

Late January-mid-February.

DU MAURIER QUÉBEC SUMMER FESTIVAL

226, rue St-Joseph Est., Québec City, 418-529-5200, 888-992-5200; www.infofestival.com

This 11-day event is one of the largest music festivals in North America. Performances are held at various locations throughout Old Québec. Major local and international artists are showcased, but the festival also serves as a springboard for up-and-coming artists.

Early-mid-July.

WHERE TO STAY
★★★AUBERGE SAINT-ANTOINE

8, rue Saint-Antoine, Québec City, 418-692-2211, 888-692-2211; www.saint-antoine.com

Explore historic Québec City from this sleek hotel housed in a building that has been occupied since the beginning of the French colony. A cannon battery runs through the lobby. Stone walls and wooden beams enhance the décor in this small hotel, located in the middle of Old Québec's Port District on the St. Lawrence River.

95 rooms. Restaurant, bar. Business center. $251-350

★★CHATEAU LAURIER HOTEL

1220 Georges 5th Ouest, Québec City, 418-522-8108, 800-463-4453; www.old-quebec.com/laurier

57 rooms. Restaurant, bar. $61-150

★★★FAIRMONT LE CHÂTEAU FRONTENAC

1, Rue Des Carrieres, Québec City, 418-692-3861, 800-441-1414; www.fairmont.com

Reigning over this historic walled city from its perch atop the roaring St.

Lawrence River is the majestic Fairmont Le Chateau Frontenac. Built as a classic, sprawling railway hotel at the end of the 19th century, the hotel features rooms decorated in a classic European style. The cavernous, wood-clad lobby is watched over by the hotel's resident canine and serviced by a friendly staff.

618 rooms. Restaurant, bar. Pool. Business center. $251-350

★★★FAIRMONT LE MANOIR RICHELIEU

181, rue Richelieu, Charlevoix, 418-665-3703, 800-441-1414; www.fairmont.com

This majestic hotel, located east of Québec City in the heart of Québec's scenic Charlevoix countryside, welcomes visitors with historic charm and world-class sophistication. Rooms and suites have a classic country appeal and are stocked with modern amenities. Guests can opt for nearby skiing and golf or enjoy the hotel's fitness and spa facilities.

405 rooms. Restaurant, bar. Pool. Business center. $251-350

★★★HILTON QUÉBEC

1100 Rene Levesque East, Québec City, 418-647-2411; www.hilton.com

Located next to the Congress Centre and a 10-minute walk to Old Town, and other local attractions, the hotel is convenient for business travelers or families. After a busy day of sightseeing, enjoy the cuisine and modern art at the hotel's Allegro Restaurant.

571 rooms. Restaurant, bar. Pets accepted. Pool. Business center. $151-250

★★★HÔTEL LE GERMAIN-DOMINION

126, rue Saint-Pierre, Québec City, 418-692-2224, 888-833-5253; www.hoteldominion.com

Old Québec is considered the cradle of French culture in North America, and Hôel Le Germain-Dominion is a wonderful base from which to explore it. This small, sleek hotel takes full advantage of the early 20th-century building's historic architectural features while providing updated, contemporary rooms with down-duvet topped beds.

60 rooms. Restaurant, bar. Fitness center. Pets accepted. $151-250

★★★LOEWS HÔTEL LE CONCORDE

1225 Cours du General De Montcalm, Québec City, 418-647-2222, 800-463-5256; www.loewshotels.com

See a vision of Paris out your window from this hotel on Québec City's version of the Champs-Elysees. Just 15 minutes from the airport, the tower has views of the St. Lawrence River, the city lights and the historic Plains of Abraham. A visit is not complete without a peek, and hopefully a meal, at L'Astral, the revolving rooftop restaurant.

404 rooms. Restaurant, bar. Pets accepted. Pool. Business center. $61-150

WHERE TO EAT

★★AUX ANCIENS CANADIENS

34, rue Ste. Louis, Québec City, 418-692-1627; www.auxancienscanadiens.qc.ca

French. Dinner. $36-85

★★★L'ASTRAL

Loews Hôtel Le Concorde, 1225 cours du General de Montcalm, Québec City, 418-647-2222; www.loewshotels.com

Each rotation of this rooftop restaurant atop the Loews Hôtel Le Concorde takes 90 minutes, which is plenty of time to enjoy its fine cuisine and the spectacular panoramic views of Québec City. Contemporary recipes such as roasted Cornish hen with kalamata olives and grapes, or grilled salmon with sweet corn foam make up the seasonally-driven menu.

French. Breakfast, lunch, dinner. Reservations recommended. $36-85

★★★LAURIE RAPHAËL

117 Dalhousie St., Québec City, 418 692 4555; www.laurieraphael.com

Owners Daniel Vézina and Suzanne Gagnon head this popular restaurant, which they named after their children, with well-known friendliness. Focusing on simple, gourmet fusion cuisine allows the flavor and taste of some of their best dishes, like Jerusalem artichoke blinis with Abitibi sturgeon egg cream, to come shining through. The impressive wine cellar includes a broad range of countries.

French. Dinner. Reservations recommended. $36-85

★★★LE CONTINENTAL

26, rue Ste. Louis, Québec City, 418-694-9995; www.restaurantlecontinental.com

Deep colors and oak dominate the rich décor and European atmosphere at this fine dining restaurant in Upper Québec. Order one of the flambé specialties for a unique tableside show. The remainder of the menu is filled with grilled steak and seafood options, and a solid list of French bottles makes up the wine list.

French. Dinner. $36-85

★★★LE SAINT-AMOUR

48, rue Ste. Ursule, Québec City, 418-694-0667; www.saint-amour.com

Family-owned and operated since opening in Old Québec in 1978, this charming restaurant is away from the bustle of the tourist beat. Fresh, local products are highlighted and the vast wine room houses more than 12,000 bottles.

French. Outdoor seating. $36-85

★★LE VENDÔME

36 Cote de la Montagne, Québec City, 418-692-0557; www.restaurantvendome.com

French. Outdoor seating. $16-35

★★★MONTE CRISTO L'ORIGINAL

3400 Chemin Ste. Foy, Québec City, 418-653-5221; www.chateaubonneentente.com

Monte Cristo is a relaxed yet modern restaurant where guests are treated to traditional and original Québec cooking that emphasizes the use of local products. Both the décor and the menu are contemporary, with dishes such as polenta with pea purée or duck tartare with wasabi on the menu.

French. Breakfast, lunch, dinner. $36-85

★★★★RESTAURANT INITIALE

54, rue Saint-Pierre, Québec City, 418-694-1818; www.restaurantinitiale.com

This modern French-cuisine restaurant is located in a former bank about one block from the St. Lawrence River in the Old Port district. Country products from local producers result in fresh, pure flavors. Service is crip and professional, and the staff can aptly recommend an appropriate wine from the lengthy list. French. Lunch (Tuesday-Friday), dinner. Closed Sunday-Monday; also first two weeks in January. Reservations recommended. $36-85

TROIS-RIVIÈRES

See also Montréal, Québec City

Considered the second-oldest French city in North America, Trois-Rivières was founded in 1634 and many 17th- and 18th-century buildings remain today. The St. Maurice River splits into three channels here as it joins the St. Lawrence, giving the name to this major commercial and industrial center and important inland seaport.

WHAT TO SEE
CATHEDRALE DE L'ASSUMPTION

363 rue Bonaventure, Trois-Rivieres, 819-374-2409

Built in 1858 in the Gothic Westminster style, this cathedral contains huge stained-glass windows, brilliantly designed by Nincheri. The cathedral was renovated in 1967.

LE MANOIR DE TONNANCOUR

864, rue des Ursulines, Trois-Rivières, 819-374-2355; www.galeriedartduparc.qc.ca

This historic structure is the oldest house in the city. It was built between 1723 and 1725 and rebuilt in 1795. When the government acquired the house in 1812, it was used as a barracks for soldiers. In 1852, it became the bishop's home. Today, the house contains the Art Gallery in the Park and features displays of paintings, pottery, sculpture, engravings, serigraphy and jewelry.

★
★ QUEBEC
★
★

187

LES FORGES DU ST. MAURICE NATIONAL HISTORIC SITE

10000 Blvd. des Forges, Trois-Rivières, 800-463-6769; www.pc.qc.ca

This site commemorates the founding of Canada's first industrial community. Visitors may see the remains of the first ironworks industry in Canada, the blast furnace and Ironmaster's House interpretation centers and a sound-and-light show at the Grande Maison.

Mid-May-mid-October, daily 9:30 a.m.-5 p.m.; after Labor Day, daily 9:30 a.m.-4:30 p.m.

NOTRE DAME-DU-CAP SHRINE

626, rue Notre Dame Est., Trois-Rivières, 819-374-2441; www.sanctuaire-ndc.ca

The site includes a small church that was built in 1714, making it the oldest preserved stone church in Canada, which was turned into a shrine in 1888. Also here is a large octagonal basilica featuring stained-glass windows made by Dutch glassmaker Jan Tillemans, as well as a neoclassic Casavant organ with 5,425 pipes. Organ recitals are held here in the summer. May-October, daily.

OLD PORT
800 Parc Portuaire, Trois-Rivieres, 819-372-4633
Here, you can see magnificent views of the St. Lawrence River. Built over part of the old fortifications, you can visit a pulp and paper interpretation center; a riverside park; and view a monument to La Vrendrye, the discoverer of the Rockies in 1743.

ST. JAMES ANGLICAN CHURCH
811, Rue Des Ursulines, Trois-Rivieres, 819-374-6010
Constructed in 1699 and rebuilt in 1754, this church was used as a store-house and a court at various times. The rectory was used as a prison, hospital and sheriff's office. In 1823, it became an Anglican church and is now shared with the United Church.

SPECIAL EVENT
TROIS-RIVIÈRES INTERNATIONAL VOCAL ARTS FESTIVAL
Bonaventure and Royale, Trois-Rivières, 819-372-4635; www.artvocal.com
This celebration of song features religious, lyrical, popular, ethnic and traditional performances.
Late June-early July.

WHERE TO STAY
★★DELTA TROIS-RIVIÈRES HOTEL AND CONFERENCE CENTRE
1620, rue Notre-Dame, Trois-Rivières, 819-376-1991, 888-890-3222; www.deltahotels.com
159 rooms. Restaurant, bar. Fitness center. Pool. Pets accepted. $61-150

★★HÔTEL GOUVERNEUR TROIS-RIVIÈRES
975, rue Hart, Trois-Rivières, 888-910-1111; www.gouverneur.com
127 rooms. Complimentary breakfast. Restaurant. Pool. $61-150

SASKATCHEWAN

SASKATCHEWAN, THE MIDDLE OF CANADA'S THREE PRAIRIE PROVINCES, IS GEOGRAPHICALLY located in the center of North America. Within its borders is more road surface than in any other province, totaling 150,000 miles (241,400 kilometers). Half of the province is covered by forest, one-third is farmland and one-eighth is fresh water, with nearly 100,000 lakes. The province is a paradise of unspoiled hunting and fishing, with extraordinary sunshine to boot.

The province is popularly explored from behind the wheel of a car or recreational vehicle—roads are easy going, amenities along the way are plentiful, and the experiences are authentic prairie. Follow the route taken in 1874 by the North West Mounted Police, forerunners of today's Mounties, when they came west to quell the whiskey trade. Take in historic sites, panoramic views, cultural icons and friendly people, along with a slew of museums celebrating everything from the province's love of the sport of curling, its wild west beginnings and its discovery of vast deposits of dinosaur fossils. Wander through what locals call "parkland," a rolling and evocative combination of "not quite prairie and not quite forest." This was fur-trade country, where rivers run clear, lakes are inviting and well-tended campgrounds are plentiful.

MOOSE JAW

See also Regina

Despite its humble beginnings as a village of sod huts and shanties, the city of Moose Jaw offers everything from high-energy adrenaline to laid-back relaxation. The city's "Tunnels of Little Chicago," an underground network of passages built to smuggle liquor during the Prohibition era, are a wink to the city's raucous history, which is well represented across several museums and sites. Take in sporting events, cultural extravaganzas, mineral spas and walking trails along with a small-town friendliness that makes Moose Jaw a must-see prairie destination.

WHAT TO SEE
BUFFALO POUND PROVINCIAL PARK/WHITE TRACK SKI AREA

110 Ominica St., Moose Jaw, 306-694-3659; www.envoirmental.gov.sk.ca

This 4,770-acre park was established in 1963 and is known for its free-ranging buffalo that traverse the Qu'Appelle River Valley. The name of the park refers to the aboriginal people's method of corralling bison by using the topography as a means to hold the animals in place. The park has a large outdoor pool, beaches, fishing, boating, mini-golf and hiking trails. It is also home to the White Track Ski Resort, with downhill skiing, as well as a number of snowshoeing and cross-country skiing trails.

CASINO MOOSE JAW

21 Fairford St. E., Moose Jaw, 306-694-3888, 800-555-3189;
www.casinomoosejaw.com

This casino has a 1920s theme and embraces Moose Jaw's unique history. It also has 20 indoor and outdoor wall murals that portray specific periods of the city's history. There are more than 150 slot machines to test your luck, as well as all table game favorites including blackjack, roulette and "Let It Ride" Bonus.

CRANBERRY ROSE GALLERY AND GIFTS

316, Main St., Moose Jaw, 306-693-7779, 800-970-7328; www.cranberryrose.com
The Cranberry Rose Gallery and Gifts shop is located in a historic house. While here, shop, enjoy a cup of tea or indulge your sweet tooth with one of the scrumptious homemade desserts.

MOOSE JAW MUSEUM AND ART GALLERY

461 Langdon Crescent, Moose Jaw, 306-692-4471; www.mjmag.ca
The permanent collections of the Moose Jaw Museum and Art Gallery feature a wide variety of works from a vast collection of local, provincial, national and international artists. The pieces from this collection are on exhibit at various times throughout the year. Don't miss the Norma Lang Gallery and the discovery center.

ST. VICTOR PETROGLYPH PARK

206-110 Ominica St. W., Moose Jaw; www.saskparks.net
At this mysterious place, there are more than 300 carvings in the sandstone of a huge exposed rock that depict stories of ancient times.

TUNNELS OF MOOSE JAW

18 Main St. N., Moose Jaw, 306-693-5261; www.tunnelsofmoosejaw.com
These tunnels between many of the buildings in Moose Jaw's downtown are said to have been dug by Chinese immigrants in the late 1800s. Rumors surround all aspects of the tunnels; they were allegedly used during the Prohibition years by bootleggers and smugglers trying to avoid the law. Two 50-minute tours can help visitors draw their own conclusions.

WOOD MOUNTAIN POST PROVINCIAL HISTORICAL PARK

206-110 Ominica St. West, Moose Jaw, 306-266-4322, 800-205-7070;
www.saskparks.net
At this historic site, learn how the Northwest Mounted Police arrived in the area and designated it as a post. The stories told during a visit through the historic buildings and sites paint a vivid picture of the important history that unfolded while people here policed the Northwest.
June-mid-August, daily 10 a.m.-5 p.m.

WHERE TO STAY

★★HERITAGE INN

1590 Main St. N., Moose Jaw, 306-693-7550, 888-888-4374; www.heritageinn.net
104 rooms. Restaurant, bar. Pool. $61-150

★★TEMPLE GARDENS MINERAL SPA

24 Fairford St. E., Moose Jaw, 306-694-5055; www.templegardens.sk.ca
181 rooms. Restaurant, bar, spa. Pool. $61-150

WHERE TO EAT
★HOUSTON PIZZA & STEAK HOUSE
117 Main St. N., Moose Jaw, 306-693-3934
Pizza, steak. Dinner. $16-35

PRINCE ALBERT
See also Saskatoon
Prince Albert is located in the broad valley of the North Saskatchewan River near the geographical center of the province, where the agricultural prairie of the south and the rich forest belt of the north meet. The province's third-largest city, Prince Albert is a gateway to the recreational opportunities in the far northern region. Its center bustles with attractions, festivals, golf courses, casinos and museums. At the Fort Carlton Provincial Historic Site in the city's southwest, see how life was lived in the days of the fur trade from the vantage point of a booming trading post circa mid-1800s, when swarthy trappers ruled along the North Saskatchewan River.

WHAT TO SEE
ATHABASCA SAND DUNES
La Ronge, 306-425-4234
The Athabasca Sand Dunes, the northernmost dunes in the world, are located along the south shore of Lake Athabasca (150 miles north of Prince Albert) in northwest Saskatchewan (and only accessible by air or by boat from the Lake Athabasca communities). This untarnished area has several dune fields that extend for approximately 60 miles. Two major rivers in the park, the William and the MacFarlane, create the unforgettable scenery here. Visitors must be self-sufficient for wilderness travel, taking along all food and supplies. All garbage must be packed out and visitors must be aware of special park regulations designed to protect the fragile environment.

CANDLE LAKE PROVINCIAL PARK
Candle Lake, 306-929-8400; www.tpcs.gov.sk.ca/CandleLake
Candle Lake has more than 19,457 acres of recreational park and is known for its beaches and sand dunes. Visitors can enjoy a number of activities in this nature park, including swimming, fishing, waterskiing, golfing, camping, hiking, biking and horseback riding. Many facilities and services are located in the nearby community of the Resort Village of Candle Lake.

LAC LA RONGE PROVINCIAL PARK
La Ronge, 306-425-4234; www.tpcs.gov.sk.ca/LacLaRonge
Lac La Ronge Provincial Park is Saskatchewan's largest provincial park, covering 851,204 acres and containing more than 100 lakes. There are beautiful waterfalls on the Churchill River, and the park is famous for its whitewater rapids. It also has excellent canoeing, fishing and hiking. If you enjoy skiing, you can bask in the beautifully diverse scenery along the 35 miles of cross-country trails, including three miles of lighted trails for night skiing.

NORTHERN LIGHTS CASINO
44 Marquis Road W., Prince Albert, 306-764-4777, 888-604-7711; www.siga.sk.ca
Northern Lights appends its casino games with monthly blackjack and slot tournaments. The casino also promotes and showcases Aboriginal artists on its stage. The Northstar Restaurant and Prince Albert Inn are part of the complex.

REGINA
See also Moose Jaw
The capital acts as the commercial, industrial and financial center of the province while still maintaining a small-town feel. Since the first pioneers homesteaded in the early 1880s, local residents have worked by hand to transform the flat, treeless prairie into a city of shaded parks and streets. Regina sparkles with rich artistic and multicultural traditions, with Canada's longest continuously operating symphony orchestra and the Globe Theatre, a company that stages innovative productions in the round. The Wascana Centre, in the heart of Regina, is one of North America's largest urban parks, measuring 2,300 acres. Regina is also the home of the Royal Canadian Mounted Police.

WHAT TO SEE
CASINO REGINA
1880 Saskatchewan Drive, Regina, 306-565-3000, 800-555-3189;
www.casinoregina.com
Casino Regina boasts more than 800 slot machines and 35 table games and features a spectacular showroom.

ECHO VALLEY PROVINCIAL PARK
Fort Qu'Appelle, 306-332-3215; www.tpcs.gov.sk.ca/EchoValley
In this 1,606-acre park (45 miles east of Regina), enjoy the picturesque Qu'Appelle Valley in addition to Echo and Pasqua lakes. Other activities such as swimming, waterskiing, sailing and bird-watching await visitors to the park. In addition, six miles of groomed cross-country trails are popular in winter and may be used in the summer for walking or biking.

GLOBE THEATRE
1801 Scarth St., Regina, 306-525-6400; www.globetheatrelive.com
View plays performed by the province's oldest professional theater company at the Globe Theatre.
September-May.

GOVERNMENT HOUSE MUSEUM AND HERITAGE PROPERTY
4607 Dewdney Ave., Regina, 306-787-5773; www.graa.gov.sk.ca/govhouse
Opened in 1891 as the residence of the Queen's representative, the house became the official residence of Saskatchewan's Lieutenant Governor from 1905 to 1945. Fourteen rooms are decorated with period furnishings and almost 100,000 artifacts.

LAST MOUNTAIN HOUSE

146-3211 Albert St., Regina, 306-787-7031; www.se.gov.sk.ca/saskparks

Last Mountain House is a reconstructed Hudson's Bay Company post from 1869. While touring the area, visitors will see the Master's House and Last Mountain House, as well as artifacts that give the history of the area and show how the fur trade in this part of Saskatchewan ended.
July-Labor Day.

MACKENZIE ART GALLERY

Wascana Centre, T.C. Douglas Building, 3745 Albert St., Regina, 306-584-4250;
www.mackenzieartgallery.sk.ca

The focus of this 100,000-square-foot, tri-level gallery is Canadian and Saskatchewan artists. The collection of 1,600 works also features contemporary American artists and 15th- to 19th-century European prints, drawings and paintings.

REGINA SYMPHONY ORCHESTRA

Saskatchewan Centre of the Arts, 200 Lakeshore Drive, Regina, 306-586-9555;
www.reginasymphony.com

Enjoy Canada's longest continuously operating symphony.
See Web site for schedule and ticket information.

ROYAL CANADIAN MOUNTED POLICE TRAINING ACADEMY & MUSEUM

5607 Dewdney Ave., Regina, 306-522-7333; www.rcmpmuseum.com

The Royal Canadian Mounted Police has been located in Regina since 1885. The museum explains the police's role in Canadian history. The tour shows visitors the oldest building in Regina, the chapel and provides a chance to view cadets in training.

ROYAL SASKATCHEWAN MUSEUM

Wascana Centre, 2445 Albert St., Regina, 306-787-2815, 306-787-2816;
www.royalsaskmuseum.ca

Visitors to this museum learn about the anthropological and natural history of the province. The museum houses earth and life science galleries and a fossil station.

SASKATCHEWAN LEGISLATIVE BUILDING

123 Legislative Building, 2405 Legislative Drive, Regina, 306-787-2376;
www.legassembly.sk.ca

The building was completed in 1912 and houses many provincial governmental activities. The building itself is worth a look, but if you take the tour, you will get a better feel for how Canadian government functions.

SASKATCHEWAN SCIENCE CENTRE

2903 Powerhouse Drive, Regina, 306-522-4629, 800-667-6300;
www.sasksciencecentre.com

Hands-on exhibits explore physics, genetics, biology, ecology, geology and space and a Discovery Lab houses an array of reptiles and amphibians. Live demonstrations of static electricity, cryogenics, lasers, sound, ecology and anatomy are given daily. The SaskTel 3D Laser Theatre (one of only 10 in the world) provides a unique experience. Visitors can also climb the 60-foot climbing wall or take in one of the many entertaining and informative stage shows. The Kramer IMAX Theatre has a five-story screen and powerful surround sound.

WASCANA CENTRE

2900 Wascana Drive, Regina, 306-522-3661; www.wascana.sk.ca
At Wascana Lake (manmade), take a ferry to Willow Island for a picnic. Swimming in the lake is prohibited, but once it freezes, ice skating is encouraged. Ski trails are groomed on the north shore from the Royal Saskatchewan Museum to Douglas Park. Call ahead for trail conditions.

SPECIAL EVENTS
BUFFALO DAYS

IPSCO Place, Lewvan Drive, Regina, 306-781-9200; www.ipscoplace.com
At this city festival, enjoy activities ranging from midway rides to livestock shows to a parade.
Late July.

MOSAIC

2144 Cornwall St., Regina, 306-757-5990; www.reginamosaic.com
Mosaic is an annual three-day festival of cultures that celebrates the rich ethnic history of the prairie settlers of this area. Experience 17 different countries and their cultures through food and dance.
Early June.

WHERE TO STAY
★★★DELTA REGINA

1919 Saskatchewan Drive, Regina, 306-525-5255, 888-890-3222; www.deltahotels.com
Contemporary and comfortable, the Delta Regina offers a range of accommodations. Have some aquatic fun at the onsite Waterworks Recreation Complex, complete with a waterslide, pool, children's pool and whirlpool. Families are particularly welcomed here with children's menus, individual check-in cards for kids and age-specific kids' essentials kits.
274 rooms. Restaurant, bar. Pets accepted. Fitness room. Pool. $151-250

★★★RADISSON PLAZA HOTEL SASKATCHEWAN

2125 Victoria Ave., Regina, 306-522-7691, 800-667-5828; www.hotelsask.com
Overlooking Regina Park, this historic landmark is elegant and welcoming to both business and leisure guests. The Cortlandt Dining Room offers fine dining and Sunday brunch and Sunday buffet. Enjoy high tea in the Victoria Tea Room or something a bit stronger in Monarch's Lounge.
224 rooms. Restaurant, bar. Pets accepted. $151-250

WHERE TO EAT

★★★CORTLANDT HALL DINING ROOM

Radisson Plaza Hotel Saskatchewan, 2125 Victoria Ave., Regina, 306-337-4316, 800-667-5828; www.hotelsask.com

Situated in the Radisson Plaza Hotel Saskatchewan, the Cortlandt Hall Dining Room offers fine dining in an elegant and relaxing atmosphere. Memorable entrée options include grilled swordfish, prosciutto-wrapped pork tenderloin and smoked duck breast. Traditional favorites are offered at the Sunday brunch and Sunday evening buffet.
International. Breakfast, lunch, dinner, Sunday brunch. $15 and under

★★★DANBRY'S CONTEMPORARY CUISINE

1925 Victoria Ave., Regina, 306-525-8777

Creative menu selections with locally produced products are offered at this casual, elegant restaurant housed in the historic Assiniboia Club building. An extensive cocktail menu is offered, as well as a cigar menu.
International. Closed Sunday. Outdoor seating. $36-85

★MEDITERRANEAN BISTRO

2589 Quance St. East, Regina, 306-757-1666; mbistro.sasktelwebhosting.com

Mediterranean. Outdoor seating. $16-35

SASKATOON

See also Prince Albert

Saskatoon is Saskatchewan's largest city, named from "mis-sask-quah-toomina," the Cree name for an indigenous berry. The jams and pies made from those berries are still local specialties. The South Saskatchewan River is the main waterway; bike, jog or take a stroll along its banks. Along the river and in the downtown area, you'll find many craft shops and galleries, a fine symphony orchestra, a plethora of summer festivals, four professional theater companies and an active amateur theater community.

WHAT TO SEE

BLACKSTRAP PROVINCIAL PARK

102-112 Research Drive, Saskatoon, 306-492-5675

This park is located on Blackstrap Lake near Mount Blackstrap. Many activities can be enjoyed on the lake such as windsurfing, waterskiing and swimming; fishing is popular as well. If you're adventurous, climb Mount Blackstrap and take in the scenery of the lake and more than 1,310 acres of park below. The hill at Blackstrap was built to accommodate events of the 1971 Canada Winter Games. There are a couple of sections for skiing along the three miles available, though the trails are not long.

FORT CARLTON PROVINCIAL HISTORICAL PARK

102-112 Research Drive, Saskatoon, 306-467-5205; www.tpcs.gov.sk.ca/FortCarlton

This is the original site of a Hudson's Bay Company fur-trading post that operated between 1810 and 1885 on the North Saskatchewan River. Today, visitors can check out a reconstructed stockade, fur and provisions store and clerks' quarters. Each of the buildings appears much like they would have in the 1860s. See, touch and smell items such as buffalo hides, beaver pelts, war

clubs, blankets, guns, twist tobacco and birch bark baskets.
Mid-May-early September.

MENDEL ART GALLERY & CIVIC CONSERVATORY

950 Spadina Crescent E., Saskatoon, 306-975-7610; www.mendel.ca
Both permanent and temporary exhibits showcase historical and contemporary art by international, national and regional artists. The gallery holds a number of special programs, including "ART for LIFE," "Something on Sundays" and the annual "School Art" exhibit, which presents the works of Saskatoon's students.

PIKE LAKE PROVINCIAL PARK

102-112 Research Drive, Saskatoon, 306-933-6966; www.se.gov.sk.ca
Just 20 minutes south of Saskatoon, Pike Lake is an escape that has something for everyone: swimming, fishing, boating, nature trails, tennis courts, golfing, picnicking and year-round camping. The Leisure Pool and Waterslide Complex are designed for all, from first-time water sliders to the more experienced.

WANUSKEWIN HERITAGE PARK

RR 4 Penner Road, Saskatoon, 306-931-6767; www.wanuskewin.com
Wanuskewin Heritage Park is set on 760 acres along the South Saskatchewan River, 10 miles from Saskatoon in the Opamihaw Valley. The park focuses on the rich native heritage of the aboriginal people who lived here 6,000 years ago through cultural, archaeological, historical and geographical interpretation. There are self-guided trails, an interpretation center and a 500-seat amphitheater where native dances and songs are performed and stories are told. As for now, the park is temporarily closed to the public due to construction work for a renewal project. Call or visit the Web site for updates before heading to the park.

SPECIAL EVENTS

CANADA REMEMBERS INTERNATIONAL AIR SHOW

101-3515 Thatcher Ave., Saskatoon, 306-975-3155;
www.canadaremembersairshow.com
This popular air show is held as a tribute to Canadian veterans. Opening ceremonies feature a parade of veterans and are followed by performances from the Canadian Armed Forces, the U.S. Air Force, the U.S. Air National Guard and the Royal Canadian Air Force.
Mid-August.

SASKTEL SASKATCHEWAN JAZZ FESTIVAL

701-601 Spadina Crescent E., Saskatoon, 306-652-1421; www.saskjazz.com
At the end of June, thousands of visitors and local residents come together to enjoy the sounds of more than 800 of the best provincial, national and international jazz, blues, gospel and world-beat musicians. Events are held in venues like the Broadway Theatre and the Adam Ballroom and require tickets, but there are also many free-staged events throughout downtown and in parks.
Late June.

SASKATCHEWAN ★★★★★

SHAKESPEARE ON THE SASKATCHEWAN

602-245 Third Ave. S., Saskatoon, 306-653-2300;
www.shakespeareonthesaskatchewan.com
This annual festival features outdoor performances of different plays written
by the bard.
July-mid-August.

WHERE TO STAY
★★★DELTA BESSBOROUGH

601 Spadina Crescent E., Saskatoon, 306-244-5521, 888-890-3222;
www.deltahotels.com
This full-service chateau-style hotel overlooks the Saskatchewan River.
Guests can relax by the indoor pool and whirlpool and children have fun here
with activities and a playground. Enjoy dinner at the Japanese steakhouse.
225 rooms. Restaurant, bar, spa. Fitness center. Pool. $151-250

★★RADISSON HOTEL SASKATOON

405 20th St. East, Saskatoon, 306-665-3322; www.radisson.com
291 rooms. Restaurant, bar. Pets accepted. Pool. $61-150

★★★SHERATON CAVALIER HOTEL

612 Spadina Crescent E., Saskatoon, 306-652-6770; www.sheratonsaskatoon.com
Located in a business and shopping district, six miles from downtown and
five miles from Calgary International Airport, this renovated hotel offers a
variety of amenities. The Carvers Steakhouse provides a wonderful steak and
seafood menu. Complimentary shuttle service is offered.
249 rooms. Restaurant, bar. Fitness center. Pool. $151-250

WHERE TO EAT
★★2ND AVE GRILL

123 Second Ave. S., Saskatoon, 306-244-9899; www.2ndavegrill.com
International. Outdoor seating. $16-35

YORKTON

See also Regina
In Yorkton, immigrants primarily from the Ukraine, who were well experienced in plains farming, settled the fertile region. These pioneers brought
with them a philosophy of community cooperation and cultural pride—and
their legacy is that the city of Yorkton still boasts a rich ethnic diversity evident in the architecture of its churches, museums and handcrafts.

WHAT TO SEE
CANNINGTON MANOR PROVINCIAL HISTORICAL PARK

Kenosee Lake, Yorkton, 306-787-2700
Cannington Manor, built in the early 1880s by a British captain who lost his
fortune in England, is located in southeast Saskatchewan. The captain wanted
to create an aristocratic society of British people living in western Canada.
Learn the history of Captain Edward Pierce and of the house itself.
Mid-May-Labor Day, Wednesday-Monday.

MOOSE MOUNTAIN PROVINCIAL PARK

Yorkton, 306-577-2600; www.tpcs.gov.sk.ca

This park features many lakes and offers such recreational opportunities as horseback riding, bird-watching, hiking, camping and cross-country skiing. Also here are two 18-hole golf courses, a 36-hole miniature golf course and a casino.

PAINTED HAND CASINO

30 Third Ave. N., Yorkton, 306-786-6777, 888-604-7711; www.siga.sk.ca

This 25,000-square-foot, Native American owned-and-operated casino features 134 slot machines and 12 table games, including blackjack, progressive jackpots, slot machines, red dog, poker and roulette. The casino also hosts major events, such as curling tournaments.

ST. MARY'S UKRAINIAN CATHOLIC CHURCH

155 Catherine St., Yorkton, 306-783-4594

St. Mary's was built in 1914 and is Yorkton's most unique feature. On the inside of the dome of the church is the "Coronation of the Virgin," painted by Steven Meush from 1939 to 1941. This beautiful painting is as similar to the Baroque painted domes in German and Italian churches as you will find in this part of Canada.

WESTERN DEVELOPMENT MUSEUM

Highway 16 W., Yorkton, 306-783-8361; www.wdm.ca

The Yorkton Western Development Museum has re-created the times and styles of some of the many immigrants who settled in Western Canada. Scenes illustrate the cultural roots of these new peoples: Ukrainians, English, Swedes, Germans, Doukhobors and Icelanders. Outdoors, the challenge of turning sod is demonstrated in the lineup of agricultural equipment, which includes the gigantic 1916 Twin City gas tractor, one of only two in North America.

SPECIAL EVENT
YORK COLONY QUILTERS GUILD QUILT FAIR AND TEA

Yorkton, 306-783-8361; www.wdm.ca

This two-day fair has been going strong for more than a decade. The quilt show is a major attraction of the event.
Early May.

WHERE TO STAY
★DAYS INN

2 Kelsey Bay, Yorkton, 306-783-3297, 800-544-8313; www.daysinn.com

74 rooms. Complimentary breakfast. Pool. $61-150

INDEX

B

★★★★★ **INDEX**

ALBERTA

216

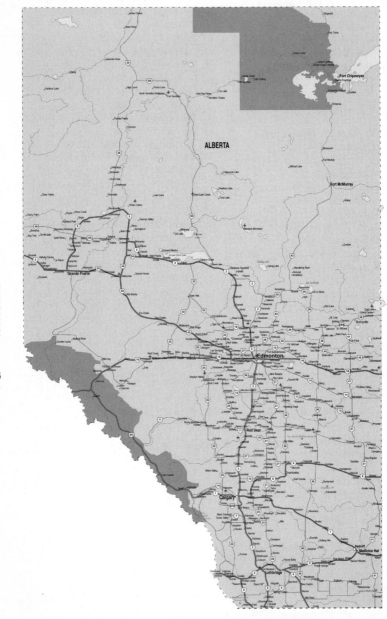

ATLANTIC PROVINCES

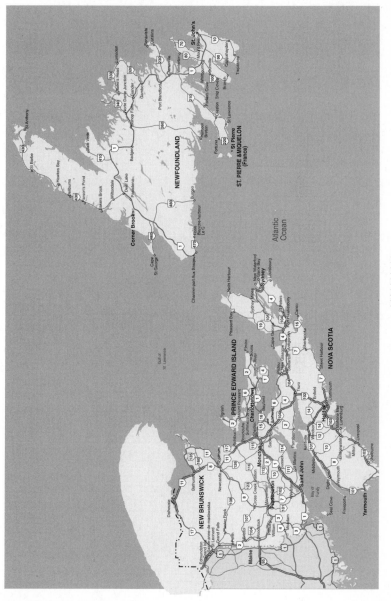

BRITISH COLUMBIA

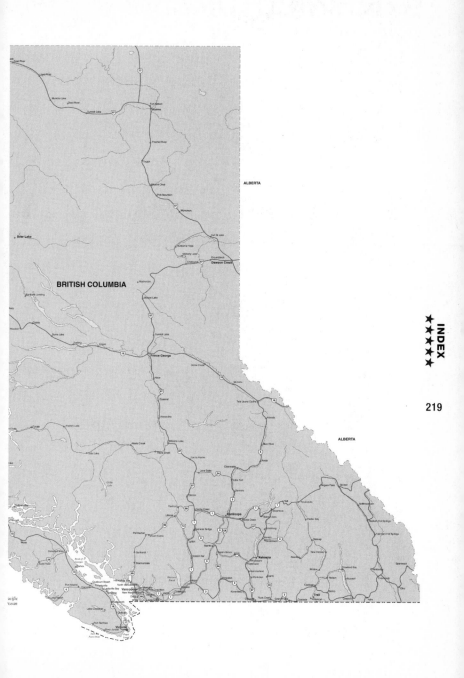

MANITOBA

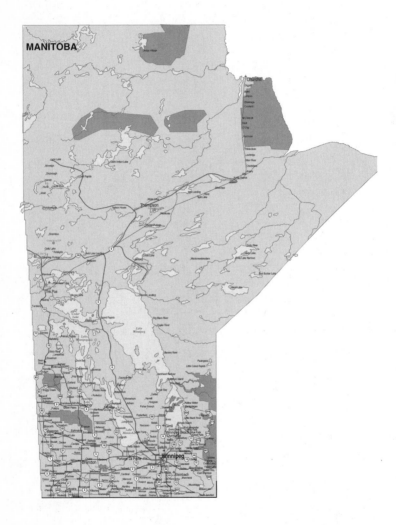

NEWFOUNDLAND-LABRADOR

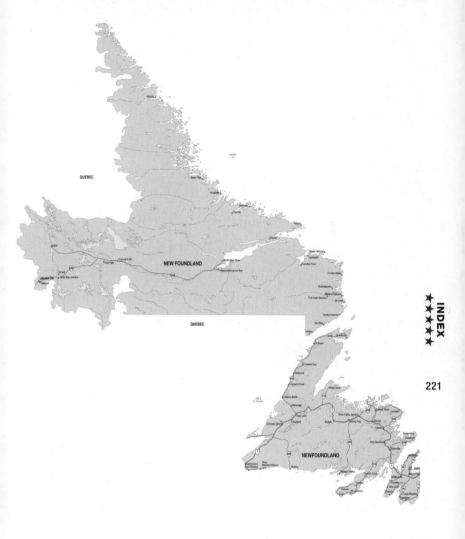

ONTARIO

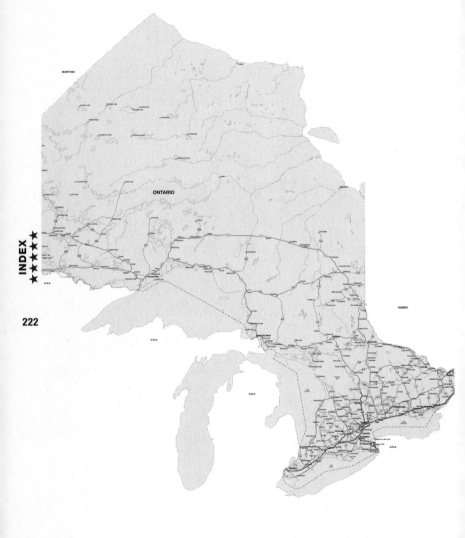

QUEBEC

NEWFOUNDLAND

NEW BRUNSWICK

QUEBEC

ONTARIO

U.S.A.

SASKATCHEWAN

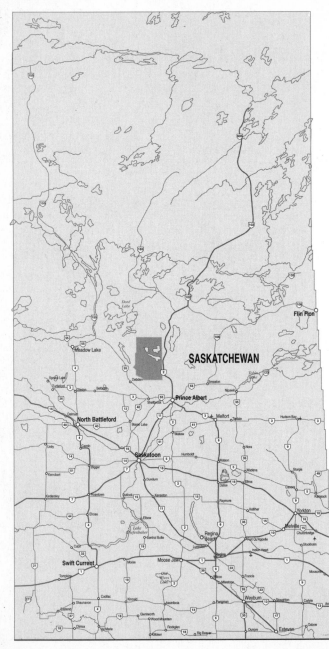